# After Authority

# After Authority

## Global Art Cinema and Political Transition

KALLING HECK

Rutgers University Press

New Brunswick, Camden, and Newark, New Jersey, and London

Library of Congress Cataloging-in-Publication Data

Names: Heck, Kalling, author.
Title: After authority : global art cinema and political transition / Kalling Heck.
Description: New Brunswick, New Jersey : Rutgers University Press, [2020] | Includes bibliographical references and index.
Identifiers: LCCN 2019008416 | ISBN 9781978806993 (cloth) | ISBN 9781978806986 (paperback)
Subjects: LCSH: Motion pictures—Political aspects. | Totalitarianism and motion pictures.
Classification: LCC PN1995.9.P6 H43 2020 | DDC 791.43/658—dc23
LC record available at https://lccn.loc.gov/2019008416

A British Cataloging-in-Publication record for this book is available from the British Library.



∞ The paper used in this publication meets the requirements of the American National Standard for Information Sciences—Permanence of Paper for Printed Library Materials, ANSI Z39.48-1992.

www.rutgersuniversitypress.org

Manufactured in the United States of America

For Mary

# Contents

# After Authority

# Introduction

## Four Angels

There are at least two versions of Jean-Luc Godard and Jean-Pierre Gorin's *Vladimir et Rosa* (1971, credited to the filmmaking collective the Dziga Vertov Group). The major version to have been distributed tells the story of the group of eight political activists charged for inciting to riot at the Democratic National Convention in 1968. Shot in the aggressive and abstract style that the pair was known for at the time, the film explores the court case but refuses to report on either the case's context or its outcome. It is instead content to vaguely allegorize the trial and to satirize the authority figures for their perpetration of what was surely a farce. Through bold colors, direct address, smash cuts, and general discord, the film, rather than directly rebuking the case, renders the trial totally incoherent, an abstract collage of competing images and dialogue that mirrors the nonsensical charges brought against the defendants.

The second version is remarkably different. The film's chief financier Barney Rosset organized and recorded a screening of the major version for two of the defendants from the actual case, the irreverent and sardonic Abbie Hoffman and Jeffrey Rubin, and recorded the results.[1] Displeased with the film, the pair laugh and yell at the screen, mocking its ambiguity and its unwillingness to accurately represent the specifics of the trial. "It's not keeping my interests," posits Rubin toward the beginning of the film, his head rested in his hand. "It's ridiculous," he continues, as Hoffman laughs. This version of the film continues by cutting between Godard and Gorin's footage and this new audience of Hoffman and Rubin, the audio of the film heard aloud in the theater linking the two spaces. The longer the film continues, the more frustrated Hoffman and Rubin become. The primary concern of these viewers moves at some point from speculation as to which characters in the film represent them and their fellow defendants—an investigation that quickly leads nowhere—to a discussion of the broader goals of the film. Hoffman at one point proposes, once familiar with the film's style, that the major function of this film is to provide coded messages to the Weather Underground—a radical leftist group. He laughs, but refuses details. While Hoffman continues to attempt to decode the film's hidden meanings, Rubin grows increasingly irritated: "The trial was more exciting than this movie," he contends summarily halfway into the film.

The major critique, however, comes via Hoffman, when responding to an unheard question: "Say we had this film made in the middle of the trial, right?" he begins. "We take it around, say we organize demonstrations at the end of the trial. We take this film, we show it to a large group of young kids, you know, I don't get the feeling that they would want to like get involved. . . . Or if we showed it at a fundraising party I don't think people would want to give us any money. I mean what could we do with the film? Say if we had it in the middle of . . .". He is interrupted by the figure who asked the question, escalating the conversation by referring to what was, presumably, an unheard accusation from Hoffman: "That doesn't make him a CIA agent just because his films don't move anybody to do anything. You gotta have a little better connection than that even for my paranoia." After a bit more discussion, the topic is again broached when Hoffman continues, "He serves the interest of the CIA with this move definitely." He is interrupted again: "So is he paid or unpaid?" the figure asks. "Yea, I would say paid," Hoffman responds. "Paid?" "Yea, I mean there's rumors of that."

That Abbie Hoffman accuses Jean-Luc Godard of being paid by the CIA to produce a film so ambiguous that it undermines the political potentials of this trial is striking, but helpful in establishing the political dynamics of ambiguity. That is, this accusation from Hoffman reveals (with some stress) the distrust that so often meets ambiguity, a distrust arising from the possibility for an ambiguous object to carry messages and meanings that are difficult to gather and even more difficult to control. This problem takes on particular immediacy in moments where political expediency is thought to be necessary. Indeed what Hoffman and Rubin's responses present are exactly the tensions that ambiguous cinema produces in moments that seem to call for a more "engaged" mode of politics, which is the major theme of this book.

For these reasons, I will address here the political potentials of ambiguity—its advantages as well as its drawbacks—by examining the history and trajectory of the cinematic mode that has taken the title of "art cinema." Ultimately, I will strive to show how ambiguity can function as a political category, a topic I further explore in the coming chapters. I undertake this study in the hopes of examining the value as well as the failings of the turn to ambiguity in the context of political turmoil, and I do so by discussing four wildly different films that employ tactics similar to Godard and Gorin's. These films were each made in and around moments of intense political change; they consist of Roberto Rossellini's *Germany Year Zero* (1948), Béla Tarr's *Sátántangó* (1994), Hong Sang-soo's *Woman on the Beach* (2006), and Haskell Wexler's *Medium Cool* (1969). While this book will largely focus on the political potentials of these films, it is important to also keep in sight the critiques, perhaps ones less conspiratorial then Hoffman's, but critiques that nonetheless contend that these films fail to meet the demands of certainty and direction that their respective contexts seem to mandate. Distrust is in fact a key feature of the approach to ambiguity outlined here, and the availability of skepticism and general rejection outlined by Hoffman is in fact a key quality of the subject under discussion.

But first the virtues. Each of the four films addressed here was made after, and in my reading in light of, the transition from authoritarianism or totalitarianism to democracy.[2] Each furthermore turns to ambiguity as a system for contending with this transition. These films in fact map a trend, perhaps a tendency, toward ambiguity in these contexts, a repeating principle that interacts with both the history of art cinema and the unique circumstances of each of these films. Ambiguity, and this is key, in each of these examples is turned to in order to both digest and deflect the effects of a wildly unchecked authority. As we shall see, for many critics contemporary with their production these films are simply "apolitical." I contend, however, that ambiguity under these conditions is itself a form of politics, as it serves in each of these examples to reject the systems of authority that have so recently in each of these cases been deposed, a gesture that ideally likewise bars the possibility for their return.

Within the spectrum of authorities rejected falls each of these films' capacity to present a coherent idea, for any clearly articulated concept must be built upon a system of meaning and argumentation derived from a hierarchical structure, which is to say an authority. This rejection of authority takes ambiguity as its corollary, and it is this recourse to ambiguity—so central, as we shall see, to the history of art cinema—which produces an antiauthoritarian politics despite the barriers to meaning that it presents. In my view, this ambiguity is essential to global art cinema, and, as this book will prove, it is furthermore linked to an antiauthoritarian stance.

The specificity of this project is derived in large part from the differences, in addition to the obvious similarities, between these films. This is to say that the four films examined here and their respective contexts allow for views of remarkably different instances of this trend in art cinema. They all turn to ambiguity, but it is the fact that each represents a different relationship to authority and democracy that makes them valuable. The chapters here have been arranged to showcase various contexts and responses to differing turns to democracy after a period of authoritarian or totalitarian politics. The case of *Germany Year Zero* is then the most unified example of post-authoritarian cinema; its rejection of authoritarian politics and hopes for democracy are more straightforward than my other examples'. As a result, this film affords the space to speak about authority and democracy more broadly, and to indeed clarify each of my significant terms (authority and democracy included). *Sátántangó*, meanwhile, troubles Hungary's transition from totalitarianism by bringing into play the idealism specific to Hungarian communism and the subsequent disappointment at its demise, a disappointment that was enflamed by the rise of democratic capitalism but also served to provide an avenue to consider the potentials of a significant economic and political transition. *Woman on the Beach* extends such disappointment by directly challenging the relationship between democracy and capitalism, and in so doing recalls some nostalgia for South Korean authoritarianism while still resisting its return. Finally, *Medium Cool* serves as a kind of counterpoint or reversal of some of these conditions, and is the farthest afield of these analyses. Made under democracy, this film proposes how it might look for a nation to transition *to* authoritarianism, and how cinema might serve to resist such a change.

This is not to say that these are the only films or contexts that might fit this study, but this selection of films is uniquely suited to map the contours and degrees of this repeated turn to ambiguity in light of the deposition of an unchecked authority. Other examples—from Chile, India, Poland, to name a few—are likewise available and certainly no less valuable. But these four films and contexts, and the distances between them, help to focus this study, allowing it to address intersections between authority, democracy, and cinema from a useful set of perspectives.

The intention here is not to propose an exhaustive account of antiauthoritarian art cinema—to do so would surely constitute a much larger project than this. Instead, this book is designed to serve two major functions: first, I will contend here that art cinema is at its core antiauthoritarian. Its beginnings, particularly in neorealism, were built upon the belief that the rejection of authority is a significant political project, and its aesthetic qualities follow from this axiom. This is not to say that these films are *correct* in their political project, but that this project locates a set of assumptions and responses that account for the aesthetic trends of global art cinema generally. Second, this book offers a new methodology for further examining the relationship between film—particularly ambiguous film—and politics. This is to say that the model presented here is valuable for identifying and evaluating the political projects of art films in general, as the tendency highlighted here has surely not yet been extinguished nor exhausted. There is a significant caveat to the method under discussion, though: the premise here is not that these films are effective political objects, but that they contain a hope for politics that might be useful, and is at the very least of interest. As will be discussed at length, the arguments for change that these films represent are not without their weaknesses. This is not then a claim about the importance of these films *for* politics—surely their effects are as ambiguous as their content—but an argument about how these films have responded to political conditions, and what uses the tendency they help to map might be put to. The goal here is not to present an overwhelming and positive account of the potentials of these films, but to think about what these films seem to have in mind (insofar as they can be said to have anything in mind) and what the effects, positive and negative, of the project of ambiguity might be.

As a method, this series of analyses hopes to provide some boundaries for understanding the elusive category of political art cinema with some certainty. The films under discussion here all fit into the industrial/aesthetic category of art cinema—a category that will be discussed at length shortly—and all encounter the tension between aesthetic ambiguity and political argumentation. To be sure, other filmmakers likewise travel these tensions—Pedro Almodóvar, Larisa Shepitko, Glauber Rocha, to name a few—and the hope of this project is to provide a lens to examine these films as well. No two films account for the tensions between ambiguity and politics in the same manner, but what the range of films discussed here reveals is a general outline of how to account for ambiguity and/as politics.

What these films together constantly push against is the insurmountable boundary between the political project of antiauthoritarianism and the means by which a particular meaning can be derived, directed, and universalized. The exchange between Abbie Hoffman and Jerry Rubin that opened this introduction illuminates some of the tensions I am describing. Hoffman's concern for direction and intention might go unmet by Godard and Gorin's film, but one might respond by proposing that these filmmakers' insist on rejecting the very systems by which direction and deliberation are formed, leaving them unwilling or unable to address Hoffman's demands without violating their own dedication to radical antiauthoritarianism. What is advantageous about the approach employed in *Vladimir et Rosa* is to be found in its relationship to possibility. Each of the films discussed here stands on the precipice of a new kind of governance, and each strives to allow an extension of the time before this new formation is cemented. What these films offer is a total rejection of the authoritarian principles that in each context resulted in some form of devastation, but what they refuse in the same gesture is the production of a new path away from this same devastation. Indeed, as Hoffman and Rubin rightly point out, *Vladimir et Rosa* presents no particular rejoinder to the wildly antidemocratic trial that it represents; but what they miss is that it is in this refusal to respond that the film finds its unique energy, its ability to point toward injustice. But to never have this gesturing verified, to never see a particular point made or position taken is always also frustrating, and this is the impossible dynamic that political ambiguity provokes.

The four films discussed in the following chapters also take up this dynamic. Rather than asking us to see anything in particular, they ask us to look and to look again, but they never exactly explain *how* or *why* we should look, or *what* we should hope to find. This is the structure of ambiguity; it pulls us always in multiple directions at once, presenting the possibility of meaning but never fully producing the conditions of its arrival. There is, then, also a tension at the heart of this project. The hope here is to generalize an approach to these films, to produce a method for further understanding films made in similar, but never identical, contexts and styles. But ambiguity is ungeneralizable; its very purpose is to resist meaning, which is to say to resist any general use. To make a project of these films is then to push against their fundamental concern: the hope for something totally new to arrive. The readings here are specific, and they specifically discuss how these films resist meaning in what I will shortly call a messianic hope for the radically different. They each do this in their own ways, but they all must return to ambiguity to render—or resist rendering—this hope. This tendency repeats in different ways, and is understood in each chapter as a variation on a central concern. Other films, those made in different contexts and under differing conditions, likewise turn to this tradition of ambiguity in order to account for, counter, and encourage political change. This project hopes to function as a guide for thinking about other films made in light of this tradition. What this constitutive ambiguity provides is a vantage from which to (re)view the devastated world, from which to see what the world is and, perhaps, how to move forward in the hopes of claiming a new solution to the misery that unchecked authority can yield. Each film here has a strong relationship to some avenue of cinematic realism, as each asks the viewer to witness and assist in ameliorating what they have seen, assimilating these experiences into their own solution to the problems of unchecked authority.

It is fair to criticize the intense atomization that this process causes. These films offer no recourse to the needs of agreement; they focus instead on individual spectators and their capacity to see new and different things *by themselves*. These films provide no system whereby these visions might be made universal or might produce some outlet into deliberation or unification, which is at least in part Hoffman and Rubin's critique. Furthermore, since the early postwar period, the forces of global capitalism have offered up exactly these same kinds of claims to openness and possibility. Indeed, it can be argued that these forces are now so deeply ingrained in our systems for rendering and evaluating meaning that the forces of global economics will inevitably be the first things to fill the kinds of openings that ambiguity provides and will regardless benefit from the disorder and difference that it produces.[3] These critiques will factor heavily into the chapters that follow. The focus of this introduction, though, is to bring into view the relationship between ambiguity, cinema in the art house tradition, and politics, and to argue that the turn to ambiguity in cinema made in moments of political transition, moments that connect all of the films here, has a coherent current: it serves as a cogent rejoinder to the effects of unchecked authority by undermining the capacity to create a singular and unified meaning. Where this capacity lies is to be found in the aesthetic tradition that art cinema offers, an aesthetic tradition that is rooted in an anti-authoritarian wish.

## Global Art Cinema

Ambiguity is a central theme in the tradition of art cinema, the origin of which is often linked to some of the films discussed here. As early as 1979, David Bordwell argued that what we think of as art cinema is in fact a relatively stable category, what he calls a "distinct branch of the cinematic institution" that is unified by a particular set of formal qualities and viewing habits.[4] For Bordwell this category has a rich and diverse history, but came into its modern form after World War II and in light of the expansion of Hollywood and its dominance over film culture, beginning, notably, with the Italian neorealists.[5] It is in fact the deviations from classical cinema that began to mark the contours of the art film, in particular the loosening of causal relationships.

Along with these loosenings of patterns of linear causation, art cinema is defined in this model by way of its strong relationship to realism, what Bordwell calls a "commitment to both objective and subjective verisimilitude."[6] Bordwell traces this category of realism to André Bazin's emphasis on deep focus, long takes, and camera movements, and to the resultant dedication to experiences of unbroken time and space. But what Bordwell is careful to note is that the interaction between photographic realism and the foregrounding of the author that is found in Bazin's work creates a tension that largely contributes to art cinema's unique qualities: "The author is the textual force 'who' communicates (what the film is *saying*?) and 'who' expresses (what is the artist's *personal vision*?)."[7] According to this formulation, the understanding of the author as master of meaning is to a degree illusory (in its supposed uniqueness) and also industrial (in that it became the tool to sell a film in the absence of genre and stars).[8] The subsequent art film mode is largely organized around realism as determined by the expectations brought about by the rhetoric of verisimilitude, but this realism must also always be ruptured, and it is these ruptures that are then used to constitute "authorial commentary," which can then be unified and reproduced to present an oeuvre.[9]

For Bordwell there is then an irreconcilable tension at the heart of art cinema: "Verisimilitude, objective or subjective, is inconsistent with an intrusive author. The surest signs of authorial intelligibility—the flashforward, the doubled scene in *Persona*, the color filters at the start of *Le Mépris*—are the least capable of realistic justification. Contrariwise, to push the realism of psychological uncertainty to its limit is to invite a haphazard text in which the author's shaping hand would not be visible."[10] To summarize: the qualities of realism and intrusive authorship are incommensurate, presenting an irreparable tension at the heart of these films. The solution to this problem, in the case of art cinema, is therefore ambiguity. In Bordwell's reading, the art film initiates a series of responses that first demand a reliance on realism and, once that response has been exhausted or interrupted, a reliance on authorship—particularly via style. As he puts it, "Whatever is excessive in one category must belong to another."[11] This trait is best exemplified by the tendency in the art film to rely on an open and ambiguous ending: "With the open and arbitrary ending, the art film reasserts that ambiguity is the dominant principle of intelligibility, that we are to watch less for the tale than the telling, that life lacks the neatness of art and *this art knows it*."[12] These endings, in other words, signify a direct link between the film and one's experience outside it: "The ambiguity, the play of thematic interpretation, must not be halted at the film's close."[13] Bordwell notes, however, the variations, departures, and disruptions at the heart of this category, and likewise discusses the way that, even as of 1979, the category of the art film seemed to be changing.[14] More recently, scholars have returned to this category, now more likely referred to as global art cinema, in the hopes of mapping its boundaries and discussing its now seemingly even more persistent presence.

Mark Betz, focusing in particular on the European context, has notably united what he finds to be the dual considerations surrounding art cinema: its status as "formal-aesthetic" category, which he associates with Bordwell, and its concurrent status as a national-institutional category, an argument that he locates centrally in Steve Neale's 1981 essay "Art Cinema as Institution."[15] For Betz, it is in fact the connection between these two divergent approaches that he finds significant: "Bordwell and Neale present two different approaches to art cinema as a distinct category of film style and production, one aesthetic and one economical/institutional. But it is their similarities rather than their differences that have proven most abiding: that art cinema is fundamentally opposed to Hollywood cinema; that it constitutes a European response to Hollywood; and that its richest vein appeared in the postwar era, especially in the 1960s."[16] The history of global art cinema is closely aligned with a need to draw a distance from Hollywood, particularly in the postwar period, and this need led to the assumption of a "national" identity drawn along the lines of language and culture.[17] But, as Betz notes, "At the same time, art cinema circulates internationally as a specialized or niche sector; it functions as 'a mechanism of discrimination' for a particular class of audience existing across nations."[18] It is indeed this tension that constitutes global art cinema as a definitional mode. Its realistic, or what Bordwell would call verisimilar, qualities arise at least in part from a need for a national orientation. When combined with its attempt to find a non- or counter-Hollywood narrative and aesthetic approach, as well as a greater emphasis on politics, this realism provides global art cinema with its unique set of principles and qualities. For Betz, who again focuses on the *European* forms of global art cinema,

> One of the striking features of modern European cinema is precisely the circuit it sets up between the spaces it frames, the time in which it sequences them, the places of its characters as viewing subjects, and the spectator, who is not so much a recipient of a unified/temporal text as a participant in a disunified one. These spaces are not generalized but very specific—and, by the time of European art cinemas proper, very urban. They are spaces of collision between the old and the new, the traditional and the modern. They signify a burst of infrastructural modernization that radically reoriented how the modern subject works, lives, and perceives her positioning in the metropole of the new Europe.[19]

Here Betz touches on the political potential of art cinema. By virtue of its emphasis on the shifting urban landscape and particularly those affected by political and economic change, art cinema took as its goal to speak generally, examining the changes underway in the middle of the twentieth century and beyond. Coupled with the disunified spectator that Betz mentions—the spectator asked to participate in the construction of meaning but provided with no protocol for unifying the results of their participation—global art cinema took and continues to assume a form that is oriented toward re-envisioning the path forward for a world faced with oppression, change, existential malaise, and outright annihilation at every turn.

Rosalind Galt and Karl Schoonover, in their significant collection on global art cinema, broach some of these same concepts, providing a kind of summation of the unique structure and orientation of this mode. According to Galt and Schoonover, global art cinema is at its core a "mongrel" category, an "unreliable label" that gathers together a diverse and flexible collection of ideas and objects. For them, "Since the term 'art cinema' has always simultaneously invoked industrial, generic, and aesthetic categories, a current reckoning of the field exposes otherwise unseen geopolitical fault lines of world cinema."[20] For these authors it is in fact this mongrel status, this unreliability, that allows global art cinema to address questions of globalization. They contend that "art cinema has from its beginnings forced a relationship between the aesthetic and the geopolitical or, in other words, between cinema and the world. Thus it is the critical category best placed to engage pressing contemporary questions of globalization, world culture, and how the economics of cinema's transnational flows might interact with trajectories of film form."[21] For Galt and Schoonover, then, it is global art cinema's unique construction as both national and transnational, both domestic and global, that provides it the vantage from which to reflect on globalization.

Of central importance to this discussion, however, is the way that *form* in global art cinema is positioned to expose these concerns for globalization as a kind of aesthetic response. Given the requirement that ambiguity mute overt meaning by virtue of its refusal to take a clear position, to still be read as critical these films' form must carry an implied critique that remains legible despite the absence of certain meaning. The category of the art film is therefore essential, as it signals toward a loosely generalizable aesthetic experience, one constituted by uncertainty. Where the lack of trajectory common to these films is registered, where slowness, restraint, and extension can be felt and subsequently given an outline, is in large part provided by way of their connection to the category of the art film, a category that substantiates these absences as critique. Qualities central to the history of global art cinema—the long take, deep focus, extended camera movements, qualities that have in fact taken on new degrees and extremes in recent years—gain new significance when one realizes, as I contend here, that they are rooted in a history of antiauthoritarian politics.[22] This can be seen most notably in the approach of the neorealists, where aesthetic ambiguity and a rejection of authority are most closely paired, and it is from this point where this tradition can be traced. It is important to note, however, that it is only when taken in context that this ambiguity can be located and evaluated. This project therefore heavily relies upon a methodological approach that pairs formal analysis and contextualization, as it is only through the combination of form and context that the ambiguity on display here can be stabilized and read, given shape, and used to find a particular understanding of these films.

Galt and Schoonover go so far as to define the entire category of global art cinema by virtue of its uncategorizability, contending that "the lack of strict parameters for art cinema is not just an ambiguity of its critical history, but a central part of its specificity, a positive way of delineating its discursive space. We propose as a principle that art cinema can be defined by its impurity; a difficulty of categorization that is as productive to film culture as it is frustrating to taxonomy."[23] I would add to this very compelling definition that this frustration arises not simply from the difficulty of its categorization—surely Hollywood cinema as a category presents these same difficulties—but from the fact that ambiguity functions as its major structuring principle.

It is this tradition of ambiguity—a tradition that arose during neorealism where it served as an aesthetic reflex, responding to the failures and destruction of fascism—that is the major concern of this book. Indeed if global art cinema takes neorealism as one of its major historical origins, as all of these theorists claim that it does, then it must be for the tradition of ambiguity—arising of course from the tension between aesthetic verisimilitude and authorship as Bordwell would insist—that it precipitated. This context is important to understanding the thrust of global art cinema as a whole, because it helps to flesh out and provide insights into the origin and course of this category. The central role neorealism played in its development imbued art cinema with an antiauthoritarian push, albeit one that only occasionally regains contact with a project similar to that of the neorealists. Given this background, ambiguity serves not only as the unifying quality of global art cinema but also the center of its political project. If, as Bordwell claims, global art cinema is necessarily ambiguous, it therefore always holds within it some antiauthoritarian promise arriving via the role that authoritarianism played in its development. The goal of this book, then, is to find again the moments where this central ambiguity constitutive of global art cinema reconnects with its antiauthoritarian grounds, and to discuss how the approaches and qualities that constitute this mode of cinema have grown and changed over time.

It must be noted that this is not, indeed cannot be, an auteurist project. If, as I contend, the dismantling of authority is at the core of art cinema's style, then it must be unacceptable to reinstitute a new authority to override the old, now under a different name. Auteurism, while perhaps a significant element of art cinema's industrial model, nonetheless troubles the political project of antiauthoritarianism, what with its central orientation around rejecting authority. Whether the authority at hand is governmental or authorial is of little importance, as ambiguity serves to at once equate and summarily reject all forms of authority.[24] This book will not claim that it is the goal of Rossellini, Tarr, Hong, or Wexler to occupy a central space of authority in order to make these films valuable. Instead, it argues the opposite: these directors' capacity to remove themselves from a central position is what makes these films truly and finally antiauthoritarian, and, in light of their contexts, political. Their status as global auteurs is, then, a bit ironic, as they must forever walk a line between asserting themselves and disavowing their own presence. This is in fact the structure of global art cinema.

Bordwell's argument that artistic intent is what fills in the interpretive gaps created by ambiguous aesthetics accounts for the industrial model of art cinema, but it is disruptive of the political project that, I contend here, accounts for the antiauthoritarian roots of this tradition. And this is therefore where I depart from Bordwell's claims. For these films to be antiauthoritarian, there must be nothing to come and fill in these gaps. Auteurist intentionality, that is, works great as a method for making sense of these films as marketable products, but it does little to account for their use to politics. For these films to make political use of their ambiguity the gaps in meaning that they produce need to linger; they need to remain open. The argument that "authorial commentary" can be said to make sense of ambiguity is a bit of a smoke screen. Commentary on what? And that accounts for what goals? The commentary in question is always empty because the supposed perspective of some great artist can never quite counter ambiguity on its own. That is, Bordwell's model can be said to provide a system for recognizing these films, but never for making sense of them; it therefore only ever tells us what films we might attend to, and never why we should do so. What I might add to Bordwell's claim, then, is that auteurism cannot solely be said to make sense of these discordant films, and that this project—while dominated by filmmakers who all fit into the auteurist tradition—is not built around the contention that the authority of a great filmmaker is what secures meaning. What accounts for these films, this book contends, is not the recourse to some great master of meaning, but the recourse to *hope*.

## Messianism

In order to discuss the political underpinnings and potentials of this history of antiauthoritarianism in global art cinema, I now turn to mapping some of its available outcomes. As Schoonover and Galt note, the art cinema spectator is asked to withstand and occupy a series of contradictory positions: "Aesthetic distance is called for, but the rigor of distanciation is constantly crushed with an emotive bodily response and a virtual engagement with the other."[25] The art cinema spectator is asked both to assume a position of distance and thoughtful analysis while simultaneously being compelled to witness and feel for the imperiled situations of people and locations on the screen.[26] This follows from the tension between verisimilitude and ambiguity outlined by Bordwell, but it also places this audience in a kind of impossible bind: unable to locate a coherent trajectory for response or to fully rationalize the events on the screen, this viewer is left to *wait* and, subsequently, to think. This is the position, I contend, of messianism.

This is not the messianism of progress and perfection that might come down and alleviate the needs of the faithful in a kind of cleansing blast that disintegrates the detritus and inadequacies of a fallen world, but the messianism most often associated with Walter Benjamin, which that disrupts perfectionism and attempts instead to find value in brokenness and an "outside" always just out of reach. Sociologist Danielle Celermajer outlines the distinction between these two forms of messianism. She begins by first discussing the former, more conservative and religious, form: "Teleological, perfectionist, potentially violent in their sacrificial logic, messianic programs seem to be precisely those that dissolve, conceptually or literally, everything false and imperfect into the path towards the final end."[27] This vision of messianism contends that a judgmental but more or less known and perceivable force is waiting with rewards for the good and destruction for those who did not obey the always available set of orders it had established. Celermajer, however, contrasts this form of messianism with that of Benjamin: "In contradistinction to a messianic trajectory that must purge the imperfect to secure its end, Benjamin suggests a wistful messianism that tenderly attends to the discarded fragments of history in their brokenness. Indeed, it is precisely in the truth of brokenness and careful attention to it, that authentic hope lies."[28]

For Celermajer, this secular messianism, what Benjamin calls "weak messianism," provides a radically different approach to politics, one that rejects both social democracy and fascism in a single gesture on the grounds that both are oriented toward perfectionism and progress-driven teleologies, particularly in relation to time. As Celermajer notes, "Like fascism, social democracy conceives of time as empty, homogenous and progressive, teleologically drawn to a perfect end and thus, implicitly, harboring a type of violence."[29] Weak messianism, however, focuses on the interruptions that might disrupt this teleological trajectory, fixing its gaze not on a progressive future, but on the possibility for change within these disruptions. For Celermajer, this different relationship to time and history is best found in Benjamin's description of the angel of history, a figure inspired by Paul Klee's 1920 print "Angelus Novus" and discussed in Benjamin's "Theses on the Philosophy of History." In this essay Benjamin describes the figure of an angel pushed forward through history by the winds of progress while facing backward, unable to see the path it is traveling, its gaze fixed instead on the destruction that progress leaves in its wake. According to Celermajer, "For this angel, messianic power lies not in bringing about the perfect future—that is the work of the impersonal, faceless wind of historical progress or the eruption of the transcendent into history that humans might passively await or aggressively accelerate. His weak messianic power comprises gazing with full presence on the broken past. Unlike historicism, where all moments and experiences are integrated into the victorious movement forward, or metaphysics that leaps out of the fray, the angel pauses in the midst of ontic being and brings consciousness to the moments that are excluded from the victor's narrative."[30] All this looking back upon wreckage begs the question of the productive potentials of this staring at and suffering with destruction itself. Unable to stop, how can this angel hope to proceed to actually address what it sees? Like the cinematic spectator, the angel is bound by time to forever see and then be pushed forward, never freed to stop and attempt to ameliorate the damage that it registers. For Celermajer, the potentials of this process are to be found in the ways that this weak messianism asks us to look back on suffering not to find something in particular, but because it disjoins the gaze from progress and asks us to find something different altogether: "We exercise our weak messianic power only when we truly separate that act of presence from any instrumentalism—when we renounce any reason for being present to the reality of the suffering of the other except being present to the reality of suffering of the other."[31] The potentials of this being present are therefore never exactly potentials at all, only attentiveness and hope; hope in its most radical form: hope that only searches to see everything, and in that seeing perhaps glimpse something different from what it suspects it can see, something new. For Celermajer, "Precisely insofar as it is *useless*, suffering is capable of shattering the closure of the subject and undoing its theory of history."[32]

The process outlined by weak messianism is valuable in its capacity to separate us from progress and perfection and in so doing to allow new histories and paths through them to emerge. For Celermajer, these openings provide new access points for radical reconfigurations of ethics. In my view, these openings are also useful in their ability to allow new and different futures for political arrangements to appear. Indeed, as the following chapters will show, the messianic gaze of each of the films discussed here looks back at a particular type of catastrophe and with a particular type of wind carrying it forward. The destruction wrought by authoritarianism is on literal display in each of the films I analyze, and the immediately available, ready-to-hand solution in each case is always a form of market-oriented democracy dedicated to rebuilding in the name of a globally oriented market-driven future.[33] But these films disrupt this process. These films are in their own rights angels, *angeli novi*, four angels, each looking backward as it is swept forward through time. What each sees, and through cinema allows us to see, is destruction, always wreckage of some sort or another. But always within this wreckage there lies the spark of something new, the possibility for something remarkably different from this path that seems so immovable. These angels nonetheless stare and in so doing hold out for the hope of some new arrival, for this is always the hope of messianism: that something new might come. If, according to the approach of weak messianism, we only look hard enough, something new might arrive, some new vision, something else altogether.

In recent discussions of art cinema, "slow cinema" has become a topic of some emphasis, and each of these films fits to some degree into this category.[34] What this slowness produces in each of these examples is the space for thought, a product of the aforementioned gaze that constantly retreats even as it produces the possibility for renewal. This dynamic connects the films discussed here: each slowly examines a post-authoritarian world, but each also moves away before this examination can yield anything in particular. As does Benjamin's angel, these films look backward as time forces them forward, never quite capable or willing to make an attempt at altering the direction of the winds of progress, for any attempt to do so would require a gesture of authority, and would violate the dedication to openness that each of these films demands. This is, then, an impossible dynamic, an absolute negativity that withdraws from any meaning—no alternative can ever be offered here because these films must always move away from their own objects of discovery. This impossible negativity reorients these films, placing emphasis on aesthetics at the fore of the experiences that they produce. Indeed, it is this focus on aesthetics that orders these films' politics; the capacity of aesthetics to ask us to reorient ourselves to difference, to encounter and evaluate new kinds of objects and impressions, is in essence what brings these films most closely to their goals. Through this process the proposed hierarchy on which authoritarianism is predicated is denied and replaced with a new horizon of political potentials, one in which difference can be accounted for and politics renewed.

There is a danger here of stumbling into the argument that ambiguity in art escapes ethical considerations, a path that might lead toward the kind of *l'art pour l'art* claims that have been proposed and as often rejected since well before Benjamin's time. Martin Jay maps just this tradition, evaluating the myriad assertions that the aestheticization of politics has been used to justify brutal acts of violence by authoritarian regimes. He ultimately sums up these critiques by positing that "the disinterestedness that is normally associated with the aesthetic seems precisely what is so radically inappropriate in the case of that most basic of human interests, the preservation of life."[35] I will not go through each of the critiques outlined by Jay here, but it is important to indicate how I am thinking of the relationship between ambiguity, aesthetics, and authority so as to at least avoid criticism of my work for lionizing art for art's sake, which is surely not my goal. The ambiguous art in this study does not aestheticize politics; it does not work to justify brutal behavior by habituating it. Nor do these films render violence beautiful and in so doing justified in whatever their means or effects. The ambiguous art in this study does just the opposite: it dehabituates seeing and asks its audience to think with and about what is being displayed, but it does so with no mechanism for governing response.

Theodor Adorno's views on aesthetics and its relationship to society are likewise valuable to any discussion of ambiguous art. For Adorno, difficult, ambiguous art is valuable in its capacity to spur critical thought. According to Astradur Eysteinsson, for Adorno the reluctance of art to adequately communicate, its noncommunication, is exactly what makes it significant. For Eysteinsson, the key to Adorno's take on art is to be found in its capacity to elide rational thought: "[Art's] social context is that of an ever-expanding, monolithic capitalist society, moving toward a system of total exchange as well as total rationality, which is equivalent to absolute reification in matters of social interaction. It is a system in which the very notion of meaning has become wholly contaminated with the capitalist ideology of total exchange. In the face of this human debasement, art's basic mode of resistance is in a sense that of opting out of the system's communicative network in order to attack it head on from the 'outside.'"[36] From this vantage, art that refuses communication is uniquely capable of addressing society thanks to its being the only thing removed from it. In regard to my project, this is quite a compelling set of claims, but it is also troubling. It begs the question of how art is to be taken up, how noncommunicative, what I call ambiguous, art is to find its way back into politics without becoming rendered useless by the rational forces shot through with fallen, pernicious logics. For Adorno, "By avoiding contamination from what simply is, art expresses it all the more inexorably."[37] What Adorno describes is how art can get at reality with greater precision by virtue of its avoiding the, for him, detestable rational world; but how it can enter back into that world, not to mention change it, remains unclear. How ambiguous art can critique society is a significant topic here, but how these critiques can re-enter the world is my major theme.

This project also therefore shares a relationship with recent explanations of the role of politics as it pertains to cinema. In his book-length explanation of the cinema of Lars von Trier, Angelos Koutsourakis defines political cinema by putting it in relation to what he calls Brechtian and post-Brechtian systems. This approach is largely built upon the process of denaturalizing otherwise familiar images, and in so doing revealing their constructedness. For Koutsourakis, "Political cinema, which is committed to questioning and not just reproducing the reality outside the narrative, experiments with film language so as to negate a static and permanent understanding of social relationships and reveal their changeability."[38] The model deployed by Koutsourakis demands that an audience reflect on what they see, and as a result think critically about the images they encounter, and subsequently the world—inside and outside the cinema—that they experience. This kind of cinema is contrasted with that which does not reflect on its own means of representation; the latter—even when explicitly political in terms of its narrative—inevitably fails as a politics because, as Koutsourakis puts it, it "reduces both cinema and politics to plot/drama, without analyzing the language that connects the reality inside the narrative with the one outside of it" and in so doing "lays the grounding for the commodification and the institutionalization of the most radical ideas."[39]

Koutsourakis, however, is careful to move beyond this Brechtian understanding of cinema and into his post-Brechtian category. Post-Brechtian films likewise rely on this process of defamiliarization (what is elsewhere called "alienation"), but they do so with no recourse to a universal claim to truth, with no master narrative or voice that might provide order to these familiar made inchoate images. To Koutsourakis, "The politicization of form aims at liberating thinking out of a motionless understanding of social reality and presenting crises and contradictions, but unlike Brechtian orthodoxy it does not offer clear-cut suggestions on how to overcome the impasse. Put simply, questions are valorized over answers so as to provide an excess of negativity, which intends to make the audience productive."[40] This is to say that the post-Brechtian film describes the process of defamiliarization, but now minus the clarity provided by a preferred political outcome.

The films under discussion here therefore share quite a bit with Koutsourakis's post-Brechtian category. They defamiliarize recognizable spaces and things, and in so doing hope to activate them as politically available. But what this connection also helps us see is the fissures presented by a political project with no ordering system. That is, without the recourse to a clear political outcome—for Brecht, leftist politics—this process is easily undermined by its own reluctance to propose anything in particular. What, we might ask, might a post-Brechtian film help us to *achieve*? Like the films under discussion here, post-Brechtian cinema hopes for a new idea, some new concept, to emerge, but it lacks the directionality of Brecht's initial formulation.[41]

In *Cinema after Fascism*—a book that shares an obvious connection with this project—Siobhan S. Craig takes a stance on the status of postfascist cinema that illuminates this dynamic between clarity and ambiguity. For Craig, postfascist films "in part through formal experimentation and a refusal to naturalize the diegetic worlds they offer, question the very possibility of representation."[42] The fascist roots of representation haunt any process that might congeal into meaning and, as a result, "What they present to us is not the possibility of knowledge or an opportunity, however, illusory, to enact a unified self in the mirror of the movie screen; instead, they posit the bankruptcy of this wish."[43] And this is where my project differs from Craig's: I contend that these films do dream of a unified whole, another available and valuable world constituted by a knowable subject. But, and this is the important part, they cannot imagine how this whole might look. To do so would work to reaffirm a master voice, a unifying principle that might sweep up the mess that is the time of political transition. They are antiauthoritarian, and they even distrust their own authority. This is an optimistic cinema—too optimistic. What it hopes for it refuses to say. But it does hope for something. The central axiom of the tendency to turn to ambiguity in the face of political change, then, can be stated thus: for a cinema to be political it must shake us, bore us, bore into us, but never remind us of any particular claim. But this is an impossible dynamic, one that never quite yields to usefulness, and as a result opens itself to co-optation and reversal.

Richard Rushton also proposes a model for political cinema, but his pushes back against the Brechtian mode of formal alienation. For Rushton, much of the discourse surrounding political cinema fits into the possible capacity of films to free an audience to think in new ways about the images presented. This tradition is found in particular among the film theorists of the 1970s who broadly fit into the category of political modernism, and who are united by the method of ideological critique. For these thinkers, who will be addressed more closely in the coda to this book, cinema in the Hollywood tradition serves largely to render certain forms of identification "normal," and in so doing largely works to reinforce racist, patriarchal, capitalist, and otherwise destructive ways of seeing the world. Rushton summarizes the assumptions of ideological critique as follows: "Under the conditions of film spectatorship I might *think* I am master of all I survey, but in reality I am being mastered by the machine—the cinema machine—to which I am being subjected."[44] For these thinkers, particularly those of the influential 1970s journal *Screen*, the task of film criticism is to unearth the mechanism that disguises ideological content, to locate and indicate the ways that cinema can appear natural, and to explain how this feeling of normalcy actually works to reconstitute dominant and destructive forms of ideology. The goal of these thinkers, and indeed for Rushton much of the tradition of film theory in general, is to find ways of escaping the constricting system of subjectivity proposed by dominant cinema. The assumption of these theorists is phrased by Rushton as: "If I am distanced from myself and from what I see on the screen, then I will not be subject to what I see and thus will not be subject to myself."[45] In this mode, films that distance their viewers are lionized, and films that do not—particularly those based on the seeming naturalism of Hollywood cinema—are derided as tools of the dominant order.[46]

For Rushton, however, the potentials of emancipation and championing of openness that derive from the alienation of a demanding or otherwise disruptive cinema have become suspect because their calls for freedom always come at the expense of commonality. Ostensibly, for Rushton, this dichotomy ultimately favors atomization over something more like democratic action. Rushton therefore argues for a return to examinations of Hollywood cinema, for in this mode of cinema "characters are faced with choices and if they make choices which take their actions in one direction rather than another, then much of the time these choices and actions in some sense reflect the kinds of choices and actions we ourselves might make—at least potentially."[47] What Rushton is calling for, then, is a turning away from the global art film as constituted by the "seer" who watches herself in a kind of disjointed narrative composed of ellipses, and what he proposes in place is a return to the motivated narrative whereby one can understand the actions of characters in relation to one's own. What Hollywood cinema produces is a world in common, a universalizable, or at least verifiable, set of observations and actions based on the agreement indicated by the legibility of certain qualities and events. There is room for difference, of course, as accounted for by one's disagreement with the decisions represented by the film, but the fact that these films are recognizable is proof of a coherent community that is based on an equality of sense experience. It is because we can understand these films that they are valuable, as this understanding proposes some common world. What Hollywood cinema does, for Rushton, is propose a society—one we can alter, but one that is nonetheless shared, for better or worse. Rushton's concerns represent a long-standing tradition for defending Hollywood filmmaking, one that is most clearly constituted by the work of Stanley Cavell and that presents a counter to the supposed advantages of dissolution presented by political modernism.[48]

Where the present discussion departs from arguments as to the freedom of thought as activated through defamiliarization, though, is in its emphasis on the historical context of these films. The films under discussion here do not propose dissolution; they are prompted by it. The year zero of politics following the deposition of authoritarianism or totalitarianism is here what accounts for the dissolution on display. Whereas for Rushton the disadvantages of ideological critique arise from the fact that it proposes no common world, the films highlighted here are drawn from the basic assumption that the common is not only suspect for its carrying with it destructive ideological content, but also for the literal destruction it has so recently carried out. The common is what has wasted these landscapes, and the distrust of it is registered in the name of revolutionary politics hopefully achieved by way of the freeing of thought.

What this discussion adds to the discourse surrounding this divide between the triumph of difference and the appeal to a common is that it relies on historical circumstances to constitute its backing of freedom. Where I deviate from political modernism—a mode of film theory with which I surely identify in many ways—is in the recourse to a political solution. As Rushton notes, "Anything that a human might call freedom requires a particular understanding of what an individual is, as an 'achievement,' rather than something natural or automatic. What it requires is an understanding of what it is to be a subject so that the notion of subjectivity emerges as very much embedded in processes of historical change."[49] This project also argues that the dissolution of a generalizable subject can be a hindrance to political action, but it does so by examining films that have no available avenue for ameliorating this concern. This position is a product of historical events, and what I contend is that these filmmakers have responded to these conditions by trying to reflect the position of dissolution and devastation back to the audience in the hopes of reconstituting some new form of political engagement. For Rushton, what constitutes politics is a searching for and recognition of a world together, one that can be verified by all parties.[50] The films under discussion here also search for this goal. The problem they encounter is that the world that might be found is so far away.

Each of the films in this book slows down cinematic narrative and arrests us in and with aesthetic experience, the fixed gaze of the camera striving to produce slow explosions of difference. This experience of aesthetic difference is where these films find their strength. The hope of these films is that encounters with unforeseen arrangements will demand that we see something new, something that might shock us and in so doing ask that we think about what it is that we are seeing. The capacity of aesthetic experience to shake us from a ready-to-hand relationship to the world and to request that whatever new experience is presented be assimilated into what we already know is the heart of this argument. The slowness of these films then exacerbates this process, allowing aesthetic differences to emerge and to multiply. As we stare, unmoored from narrative and trapped within a film unwilling to say anything in particular to us, at the ruins—literal and otherwise—brought about by unchecked authority, we are asked only to occupy and support this gaze, to take it and to use it, to see anew and to be ourselves slowed, to be examined by it and to examine along with it. These films are the eye of the storm of political transition, the vantage from which we can see the events that otherwise seem to happen with such speed and rage. This is the task that finally renders the tradition of art cinema aesthetics consistent: it asks us to wait and see but never provides any order or operation for what is experienced.

This tradition finds its origin and its most valuable form in these moments of transition, where things are on the precipice of change and where, finally, cinema can offer a rejoinder to the tumult of the world outside the theater. These films and the aesthetic approaches that they employ slow things down and ask their audiences to think anew about the path by which the winds of history carry them, and ultimately whether the ready-to-hand solutions that appear are indeed the ways that are best to take. They do this, though, while adamantly refusing their own capacity to tell us what they think of what is happening. This is their gift and their curse, forever asking us to watch and to wait.

## Chapters

My first chapter focuses on Roberto Rossellini's *Germany Year Zero* in order to more specifically address issues of authority, authoritarianism, and ambiguity as it pertains to the conditions of post–World War II Berlin, all as borne out by the aesthetic approach of this film. What makes *Germany Year Zero* unique in regard to other neorealist films is the difficulty of its national origin; that is, its having been shot partly in a rubble-reduced Berlin and partly in Rome (where its interiors were largely filmed). This confused spatial arrangement likewise confuses the national identity of this film, and allows it to move from a form of nation building—the task that is often taken, by many accounts, in other neorealist films—to a larger discussion of the ways that cinema is capable of responding to authoritarianism; to the ways that the vacuum found at the center of the transition from authoritarianism to democracy can be extended and, perhaps, used to produce the space for new and novel political arrangements.

The second chapter builds on the first but focuses in particular on the developing aesthetic qualities of antiauthoritarian cinema. Here, I focus on post-Soviet Hungary, and in particular on Béla Tarr's *Sátántangó*, a seven-hour-plus film that was produced during the transition from communism to capitalism in Hungary. This film directly addresses the effects, hopes, and difficulties of this transition but, for the purposes of this book, it is the aesthetic approach of this film that is of particular value. Consisting of extremely long tracking and still shots, this film famously extends the time of each event to drastic and demanding proportions. Fitting clearly, and quite notably, into the slow cinema approach that has developed throughout the history of art cinema and has taken on new emphasis starting in the late 1980s, *Sátántangó* extends each moment and demands that its audience endure its extreme slowness. Given the context of post-totalitarianism, this aesthetic approach takes on new qualities. The endless watching and waiting here serves to extend the moment of transition, slowing its pace so as to allow—as with *Germany Year Zero*—new formations to take shape. Where this film differs from the first, however, is in the extreme demands it makes on its audience; indeed it asks them to suffer with and against *boredom*, a quality that it uses to disrupt the coherent divide between audience and film.

If *Sátántangó* and *Germany Year Zero* provide something of a relatively unified vision of post-authoritarian or post-totalitarian cinema, the topic of chapter 3, Hong Sang-soo's *Woman on the Beach*, presents a significant departure. Made well after South Korea's authoritarian government was deposed and replaced with a democracy, and indeed made in relation to—if not in the spotlight of—the immense rise in popularity of the South Korean "Hallyu" (the popular media explosion also known as the "Korean Wave"), *Woman on the Beach* deploys some of the qualities of post-authoritarian cinema outlined in the first two chapters, but it does so in such a way that greatly broadens the spectrum of what these qualities are capable of challenging. Through its restrained style, extended conversations, and deplorable-yet-reflective major characters, *Woman on the Beach* expands the degree of critique wide enough to reject democracy as readily as the other films reject authority. That is, this film disallows its own authority and introduces ambiguity in such a way as to reject meaning, but it is also careful to show the damages wrought by democracy when paired with capitalism, particularly as it regards the way that this combination incentivizes brutality and self-obsession. Democracy and capitalism, this chapter contends, greatly reward those willing to insist on their own genius, particularly if they are simultaneously willing to take advantage of the gaps in meaning and authority inherent to democracy. In this way, the film provides the position from which to evaluate how contemporary capitalism preys upon the same evacuation of meaning that both *Germany Year Zero* and *Sátántangó* celebrate. However, *Woman on the Beach* renders this critique from the position of having relatively recently experienced the damages of authoritarianism, and declines its return as an alternative. *Woman on the Beach* is perhaps the most radical of the films discussed so far, as it dismisses both authoritarianism and democracy in a single gesture, and yet, like *Germany Year Zero* and *Sátántangó*, provides no alternative—producing the most extreme emptying of meaning and perhaps subsequently the most hope of any of the films addressed here.

Finally, chapter 4 rearranges these conditions so as to discuss antiauthoritarian cinema made in a different context altogether. *Medium Cool*, directed by notable American cinematographer and director Haskell Wexler, was shot at and around the political actions surrounding the 1968 Democratic National Convention in Chicago. Consisting of both fictional and documentary footage, the film mingles a narrative familiar to contemporary global art cinema (particularly to those acquainted with Federico Fellini's *La Dolce Vita*) with footage shot at the convention. Taken inside and, more significantly, outside the convention venue, this footage clearly shows the intense police response and police violence that met the protestors. This chapter uses this film to discuss the potentials of antiauthoritarian cinema in a moment of perceived transition from democracy to authoritarianism. That is, it reverses the trajectory of the films discussed earlier and evaluates *Medium Cool* in the hopes of understanding the role antiauthoritarian cinema—and global art cinema more broadly—can play in combating the rise of an oppressive centralized power. *Medium Cool* is unique among these films in that it shows an authoritarianism taking shape within a democracy, and therefore provides a wealth of insights into how cinema is suited to respond to these conditions.

Throughout this examination, I strive to both articulate and evaluate a longstanding trend in global art cinema—a trend that has largely shaped postwar filmmaking. Furthermore, this book shows how the elusive qualities that are so central to global art cinema in fact constitute something of a coherent political project. These qualities circulate around both narrative and, particularly, aesthetic, ambiguity, which are bound up with multiple approaches to antiauthoritarianism. What I present here is not an exhaustive account of how art cinema responds to the rise and subsequent deposition of authority, but an explanation of how we might think of the role of art cinema under these conditions. A brief note on my own methods: this project will drawn upon, and indeed has already drawn upon, a wide range of theorists, some of whom disagree or are at times incommensurate with one another. The task here is to survey ambiguity in art cinema as a political category, and the approaches to this subject are varied. What I have tried to construct here is not a singular argument about politics and ambiguity in cinema, but a series of images of this issue that are composed of different and at times contrary perspectives. What is stable here is the subject, and this composite of different viewpoints strives to survey it from a number of angles, presenting ambiguity in cinema both as a positive project and also as a form of political cinema that is too easily co-opted or otherwise undermined.

What is provided here, then, is a system for thinking about these four films and, it is hoped, other films that fit into the art film tradition. This is then a project that locates films made in this mode and maps how we might think of them; it does not address *all* the films made in these conditions, but what it provides is a method for thinking about cinema and political transition broadly, and in so doing gestures toward the possibility for understanding the potentials of ambiguous cinema in relation to politics in general. Ultimately, the wager of these films rests upon the hope that in and through their ambiguity something new might be discovered, some new way of thinking about the changes that are taking place. This is the political potential of ambiguity.

# 1

# Authority Year Zero

## On *Germany Year Zero*

Chief Nazi propagandist Joseph Goebbels put heavy emphasis on the relationship between art and politics. In fact, he equated the two and fixated on the central role of art in constructing his idealized vision of a public unified around the Nazi Party. According to Goebbels, "Politics, too, is an art, perhaps the highest and most far-reaching one of all, and we who shape modern German politics feel ourselves to be artistic people, entrusted with the great responsibility of forging out of the raw material of the masses a solid, well-wrought structure of a *volk*."[1] The key to Goebbels's claims here is the relationship between raw materials and the solidity of a unified body or *volk*. For Goebbels, and indeed the totalitarian enterprise that he represents, the function of art (and for him its compatriot: politics) is to bring into being a cohesive and singular formation that can function and move with unified purpose. Indeed, as Rainer Stollmann observed, one of the primary functions of Nazi art seemed to be the unification of the inchoate actions and events of a national social life into a coherent and singular body.[2]

Given the context of the Nazis' attempt at constituting an art dedicated to a unified front, the postwar cinema of Roberto Rossellini—and in particular his *Germany Year Zero* (1948)—takes on a very particular series of significations. It was Rossellini's goal, this chapter contends, to undermine the centralized, unified, and ordered totalizing principle that Goebbels's vision relied upon, and to replace it with a return to the inchoate raw material that the Nazis so wished to tame and direct. As we will see, one of the ways that this goal is achieved is by confusing the boundaries of the national, as this film is uniquely situated to respond to the differing contexts of the Nazis and the Italian Fascists, never exactly equating the two but proposing ambiguity as a rejoinder to both arrangements.

Susan Buck-Morss also touches upon the dark pursuit of making a coherent and legible whole by way of art. Speaking of Leni Riefenstahl's seminal Nazi propaganda film *Triumph of the Will* (1935), Buck-Morss proposes the following: "The mobilized masses fill the ground of the Nuremberg Stadium and the cinema screen, so that the surface patterns provide a pleasing design of the whole, letting the viewer forget the purpose of the display, the militarization of society for the teleology of making war."[3] Again, a metaphoric body is built around a coherent, and in this case supposedly pleasing, series of images that unify a group of subjects and direct them to action. In opposition to this reading of Nazi cinema, *Germany Year Zero* proposes no pleasing pattern; it pushes the audience to pay attention to the circumstances on display but without the ordering function upon which Nazi cinema so heavily relied.

This chapter proceeds by introducing *Germany Year Zero* and exploring the openings to contingency and change that this film proposes. I then move to an analysis of the specific status of the ruin in Rossellini's film and the way it orients audiences toward a particular (and perhaps productive) relationship to time and rebuilding. I follow this discussion of the ruin with an examination of Karl Marx's own figuration of the inchoate masses and their historical formation into a public. Finally, the chapter ends with an investigation of the failures and drawbacks of Rossellini's dedication to openness—focusing in particular on the way that the intense marketization that has come to be called neoliberalism has aimed to take advantage of just these claims to potential and change. This final section is central to this study, as it marks the beginning of the countermove that occupies much of this book: while hopeful, the flight from order of each of the four films analyzed makes them particularly vulnerable to the forms of authority—now a kind of absent authority—that have arisen in recent years.

Ultimately, this chapter examines the most clear and direct example of a post-authoritarian response. It is, however, the nuance of this particular film and the ways that it navigates the circumstances that contributed to its stance against authority that highlight post-authoritarian cinema's unique systems for encountering and subsequently countering authority.

## Germany Year Zero

*Germany Year Zero* is the third entry in what is commonly referred to as Roberto Rossellini's war trilogy. Shot in Berlin and Rome, the film fits squarely into (what might be called the later portion of) the postwar Italian film movement known as "neorealism." At once an exemplary work (in terms of the aesthetic principles of the movement) and an outlier (in terms of its concern with coherent nation building) of neorealism, *Germany Year Zero* provides a glimpse of rubble-strewn postwar Berlin and fulfills much of the documentary/narrative promise that this movement hoped to provide. But what is truly valuable about this film, I propose, is its reluctance to present a particular answer to the problems that it poses. It is this reluctance that allows *Germany Year Zero* to question after not only what is to be done with rubble-reduced Berlin (and the postwar world more broadly), but also what might be valuable about occupying a space that is yet to be rebuilt, and occupying a politics that is yet to take form.

Marsha Landy defines the "major project" of neorealism as "the demystification of the ideology and practices of fascism."[4] Of this relatively loose grouping of postwar Italian films, she writes, "In their content, they explored authoritarianism; bureaucracy and power; violence; consensus and conformity; the oppression of workers, and passive obedience to tradition, the law, and the state."[5] Similarly, Angelo Restivo, borrowing from Benedict Anderson, argues that "neo-realism can be looked at as . . . an attempt to create an imagined community to replace the (equally media-constructed) imagined community of the fascist period," and he further traces the origin of this moment to "the collapse of a coherent national narrative that could be taken as meaningful by Italians."[6] Indeed Restivo argues that *Rome, Open City* (1945)—the first film of Rossellini's war trilogy—"allegorizes the birth of the aesthetic of reality out of the bankruptcy of the fascist aesthetic,"[7] and that "it is with *Paisa* [1946, the second film of the trilogy] that the new aesthetic seems to have achieved its full realization."[8]

Of course, after *Paisa* and at the end of this lauded triptych lies *Germany Year Zero*. Whereas, for Restivo, the first two films of this trilogy serve as "a picture of the nation in the radical process of *becoming*,"[9] *Germany Year Zero* relocates this process to a new setting, Berlin. Because of this move this film, rather than presenting a new imagined community, produces the moment before this imaginary, questioning after the damage that the process of imagining might entail. Its *demystification*, to return to Landy, surely concerns fascism (and authoritarianism more broadly), but it levels its critique not merely on the basis of the particular brutality of fascism, but on the unavoidable damage caused by the exclusions inherent in any political arrangement. This is not to say, of course, that the differences of particular political configurations are flattened, nor that democracy and fascism are equated here, but this argument does contend that the particular vision of the world presented in *Germany Year Zero* shifts the elsewhere-defined neorealist project from the re-evaluation of the Italian national identity to a more abstract politics that accounts for authority more broadly. The vantage of *Germany Year Zero*—looking backward as it does from a democratic moment only just developing to an authoritarian one—provides a unique opportunity to envision the potentials of a moment after an authoritarian regime but before democracy has fully arrived.

Whereas *Rome, Open City* and *Paisa* are clearly located within the borders of Italy and, as Restivo notes, concentrate on a particular reimagining of that nation, the locale of *Germany Year Zero*, Berlin, helps in expanding the purview commonly associated with neorealism (Italy) and the forging of a new national identity that it so commonly connotes. The unusual production process of this film—its interiors being shot in Rome and its exteriors in Berlin—serves to elide national specificity, and in so doing it depicts a world after authoritarianism, allegorizing the rubble of Berlin to broaden its perspective. This is a film, then, that allows for the thinking of political claims and political differences at the moment before they concretize into something new—the moment before a coherent narrative has taken hold. Its confused national allegiances help to extend the moment of contemplation by holding the ordering functions of narrative at bay and in so doing disrupting the possibility for a clear and singular reading. The asking of the question of whether this film is about Italy or Germany, then, guarantees a pause that the film strives to occupy, and the reluctance to produce an answer or a closure to this pause is one of the many systems whereby *Germany Year Zero* refuses to render a particular political project or solution.

But this reluctance to render a coherent answer to its political concerns also leads many to posit that Rossellini's work (broadly) is better thought of as apolitical. Indeed, Geoffrey Nowell-Smith notes that much of the praise for Rossellini, particularly that of the critics of the *Cahiers du Cinema*, lionized the director on the basis of "aesthetic grounds" and likewise found that "his neorealist trilogy stands aloof from the politics of the resistance and postwar reconstruction."[10] Nowell-Smith posits that, for those who find Rossellini to be lacking in terms of a politically or ideologically clear stance, "Rossellini's great misfortune . . . was to be born into a world that was too political."[11] Much of the grounds for this apolitical understanding of Rossellini's cinema are based on André Bazin's positioning of him as a "spiritual" filmmaker.[12] But Nowell-Smith contends that it is in fact Rossellini's political identity that unifies much of his work.

According to Nowell-Smith, Rossellini's politics are derived from a kind of intuition that does not adhere cleanly to the guideline of a postwar neorealist and antifascist left. For Nowell-Smith, "In a world marked by noncommunication, suddenly something would be communicated, a flash of insight enabling the audience to see what these characters themselves saw or maybe were too blind to see, or enabling the characters themselves to go forward from an impasse."[13] It is this idea of noncommunication that is punctuated by sudden clarity that, for Nowell-Smith, serves to guide Rossellini's project.

But my contention posits that Rossellini, at least in the case of *Germany Year Zero*, is concerned not with the spirit or power of communication, nor with the overcoming of its difficulties. What is invaluable about *Germany Year Zero* is its presentation of a damaged world that finds the very prospect of communication troubling. As Sandro Bernardi argues of the film's landscapes, "The picture that Rossellini tries to give us is that of a world destroyed, whose shattered monuments are no more than the ruins of a culture swept away by an infernal ambition."[14] The world on display in this film is one destroyed by what Bernardi calls "the catastrophe of ideology", a world ruined by violent attempts to orient meaning in a particular way.

Karl Schoonover argues that Rossellini's war trilogy—*Rome, Open City* and *Paisa* in particular—facilitate a politics by engaging its characters, and indeed its audiences, in a certain style of looking. For Schoonover, "By placing ocular witnessing at the center of their narratives, these films seem to transform seeing from a passive state of consumption into a powerful means of moral reckoning."[15] For Schoonover, this positioning engenders a specific global view, and in so doing "these films promote a universalist conception of human compassion by reifying a particular response to violence as the exclusively moral one."[16] Ultimately, according to Schoonover, this system solidified a particular response to fascism that unified divergent critiques and addressed them outward in the hopes of supporting the Marshall Plan and other forms of international aid.[17] Schoonover is speaking, though, primarily of *Rome, Open City* and *Paisa*. *Germany Year Zero*, I contend, defies this reification of a particular violence and instead leaves unarticulated the "appropriate" moral response to the horrors that guides the film. What differentiates *Germany Year Zero* from its predecessors, then, is that, through its spatial and narrative ambiguity, it refuses the figuration of a particular plea and instead asks after how to proceed at all. It does this by providing and attempting to expand an opening, an indeterminate moment, whereby actions (and responses) are left in stasis.

It is the promise of these kinds of stunted moments, these pauses, that this chapter focuses upon. I argue that this reluctance to forge a particular—this open-endedness and "apolitical" moment of noncommunication—serves as a politics all its own. Indeed, that the film refuses to render a particular future and insists instead on decay is exactly what makes it a political film, for through these pauses and disruptions *Germany Year Zero* casts doubt on those who might present a solution. It questions, that is, the authority that might propose to solve society's problems, and in so doing brings into light its own relationship to authority and the possibility (always fleeting) of democratic art. Authority is of particular historical significance to this film by virtue of its having been made in two countries, Germany and Italy, who were in the throes of a transition from, respectively, totalitarian and authoritarian systems to democratic governance. This argument is complicated, though, by the relationship that art (and the meanings that it at times enfolds) has to authority itself. What this film can be said to examine, then, is not only what to do when authority fails, but how a film can be made without reinstituting authoritarian logics.

## Authority

In the final shots of *Germany Year Zero*, Edmund, the thirteen-year-old protagonist of the film, looks out of what was formerly a window (and is now simply an opening) of the demolished building that he currently occupies. Across the street he sees the apartment where his family—along with a number of other families—currently resides. He watches as a small truck pulls up and quickly learns what it carries: a well-stacked collection of coffins. Edmund continues to look as those in the truck enter the building and then exit carrying another coffin; they place it with the others and then leave. After staring again briefly at his destroyed home, Edmund carefully hangs his jacket from an errant metal pillar. Disillusioned as he is, and as he has carefully been shown to become, by the prospect of existence in post–World War II Berlin, Edmund slides down the stanchion to a lower level of the building. He takes a final brief look again at his family's apartment; framed against the rubble, he is shown gazing out on a world that has been reduced to amorphous gray masses of concrete (see figure 1). He then closes his eyes and jumps from the building. The artificial

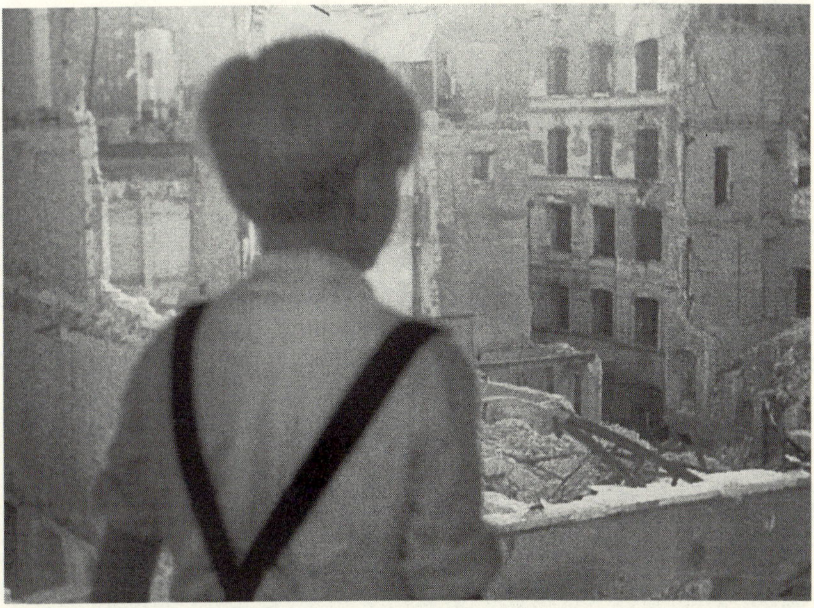

FIG. 1 Rubble-reduced Berlin seen over Edmund's shoulder in *Germany Year Zero*.

speed of his fall—created by the lowered frame rate of his descent—lends the jump a kind of oneiric quality that only aids in fostering the understanding of war-torn Berlin as a rubble strewn alien world. The film ends with his dead body being found a few seconds later by a woman walking by.

What Edmund had just witnessed, and what indeed caused him to make this jump, was his elderly father's body being removed from his apartment. Earlier in the film, Edmund, under the advice of his former teacher, had poisoned his bedridden father in the hopes of allowing his remaining family—himself and his two much older siblings—to more easily survive. The advice given by Henning when approached about what to do in the face of Edmund's lack of food and ailing father is as such: "Stop this now, you can't change things. Everything isn't about you and your selfishness. Afraid that daddy will die! Look at nature. The weak are destroyed so that the strong survive. *One must have the courage to let the weak die.*" The manipulative Henning, one of the few characters of the film who is directly associated with the Nazis, has presented the destructive rationale that this film strives to critique, but what here is emphasized are the parricidal and survivalist strains of his Nazi values. Henning's status as Edmund's former teacher and his allegiance to the Nazis—he had, according to some earlier dialogue, wished he had been more critical of Edmund's parents when they avoided entering him into the Hitler Youth—make clear his role as surrogate for the doctrines of the Nazi Party. But Henning, in addition to being a Nazi, is also presented as the only figure that provides Edmund with any system by which to survive in this world. Henning's reliance on black market profiteering and, disturbingly, what seems to be the collecting of young boys for the pleasure of the strange mansion owner who supports him escapes Edmund's youthful appraisal of this teacher, and so he heeds his advice and engages in a very deliberate plot to kill his own father.

The value system that Henning represents, though, comes unbound as the film progresses. Indeed, when Edmund returns to him after committing the murder in order to confess (or perhaps report back), Henning immediately becomes furious. "I didn't tell you to do anything, you little monster!" he yells as he slaps Edmund. "People will find out you've been coming alone here. I never told you to do such a thing! Never!" At this Edmund snaps and runs off, beginning the journey that will culminate in his suicide.

To proceed with my analysis of this exchange it is perhaps best to discuss authoritarianism in general. Writing in 1959 and concerned in many ways with the same historical moment as Rossellini, Hannah Arendt delineates the idea of authoritarianism, and in so doing brings to light her concerns for living in a world free of the hierarchical structures and calls to abstract sources of power that this governmental system entails. For Arendt, "The source of authority in authoritarian government is always a force external and superior to its own power; it is always this source, this external force which transcends the political realm, from which the authorities derive their 'authority,' that is, their legitimacy, and against which their power can be checked."[18] Thus it is always the call to some kind of outside and unquestionably correct vision of the world, be it supported by religion or, as in the case of the Italian fascists, tradition, which accounts for the authoritarian government's ability to render particular judgments.

Given that we are talking about a precise moment, it should be noted that Arendt differentiates Mussolini's Fascism from Hitler's totalitarianism. Arendt notes of Mussolini that "his one-party rule was in a sense the only one still intimately connected with the multiparty system [unlike Hitler's and Stalin's]. He carried out what the imperialist-minded leagues, societies, and 'parties above parties' had aimed at, so that it is particularly Italian Fascism that has become the only example of a modern mass movement organized within the framework of an existing state, inspired solely by extreme nationalism."[19] The distinction, then, is that Mussolini's Italy worked within the boundaries of a previously established state, pulling it toward its extremes but still relying on its formerly negotiated and relatively coherent outline.

By contrast, Arendt defines totalitarianism—which is, to her, exclusively a more recent occurrence and is better exemplified by the nations governed by Hitler and Stalin—by its cutting itself off from national traditions and providing a novel governmental form that is much less coherent. To Arendt, "Wherever it rose to power, it developed entirely new political institutions and destroyed all social, legal and political traditions of the country. No matter what the specifically national tradition or the particular spiritual source of its ideology, totalitarian government always transformed classes into masses, supplanted the party system, not by one-party dictatorships, but by a mass movement, shifted the center of power from the army to the police, and established a foreign policy openly directed toward world domination."[20] This difference amounts to a distinction between a call to tradition and the efficacy of one-party rule (for the authoritarian state) and the creation of a new (and terrifying) ideological unity (that of totalitarianism).

Likewise, there is a difference in structure for these two systems. Whereas totalitarianism is structured like an onion—with a leader at the center that is insolated by layers that, to the outsider, seem to decrease both in power and extremism the further they are from the center—authoritarianism is better described as a pyramid. For Arendt, the structure of authoritarianism is as follows:

> The pyramid is indeed a particularly fitting image for a governmental structure whose source of authority lies outside itself, but whose seat of power is located at the top, from which authority and power is filtered down to the base in such a way that each successive layer possess some authority, but less than the one

> above it, and where precisely because of this careful filtering process, all layers from top to bottom are not only firmly integrated into the whole but are interrelated like converging rays whose common focal point is the top of the pyramid as well as the transcending source of authority above it.[21]

Arendt's distinctions between totalitarian and authoritarian governance are helpful in revealing how Rossellini's film presents its Nazi characters in a way that brings to mind Italian authoritarianism more than German totalitarianism. Henning, rather than being drawn as a monstrous ideologue with an unflinching certainty in his beliefs, is presented here as wavering, weak, and primarily concerned with maintaining his bureaucratic position—he is a rung in a larger pyramidal arrangement rather than an absolute believer insulated by subsequent layers of certainty. This point is proved by the way that Rossellini presents the relationship between Henning and Edmund.

Henning is situated as a point of authority above Edmund, but through this diffusive structure Edmund still feels empowered to take the admittedly extreme action of killing his own father. His is not the ideological certainty of a denouncement-obsessed Nazi youth but that of a deindividualized fascist in search of an authoritative system through which to reproduce a hierarchical order. But Henning too is located within a greater power hierarchy because the mysterious wealthy pedophile for whom he works and whose presence is only ever in the periphery is constantly deferred to as the seat of authority for Henning's economic, moral, and even pleasurable concerns (it is hinted, after all, that Henning is a pedophile himself, although his desires are never clearly stated). There is, then, a deferral of authority in play here that signals upward, toward some greater source. Rather than presenting Henning to be a totalitarian, self-justifying "layer," he is only a transmitter of authority, and his cowardly reaction to Edmund's following his advice reveals that the seat of power that he at first appears to occupy is in fact centered elsewhere. This is not to say that Rossellini's film serves to draw the same distinction between totalitarianism and authoritarianism as Arendt, but that his understanding of this moment anticipates Arendt's claims. Whether this is a critique of Germany or Italy (or whether, for this film, these distinctions are even available) is not at issue here—and indeed the disassociation of these two countries from each other is complicated by the film's confused and confusing relationship to the national. Instead, Arendt's conception of authoritarianism is helpful because the film's depiction of power seems to match this arrangement in certain ways, and deviate from it in others (as we shall see).

Henning's failure to endorse his own advice is caused by the general failure of authoritarianism in this context. For Arendt, religion, tradition, and authority are the central triumvirate that holds together power structures—be they authoritarian, totalitarian, or democratic—and in the absence of any of these three factors the other two are inevitably brought into question.[22] Here all three are presented as unstable and failing, and this inability to maintain an interconnected structure for power leads to an instability at the heart of the characters' claims for a political future, and more specifically also leads to Henning's disavowal of his own views—his ability to justify the power structures that he attempts to reproduce fails him totally. His supposed authority is immediately revealed to be merely a series of hollow claims to a higher power that cannot call to any system of justification other than force.

For Arendt, though, a world without authority also creates a variety of problems:

> If I am right in suspecting that the crisis of the present world is primarily political, and that the famous "decline of the West" consists primarily in the decline of the Roman trinity of religion, tradition, and authority, with the concomitant undermining of the specifically Roman foundations of the political realm, then the revolutions of the modern age appear like gigantic attempts to repair these foundations, to renew the broken thread of tradition, and to restore, through founding new political bodies, what for so many centuries had endowed the affairs of men with some measure of dignity and greatness.[23]

For Arendt, this triumvirate grants politics a unified and, more importantly, externally justified body whereby meanings can take shape and decisions are subsequently made. But it must also be noted that this is one of the few moments in this essay where Arendt divorces the terms "authority" from "authoritarianism," as here "authority" seems to describe a process whereby decisions and actions are deferred to a higher figure in the hierarchical arrangement, and ultimately to a greater external authority with some capacity to render meaning. This arrangement alone, however, does not constitute authoritarianism for Arendt. This is to say that authoritarianism is a form of governance in which the systems of authority are monstrously oversized, but it is important to note that authority, for Arendt, is an essential structuring principle, without which *any* form of governance has no system for securing itself.

The crisis of the postwar world, for Arendt, is derived from the failure of these three factors to maintain a hold on the world and negotiate a transcendent system that justifies any set of decisions.[24] The revolutions that she speaks of fail to take hold, then, because they fail to establish anything other than an unmoored authority and are therefore always left open to the possibilities inherent in disagreement and difference.[25] For Arendt, without access to a stable claim as to a general truth authority can never find purchase. These fascist and totalitarian movements are attempts to create and centralize their own authority in response to these conditions, but their failures are revealed in the aggression with which they figure their claims to authority. They know, that is, that their truth claims are unstable. As a result, they overcompensate and, what's much worse, lash outward in attempts to reaffirm their authority through violence and control; this, to return to the film, is exactly how Henning operates.

## Ruins

*Germany Year Zero*, however, deviates from Arendt's pessimism toward the post-authoritarian world and instead presents the crisis at the end of authority as one valuable to the reformation of these countries. The failures of authoritarianism—and the horrors that have been unleashed by the ascension and subsequent destruction of this mode—are displayed here, and the potential effectiveness that this kind of authoritarianism had promised has been reduced here literally to rubble. In effect, *Germany Year Zero* argues the necessity of the crisis that comes at the end of authority by focusing squarely on the horrors that authoritarianism has wrought. One of the primary ways that it establishes this unique orientation to the absence of authority is through its emphasis—indeed its insistence upon—ruins. That is, the ruins that this film so often fixates on signify both the death of authoritarianism's dark promise and an uncertainty pertaining to how to rebuild. It is this dynamic that constitutes the politics of this film.

In order to address the ways that ruins function here to create a particular temporal relationship to the origins and effects of the war, it is necessary to begin by exploring how ruins were defined by two significant thinkers of the topic: Walter Benjamin and Georg Simmel. Benjamin discusses ruins in a number of ways; one of the less examined occurs in his essay "The Storyteller." In a moment where he addresses and describes the perhaps lost artisanal qualities of storytelling, Benjamin proposes: "One can go on and ask oneself whether the relationship of the storyteller to his material, human life, is not in itself a craftsman's relationship, whether it is not his very task to fashion the raw material of experience, his own and that of others, in a solid, useful, and unique way."[26] This is to say that storytellers are craftsmen of sorts due to their undertaking the basic task of forming from human experience something like a particular—Benjamin says "unique"—arrangement from the unorganized mass of unmolded experience. There are then two states at play in Benjamin's model for storytelling: first, the state of raw experience and, second, the story drawn from that raw experience and which arranges it into a coherent model. We can think of the quote from Goebbels that began this chapter, I think, as a kind of dark variation on this same process of forging particularities from an unmolded mass.

Benjamin continues by introducing a third state of experience so as to provide a useful extension for this model for storytelling. He says of this task of organizing experience into story: "It is a kind of procedure which may perhaps most adequately be exemplified by the proverb if one thinks of it as an ideogram of a story."[27] Benjamin brings in the figure of the proverb to further concretize the task of the storyteller, and it is this third model that produces the most clearly delineated explanation of experience. The story becoming proverb exaggerates the storyteller's capacity to distill experience down to a coherent singular principle, and Benjamin indeed goes so far as to connect these storytellers to teachers and sages for their shared capacity to present and communicate concepts.

It is in the figure of the proverb that we find the point of interest for this discussion. Benjamin continues: "A proverb, one might say, is a ruin which stands on the site of an old story and in which a moral twines about a happening like ivory around a wall."[28] He proposes this metaphor so as to account for the ways that a proverb, as an extreme distillation of a story, brings coherence to experience. But it is the figure of the ruin that complicates this passage. It is worth noting here that in German Benjamin uses the word *Trümmer*, which, in addition to "ruins" (in the German it is plural), can translate to "fragments" or "broken pieces." These alternative translations heighten the metaphor in use here as they parallel and in fact amplify the relationship that proverb has to story. The translation of "fragment" emphasizes the fact that the proverb is itself ruinous, its presence indicating that the story—and furthermore the experience that the story has filtered—has broken apart and what remains is a simplification that holds only a section of the shattered original. This distinction in fact tells us a lot about what, according to this logic, a ruin is: a fragment of a whole that holds within it some semblance of a former state but that fails, due to its highlighting only a single part, to account for the entirety. A proverb, according to this passage, is not simply a distillation, but a distillation that occurs only at the site of disintegration of a former structure, a ruin. The errand of this discussion is to reverse this analogy. The task at hand is not to ask "How is a proverb like a ruin?"—as indeed Benjamin proposes an answer to this question—but "How is a ruin like a proverb?," and, furthermore, what does it means for a ruin, or an image thereof, to take this status as proverb? Rossellini's *Germany Year Zero*, I contend, takes up this question.

In *Germany Year Zero* there are many ruins—one might even say that there is nothing but ruins—but in one particular sequence the status of the ruin as fragment is emphasized, and indeed complicated. When early in the film Edmund, acting under orders from Henning, is enlisted to sell a record to some allied troops, the damages caused by authoritarianism, and the necessity of never turning back, are made totally clear. In this scene Edmund demonstrates the qualities of the record by playing it aloud on a small player. The sounds of the record begin to echo through the ruined building that the group occupies. The speech by Hitler that the record contains initially confuses a small boy and his elderly guardian strolling nearby, who look up, surprised (see figure 2). The camera quickly leaves the particularity of this ruined building and a wide, high-angle shot of the demolished city is presented. A slow pan reveals more and more demolished structures, before finally tilting up toward the sky (see figure 3). The speech concludes with the need for the German people to "raise up," and the elderly man and child slowly walk off screen as Hitler is yelling about the victories that await.

This moment serves to concretize the film's pessimism toward the post-authoritarian world while simultaneously presenting the crisis at the end of authority as one valuable to the reformation of these countries. The failures of authoritarianism—and the horrors that have been unleashed by the ascension and subsequent destruction of this mode—are displayed here, and the potential effectiveness that this kind of governmental approach had promised has been reduced here literally to rubble. To return to Benjamin, what is distilled in these images and calcified into proverb is the terror that Hitler has unleashed. But not only the damage that has been done to Germany survives in these images. These ruins point toward the similar ruins produced elsewhere by this same conflict. These downed buildings and the hateful speech that here accompanies them point backward to the war to produce a relatively straightforward denunciation, and Edmund's later actions—particularly his poisoning of his ailing father at the behest of Henning in the name of securing more rations for his family—are also condemned in this gesture.

The juxtaposition of Hitler's speech with the wrecked buildings serves as an effective if obvious criticism of his monstrous actions, but also haunting this scene is the question of how to rebuild. Arendt ends her discussion of authority with a flourish: "To live in a political realm with neither authority nor the concomitant awareness that the source of authority transcends power and those who are in power, means to be confronted anew, without the religious trust in a sacred beginning and without the protection of traditional and therefore self-evident standards of behavior, by the elementary problems of human living-together."[29] This film asks what is to be done with *and* without authority, but it asks it from the perspective of the damage that efforts to reinscribe authority have wrought. That is, this film functions to force the confrontation that Arendt predicts; it asks how one is to see and understand the problems of living together, but it asks these questions from the literal view that Edmund occupies just before he jumps. His is the high-angle view that looks down upon rubble, the very rubble caused by others' attempts to answer these same questions through a reclaiming of authority—attempts that have led to levels of destruction never before seen. The title of the film asks where to go from here,

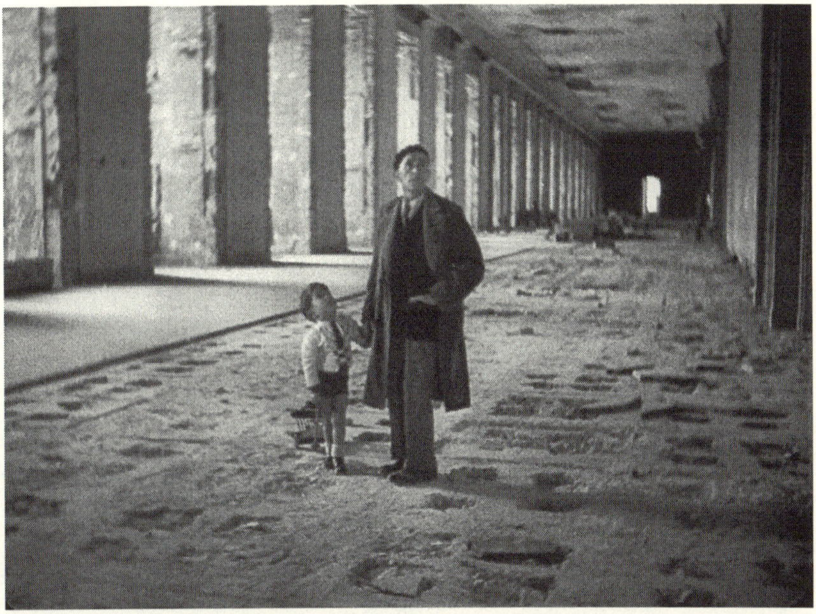

FIG. 2 A boy and his guardian look up, confused, when they hear a speech by Hitler played aloud in *Germany Year Zero*.

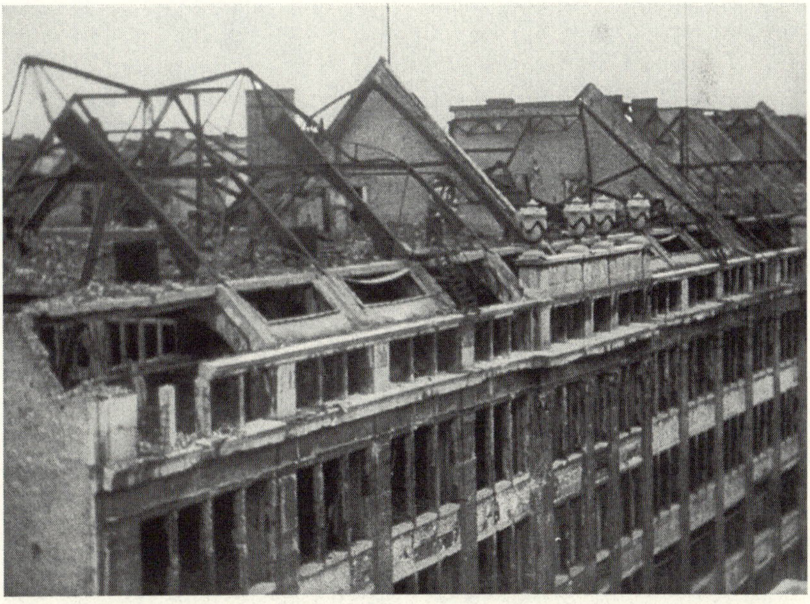

FIG. 3 Demolished structures shown as a speech by Hitler plays aloud in *Germany Year Zero*.

but the "here" is a zero point, a point where the triumvirate of authority, religion, and tradition has been broken apart from every side and has been reduced to the worthless waste of a misguided attempt to render the world coherent.

In light of Benjamin's metaphor, then, it becomes clear that something like ambiguity has crept into the easily read proverb that these ruins provide. The distillation and renunciation of Nazi ideas and practices is clear, but another quality of ruins and their coherence is that their relationship to a former glory no longer available necessarily stands them apart from the past. In light of the speech on the record and the wrecked buildings, Edmund's approach to reconciling his family's needs through a single brutal decision appears simply outmoded, a ruin as repellent as the views reproduced on the record. But what arises in these moments is the questions of humans living together, how to account for others, and how to produce meaning without re-erecting the hierarchies of authority that have here so recently been deposed. This is all to say that these ruins also point forward, albeit to an unfigured future. These bombed-out landscapes indicate how ruins, like proverbs, can point toward their own boundaries; in this case, how they can motion toward some other way of living together that can produce different kinds of structures and different forms of logic.

As Svetlana Boym notes, ruins tend to propose particular visions of both the future and the past. According to Boym, "Ruins make us think of the past that could have been and the future that never took place, tantalizing us with utopian dreams of escaping the irreversibility of time."[30] In the case of *Germany Year Zero*, in which asking what could have been is a dark question, it might be better to think of these ruins as signifying a dystopia avoided. The terrifying path so narrowly escaped figures the ruins here as a kind of relief; rather than cement the loss of a positive future, these ruins provide a devastating but in a way triumphant background. These are after all in a sense the ruins of fascism, so the future that could have been functions here as a kind of dark specter.

The ruins of *Germany Year Zero* never haunt us with former glories, and the only future they signal toward is one we are glad to have avoided. But within these collapsed spaces there persists human misery, and this film suggests that it is among these miserable circumstances that something like the ruinous potential of fascism can rise again—as best evidenced through Edmund's actions. This is effectively the dynamic of the film: a renouncement of the fascists and a kind of sad relief at the depths of destruction here in the heart of fascism. But accompanying this there is a profound sadness for those occupying what is no longer a hospitable space. The question that arises in light of this intolerable dynamic increases in line with the acceleration of Edmund's demise: What new structure can arise to account for what we have seen here? What kind of building can be built to house these characters, and how might it dissuade future returns to violence? This film is, of course, either unwilling or incapable of answering these questions. It instead suspends them, creating a gap that seems to interrupt the inevitable project of rebuilding by proposing and dwelling upon the question of how to proceed.

In a different examination of the subject, Benjamin touches upon the ruin's capacity to disrupt the apparent unity and coherence of historical progress: "In the ruin history has physically merged into the setting. And in this guise history does not assume the form of the progress of an eternal life so much as that of irresistible decay."[31] Given the context of Mussolini's obsession with the glory of Italy embodied by the splendor of the Roman past, the location of Berlin functions here as a deliberate riposte. There is no irresistible historical victory to Rossellini's Berlin, only misery, failure, and death.

It is precisely this gap between the question of how to proceed after such destruction and the subsequent production of an answer that this film attempts to extend. If the ruin serves here to provide a vision of history predicated on destruction rather than progress, then it also highlights the possibility of differing directions for renewal. For Benjamin, the ruin also serves as a reminder of the constructedness of history, of its failures and its missteps.[32] It is within this dismissal of inevitability and the potential turn to something radically different where optimism and opportunity persist.

Georg Simmel discusses ruins at length, and in particular highlights their capacity to produce a relationship to time that draws attention to the array of options available in the present. While Simmel distinguishes the ruins generated by human destruction from those that result from time and what he calls nature, elements of his ideas on ruins are nonetheless useful in the case of *Germany Year Zero.* According to Simmel, "Between the not-yet and the no-longer lies an affirmation of the spirit whose path, it is true, now no longer ascends to its peak but, satiated by the peak's riches, descends to his home."[33] Thus the ruin has the capacity to place those who encounter it in a position focused on a present defined by a fallen past and a failed future. By virtue of their serving as an emblem of a given course that has crumbled away—its goals exhausted or, as in this case, thwarted—ruins renew the possibilities for seeing and exploring different paths and methods for existence.

Simmel puts the moment of the ruin in opposition to what he calls the "fruitful moment"—the time when the riches that predate the ruin are still in sight.[34] The presentation of ruined spaces from *Germany Year Zero* exemplifies just this dynamic. The ruinous moment has arrived in full force, and here it is presented as direct counterpoint to the "fruitful moment" perceived—and indeed reproduced in the form of the record—by Hitler and his cronies. What takes shape, thanks to this juxtaposition, is a widening of possibilities. The vacuum created by such spectacular hatred and its resounding defeat creates a ghostly figure that gestures outward toward reconfiguration, but Rossellini refuses to give this figure form, to configure a path forward. What he produces in this absence of clarity and figuration is an abstract form of hope, the possibility for difference and change but a refusal of its direct representation.

Simmel continues with a final summation of his views on the ruin: "The past with its destinies and transformations has been gathered into this instant of an aesthetically perceptible present."[35] Rossellini strives to present his ruins as *all present*; they reject the past, its failures as well as its legacy, and refuse a future. This endeavor finds its full force in this sequence's juxtaposition of the mad grasp for glory (the speech on the record) and the destruction that it has produced (the ruins). In this moment past and future are simultaneously negated. For Simmel, in the ruin "such profound and comprehensive energies of our soul are brought into play that there is no longer any sharp division between perception and thought."[36] And it is this capacity to crystallize the present while simultaneously severing its relationship to the past and denying its future that is key for Rossellini's film. Here is a film in which all elements, including the very spaces that the characters occupy, transform experience into a unified question: How is one to proceed in light of this destruction? This is the proverb that has been produced, the experience that has been distilled. But it provides no easily assimilable message. *Germany Year Zero*'s quandary stands as unanswered and perhaps unanswerable, a coherent point that provokes no particular rejoinder. What Rossellini is trying to do is make *seeing* political, and it is his refusal of a cogent and particular approach that produces this condition. Hence the meaning of the title; this is year zero, where perception and thought collide.

## Freedom and Authority

But this film does more than thematize these concerns; it asks after them on the level of its very grounds for constructing meaning. That is, *Germany Year Zero* refuses to render any particular solution, it neglects to signal toward how "Germany Year One" might look, and it instead ends only with a further counter to the resurfacing of any authoritarian rule. Rossellini, the "author" to whom we might ascribe credit, recognizes his own status as authority and outwardly works to undermine this position.

This can be seen, for instance, in the long sequence where Edmund is seen at play in the rubble. Just before he admits his murder to Henning, Edmund, dejected, wonders the streets. During this extended sequence he is shown, first, in a long take playing near what appears to be a destroyed statue; the skeletons of buildings loom (as always) in the background. This image fades fully to black and another fades slowly in. This second image presents Edmund in silhouette, perhaps against a body of water, a dark railing separating him from the background (see figure 4). This grainy shot, combined with his

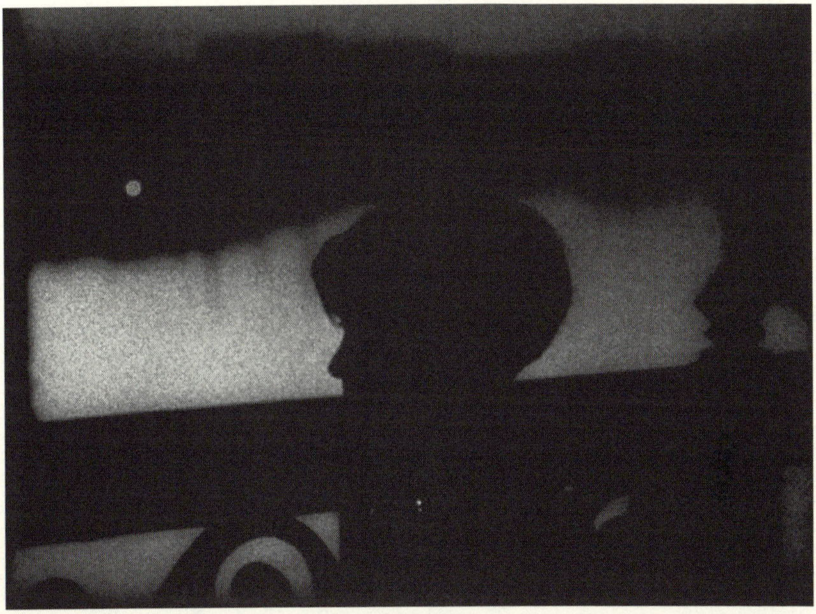

FIG. 4 Edmund in silhouette in *Germany Year Zero*.

playing in the rubble, presents a moment that gestures toward an interiority but refuses to provide it; it stands on the edge of meaning but keeps it at bay. This image serves to undermine its own meaning, negating any coherent understanding of Edmund's subjectivity by abstracting his understanding of the world—and even his own surroundings. The answer to Edmund's turmoil, the coherent concept that will provide him with a way to understand the world and to again take part in it, is refused. Instead, what is presented are images that tend toward the impossibility of meaning, for meaning here would inevitably come from an authority, and it is exactly authority that this film so vehemently denies. Rossellini's film, then, strives to connect the authoritarianism of Mussolini's Italy with the authority rendered in any act of authorship, and it is through this process whereby this film begins to critique the very systems of interpretation that render art coherent and capable of presenting meaning.

The restraint in *Germany Year Zero* here is indicative of the film's greater attitude toward resolution, for the presentation of a particular meaning would also serve to assert a new master of meaning, and therefore a figure of authority. Given that this is a film about the damages authority can inflict, to present a solution (a positive future or even a dystopic hellscape) would be to seize a role that would undermine the film's central concerns. This presents, of course, an impossible conundrum: How can one speak without presenting a masking that disrupts other avenues of thought? How can one live, to return to Arendt, in a political realm without any universalizing, self-evident truths?

In a remarkable moment of his *Capital: A Critique of Political Economy*, Karl Marx encounters this same problem. In a striking chain of declarations, Marx digs into the systems through which capitalism serves to normalize and subsequently perpetuate itself. By outlining a series of increasingly brutal laws that, in essence, illegalized "vagabondage" in England and France—a process through which labor became instituted as morally, as well as economically, productive—Marx broaches a discussion of minimum and maximum wages. Imbricated throughout this discussion, though, are some of Marx's more significant thoughts on the linkages between productive labor and the will.

Marx begins these thoughts by excoriating the historical developments that led to some of capitalism's now invisible disciplinary maneuverings: "Thus were the agricultural folk first forcibly expropriated from the soil, driven from their homes, turned into vagabonds, and then whipped, branded and tortured by grotesquely terroristic laws into accepting the discipline necessary for the system of wage-labour."[37] Here Marx sums up, in rather fiery terms, the process that the laws he has just described delineate. That there is a historical trajectory that has culminated in the workers being forced into this position is no surprise, but the system by which this was accomplished—the process whereby the workers were forced to "accept the discipline"—is of particular import. Marx continues shortly thereafter, "The advance of capitalist production develops a working class which by education, tradition and habit looks upon the requirements of that mode of production as self-evident natural laws."[38] Herein lies a fragment of a discussion of how capitalism comes to constitute a particular subject. That capitalism is a system that reinforces itself, first, through laws and, second, through the trace of these laws—now forgotten—into an arrangement of tradition and habit is what allows this system to perpetuate itself without need for force. As Marx contends, "The organization of the capitalist process of production, once it is fully developed, breaks down all resistance."[39]

Marx notes that "direct extra-economic force is still of course used, but only in exceptional cases."[40] The rest of the time, the self-evident codes of conduct that this schema has produced in effect keep everything in check, and they minimize the need for force or, really, any strenuous intervention. However, during earlier stages of capitalism, Marx is careful to note, this self-evidence is not yet set and it is up to the state to use force to institute these future norms (as in the case of the laws against vagabondage mentioned above).[41]

Of particular importance to this discussion, though, is Marx's use of the term "free and rightless" (*vogelfrei*) to describe those who initially provided the conditions that these laws correct. The free and rightless proletariat are those who, having been recently forced from their agrarian practices but not been absorbed into the urban workforce, are free insofar as they are "outside the human community and therefore entirely unprotected and without legal rights."[42] The task of these laws, then, was to quantify these new editions to the urban setting and to provide them with a directive that yielded increased production.

*Germany Year Zero* explores this same moment; what is to be done, it asks, with a subject who occupies a space outside the strictures of this forgotten code, and how can a society rebuild from a zero point where these restrictive systems no longer hold sway. What Marx's vision of the free and rightless affords this discussion is a system whereby the political concerns that I located in Rossellini's work can take form. For Marx, of course, the free and rightless are a grouping of people that existed before their assimilation into the capitalist system. This assimilation takes the form, in Marx's account, of a set of arbitrary and forgotten laws that call to an a priori and stable set of external values. Marx's absorption of this group into capitalism assumes the hierarchical logics that Arendt's account of authoritarianism supplies. For Arendt, the absence of authority brings about a range of problems for modern society, but for Marx this absence brings about a very different set of concerns.

The free and rightless are free in the sense that they provide an "outside" to not only capital, but also society in general. The agrarian societies that the free and rightless arose from were not the privileged holders of an otherwise impossible freedom; instead, the "freedom" that this state entails arose only as a result of being forced halfway into a new relationship to governance and economics. That is, the "freedom" of this state serves as readily as a restriction as it does an advantage. The other half of this term, the rightlessness, clarifies this dynamic. The free and rightless are free in the sense that society has no system to account for these individuals and their actions, and this freedom means that they are also restricted from engaging in the social contracts that might allow these people to subsist. Marx is positing, then, that the outside of capital, the position of the free and rightless, is no viable system of escape, for any freedoms that it affords are always tempered by the inability to guarantee any consistent social arrangements.

To be free and rightless is to potentially occupy a transitional state. That moment *between*, where a figuration is yet to take place and where the people that occupy this state are not yet absorbed into the capitalist (or any other) apparatus. What the free and rightless represent is a kind of indeterminate grouping that can recombine in any of a variety of formations. For Marx, of course, the assimilation of the free and rightless into capitalism was a brutal and deleterious process, but the persistence of this transitional moment also implies the potential for a return, a new transition where new configurations are available.

The term "free and rightless" then serves a double purpose here. On one register it reveals how the brutal and destructive effects of capitalism directly and deliberately, in Marx's account, operate to generate a subject position conducive to capitalism. But it also grants a vision of an indeterminate moment where any of a number of potentials are available. In this moment, though, the advantages that the ability to organize and decide provides—perhaps the advantages granted by hierarchy and authority—are erased, and the rights that the social order might produce are hollowed out and rendered ineffective.

This state between is exactly the zone that Rossellini's film strives to occupy. Where the ideas that *Germany Year Zero* presents deviate from those of Arendt and Marx, then, are in its attempt to extend this moment, to think through the indeterminate stage and try to sustain the very space of transition. Before a space can be rendered knowable, before, perhaps, foreign aid can arrive to help in determining how Italy or Germany is to be reconstructed, before the logics of authority can take hold, there is that moment where no course has yet been taken. This time, this pausing and taking a breath, is what Rossellini's film attempts to figure, and this attempt to extend this pause comes via Edmund's consistent failure to constitute an understanding of the world. To be clear, this in-between moment coincides with the postwar world at its most desolate (the time, in very real terms, before help in whatever form has arrived), but it is also the moment brimming with the most potential. This dynamic exactly accounts for this film, and the project of antiauthoritarian art cinema as a whole. To be free and rightless is exactly the position of greatest opportunity. The world is aglow with openings for renewal and previously unforeseen configurations for governance, but there is no mechanism for making these things come into being. Furthermore, those occupying this position are easily subject to pernicious modes for order that have access to the powers of authority, either through exterior pressures or the ready-to-hand logics that might prematurely put an end to all this openness.

When Edmund carefully hangs up his coat, slides down the stanchion, and jumps to his death, this delay is ended. A decision has been rendered, and his course for figuring the world has been (rather pessimistically) determined. But death here is not simply one of a number of outcomes: it is the only option that seems to persist in resisting. After Edmund kills his father he asks, "Is he free now?" What he was asking after, it now seems, was whether the course that Edmund himself had tried—and failed—to navigate had finally been negated; whether the authority that Edmund had attempted to muster had really finally been disproven; whether the Nazi logics that Henning and his actions represented had indeed finally been separated from the authority they claimed to hold. Was he free to remain free and rightless?

The starts and stops that the film presents, its criminal logics and cowardly missteps, seem to signal toward an attempt to find (or refind) some way to shape the world, but its refusal to figure a positive future (there is no heroic martyr here) stands as a direct attempt to think through the democratization process that awaits. The pessimism that concludes this film signals the degree of destruction that must come before any extensive rebuilding, as well as the agony of living free and rightless. To assimilate into an arbitrary arrangement that will, far in the future, come to account for meaning, or to die and, hopefully, persist in a freedom outside of the social is the decision that Edmund is forced to make, and it is this decision, at the moment when it is more available than ever, with which this film is concerned.

The difficulties that a forthcoming democracy holds—where and how decisions are to be made and what actions are to be taken—haunts this film. The discovery as to whether the world can persist without authoritarian logics and how one is to find meaning in this landscape is the task that occupies Edmund. But to make meaning on film also implies some knowledge that is otherwise unavailable, some authority to which the film's makers have some kind of access. For *Germany Year Zero*, the question posed is not only how to proceed in a world without authority (and whether such a task is possible), but also how to make art that can attend to and extend the tenets of democracy, a difference that distinguishes Rossellini's project from that of Arendt and Marx. The solution, here, seems to come via a return to ambiguity, an unwillingness to take a stance or to render a solution. This film, I contend, participates in an active engagement with just these questions. What it means to stop at the moment before decision and whether one can proceed in this stoppage is the question at hand, and the answer as to how meaning is to come and fill these empty streets again is what this film is so generously unwilling to provide.

## The End of Openness

But what becomes visible thanks to our remove from the world of 1948? If we take the goals of this film to be radical change by virtue of the creation of an opening for the constitution of something remarkably different, then it is difficult to call this film a success. The opening that Rossellini here strives to provide and the refusal of figuration that he heroically produces never did generate radical difference. Instead, what came to fill in the openings and gaps of Rossellini's year zero was simply another form of authority, another set of troubling ready-to-hand logics, defined not by a unified solidity and ease of identification but characterized instead by fluidity and an ability to escape opposition.

While Rossellini's approach as outlined in this chapter might well serve as a coherent and perhaps effective response to a calcified and crushing authority, it might likewise might be called shortsighted in regard to the potential formations of capitalism that could, and indeed did, begin to form in the years following the war. What Rossellini did not foresee, that is, is the possibility of a kind of capitalism that counters—or indeed thrives upon—the openness and uncertainty that his film proposes.

In *Liquid Modernity* sociologist Zygmunt Bauman outlines the ways that dedication to openness and contingency has been reabsorbed into the logic of capitalism. For Bauman, many of the oppositional thinkers of the first half of the twentieth century, in particular those unified under the loosely arranged banner of "critical theory," were writing against the overwhelming terror of totalitarianism and authoritarianism. These governmental and institutional arrangements were constituted by solid controlling systems of thought set upon shattering individuality and difference, and included a range of foes that extended from the fascists to the Fordists, forces that sought to establish control of society in the name of efficiency and profit.[43]

Rossellini's film, as this chapter has shown, is exactly in line with this mode of critique. *Germany Year Zero* strives to cede control, and in so doing to withstand the onslaught of hierarchical order and authority that the Nazis and Fascists sought to impose. Rossellini's cinema stands in clear opposition to the climate that culminated with World War II, what Bauman calls a modernity defined as "a sworn enemy of contingency, variety, ambiguity, waywardness and idiosyncrasy, having declared on all such 'anomalies' a holy war of attrition; and it was individual freedom and autonomy that were commonly expected to be the prime casualties of the crusade."[44]

But the authority that developed in response to attacks like those of Rossellini harnessed for its own advantages just the kinds of relationships to contingency that Rossellini lionized. Far from the old logic of stopping to build a moment and a movement, Bauman's new postwar modernity is that of the fresh beginning that promises no particular outcome other than open potential and contingency. Bauman's modernity is that of the "collapse . . . of complete mastery over the future—so complete that it puts paid to all contingency, contention, ambivalent and unanticipated consequences of human undertakings."[45] And it is in this regard that this new modernity and *Germany Year Zero* overlap; these are both oriented toward freedom and contingency, toward an inchoate becoming that holds within it the possibility for something new.

Bauman's modernity, however, uses these openings to produce something entirely counter to Rossellini's hopes, and indeed critical theory's championing of justice and equality. According to Bauman, the major political platform of this new modernity is "the deregulation and privatization of the modernizing tasks and duties. What used to be considered a job to be performed by human reason seen as the collective endowment and property of the human species has been fragmented ('individualized'), assigned to individual guts and stamina, and left to individuals' management and individually administered resources."[46] This characteristic of contemporary modernity—what is elsewhere called neoliberalism and is qualified as the thrust for total privatization of the economy and the subsequent tendency of the logic of rationalization and privatization to come to account for human decisions in every aspects of life—preys upon, and is indeed uniquely suited to consume, just the kinds of hopes that *Germany Year Zero* encapsulates. The openness and freedom to choose and reconfigure that serves as the heart of Rossellini's film is built on the unsteady trellis of chance and difference, and the neoliberal logics of privatization, individualization, and uncertainty transform this openness into an opportunity to produce a lifestyle of individualistic, flexible labor under the destructive rhetoric of freedom.

As Bauman notes, it is this rhetoric of freedom that has in fact come to constitute the available set of outcomes for political discourse. For Bauman, this change in contemporary society "has been reflected in the relocation of ethical /political discourse from the frame of the 'just society' to that of 'human rights,' that is refocusing that discourse on the right of individuals to stay different and to pick and choose at will their own models of happiness and fitting life-style."[47] This is not to say that the projects of human rights are not worthwhile, but that they are consistently being sectioned off from projects that pertain to society's capacity to change things for the good, a system that has been deliberately developed to counter political approaches predicated on contingency and change—ostensibly, and by many accounts minimally, appeasing calls for change without radically altering the grounds of society. This creates an arrangement whereby the responsibility of government is restricted to acknowledging and, at its most aggressive, helping society at large to recognize the rights and values of previously alienated or unrecognized individuals. What is lost in this—at times very noble and valuable—process is the hope that there is something other than marketplace unity as the endpoint for any and all identities. The term "human rights" implies a world where every human is free to take part, but here it loses hold of the idea that the grounds of society are contestable. The openings that Rossellini provides, then, are in the contemporary moment reabsorbed into a capitalist system through acknowledgment, and in this process stripped of their revolutionary wish.

The freedom to choose that *Germany Year Zero* offers—the ending of authority signifying the opportunity to rebuild society in any of a number of new ways—with its adamant insistence about freezing this moment of choice and projecting it back to an audience, strived to produce a cogent and valuable instant of freedom, but it is this very rhetoric of freedom that has since become suspect. In the eyes of the statistics-based society that has developed after the moment of unbound authority that culminated in postwar cinema, "the loose, 'associative' status of identity, the opportunity to 'shop around,' to pick and shed one's 'true self,' to 'be on the move,' has come in present-day consumer society to signify freedom."[48] The freedoms that flowered in the wake of Hitler and Mussolini, the freedoms that accompanied such misery, which haunted

Edmund to his death and which through the image of the ruin proposed an infinite range of possibilities, are maintained and in fact encouraged under neoliberal capitalism. In this new world Edmund's choices remain his own; he can be a Nazi or a progressive or something else entirely. He can be all of these things and none of them, as long he does not demand any sort of rethinking of the grounds of society: the market. What is particularly frustrating and pernicious about this new arrangement is that, while this capacity to radically reshape the structure of one's identity at any moment benefits from and reinforces the long-fought-for freedoms of individual expression, it is just these freedoms that have now been co-opted by the new authority of market logics. Ultimately, in any of Rossellini's fissures and openings the first thing to come in and fill the gaps must, in the contemporary moment, always be individualized, market-oriented freedom, for it is just the idea of "freedom"—indeed the central idea of Rossellini's quest—that has already been corrupted.

The world that has overtaken the ruins so prominently figured in Rossellini's film has built no monument to itself, for it must slip away from any calcified formations. This is a world where the figures of authority have ceded control, as Rossellini foresaw and indeed tried to facilitate. But what has taken the position of the traditional authority is no less pernicious, and many times more elusive. What has filled in the openings that Rossellini sought is a market-oriented logic unmoored to tradition and seemingly immune, thanks to its liquidity, to contestation. Bauman places the roots of this liquidation as far back as Marx, but Rossellini's approach and context crystallize the problem of fighting this new modernity. Rossellini's film sought, to use Bauman's terms, to "melt the solids" of concretized hierarchical order in the hopes of allowing other formations to emerge, but, as Bauman notes, "The melting of solids led to the progressive untying of economy from its traditional political, ethical and cultural entanglements. It sedimented a new order, defined primarily in economic terms."[49]

It is this logic of pure economy that haunts the style and narrative of Hong Sang-soo's films, which are discussed in chapter 3, but its origin is here made visible in Rossellini's cinema. If it is a response to authoritarianism that generated these circumstances, then indeed the rejection of authority present in Rossellini's film created exactly the conditions upon which neoliberalism preys. The economic logic that fills the gaps of freedom and any openings to change is furthermore nearly impossible to locate. Rather than the monumental structures of authoritarianism, the neoliberal logics that came to respond to its collapse function as an "absentee-landlord," looming just around every corner but always just out of sight, unconcerned with the conditions of its property except insofar as it effects the bottom line.[50]

This new modernity is reliant on the perpetual disappearance of its own authority; it refuses a structured position but always lurks at the bottom of any arrangement, consistently undercutting the possibility for organized critique by constantly obscuring the object that would be opposed. If *Germany Year Zero* refused to figure its oppositional stance in the name of contingency, it neglects to account for the possibility that the inchoate unfigured void that it champions could come to reinscribe the misery and oppression that had previously been the domain of unbridled and obvious authority. But the question of how to oppose this unfigured mess remains very difficult to answer. Rossellini's heroic resistance, his refusal to name a way forward or to figure an opposition to be dispatched, tragically finds itself complicit with the wishes of the new modernity: openness and indecision have become a tool for a new kind of oppression.

Given the hindsight of some seventy years, Rossellini's bind feels nearly impossible to overcome. On the one hand his project—melting the rigidity of authoritarianism in the name of the possible—is a valuable one, and his insistence on refusing to figure the path toward a more just society is a cogent and valuable intervention that makes sense given the contemporary context. The downside of this approach, and what time has revealed to us, is that the forces of consolidated capital and inequality are all too capable of reorganizing and taking hold of these openings—a process that seems to have taken place and indeed continues to accelerate in the time since Rossellini's film.

Moving forward just some forty-five years, to just after 1989 and the end of a clear alternative to capitalist democracy, provides a striking example of a filmmaker attempting to produce a similar set of themes. The post-Soviet world—and the particularities of Béla Tarr's disjointed and unidentifiable representation of Hungary—provides a valuable vantage from which to probe problems similar to those examined by Rossellini, now with an eye turned to the aesthetic response made available by the failure of a new, but not altogether unrecognizable, form of authority. This is the subject of chapter 2.

# 2

# The Image That Waits

## On *Sátántangó*

Forty-six years after Rossellini's neorealist trilogy concluded—a 46 years that spanned a heated period of conflict between economic policies and their often brutal representatives—Hungarian filmmaker Béla Tarr returned to some of the central themes of *Germany Year Zero* (1948). The cinema of Tarr, who was equally concerned with the project of resisting authority, produces two important expansions of Rossellini's project. First, Tarr's cinema—and in particular *Sátántangó* (1994)—extends, in a quite literal sense, the aesthetic qualities that support my claims about antiauthoritarian art cinema. The takes in *Sátántangó* provide unbroken and extended swaths of time that generate a kind of waiting that pushes forward the political approach—apolitical approach? political "inapproach"?—that I located in Rossellini's film. That is, Tarr's long takes serve to *extend* the refusal at figuration that Rossellini demanded. These takes crystallize the aesthetic dimension of these two directors' relationship to possibility, and indeed possibility's failures.

The second of Tarr's additions to cinema's capacity to reject authority arises from the time that has passed between these two films. If *Germany Year Zero*—somewhere in its unfigured cone of potentiality—still proposed as a possibility the capacity for communism to aid in a rebuilding that might lessen misery, *Sátántangó* jettisons this possibility entirely. This is to say that, having survived it and its seeming conclusion, Tarr's cinema rejects communism. This difference is responsible for the hopelessness and confusion that underwrite *Sátántangó*, but as the strength and scale of its hopelessness increases, this chapter contends, so too does the luminosity of hope—its light seeming to intensify as the availability of a new and better outcome recedes.

This chapter begins by outlining *Sátántangó* and some responses to it. It then briefly explores a connection between the functions of the long take proposed by film theorist André Bazin and Tarr's own views on habituated vision. It proceeds by discussing the specific significance of this film in regard to the historical circumstances of post-authoritarian Hungary. Next, it addresses the concepts of waiting and boredom: their political potential and their specific relationship to this film. The chapter then transitions into a discussion of two recent books on Tarr's cinema and how these provide different directions for analysis, ultimately exploring how politics interacts with waiting and proposing possible paths for and barriers to political change. Finally, this chapter concludes with an examination of the ways that hope and waiting interact, and the forms of action that this film both produces and denies. In all, this examination of *Sátántangó* extends the argument I wish to make about the realization of an antiauthoritarian cinema by way of ambiguity, and does so through an analysis of the aesthetic approach and historical context of this unique film.

## Ambiguity and the Long Take

In the foreword to *A Companion to Eastern European Cinemas*, an edited collection on film in post-Soviet Europe, Dina Iordanova outlines the two common understandings of the paths taken by post-Soviet countries in the wake of the revolutions of 1989. According to Iordanova, "Some of us, mainly based in the social science disciplines, maintain that, once emancipated form Soviet tyranny, the countries of the former Soviet bloc promptly readjusted their political and economic course and soon caught up with the democracies of old Europe, joining a position where they always belonged, historically and culturally. Others, mainly from the humanities camp, focus their attention on the hiccups, the failed enthusiasm, and the disillusionment."[1] The function of this chapter is to forge a link between these binary appraisals of post-Soviet Europe and to explore how these two understandings are functioning in relation to each other. Indeed, this chapter argues that these hiccups in what would be an otherwise continuous transition serve not only as a symptom of the re-entry of post-Soviet nations—and for my purposes Hungary in particular—but actually allow a space for thinking through the function and formation of the democracies in question, and subsequently democracy in general. This chapter therefore contends that it is these hiccups and failed enthusiasms that are vital to the task of political transition, as the interruptions they provide allow for a rethinking of the change underway. What *Sátántangó* does is extend these interruptions, and in so doing the time of indecision. The key to these hiccups and failed enthusiasms is their relationship to *waiting*—the moment just before figuration when the particularities of action are yet to fully take form.

In order to address these ideas, I focus on Hungary in the early moments of post-Soviet transition. Tarr's *Sátántangó*, released in 1994 but produced throughout the early 1990s, allows the kinds of waiting that generate the disillusionments that Iordanova describes. It produces these moments, though, not in the hope of generating a nostalgia for a lost Soviet past but in an attempt to slow the transition at hand. The goal here is to arrest the momentum of change, asking the film's audience to contemplate one last time the coming democracy in this moment just before it enters into view.

According to Iordanova, "The more effectively one deals with change, the more likely one is to thrive, management wisdom has it. Just like the natural world, societies and individuals encounter changing conditions that are beyond their control; successful adaptation to change is crucial for the success of the enterprise."[2] Iordanova labels this attitude to change "change management," and argues that it describes an "approach to shifting individuals and groups from a current to a desired state, empowering stakeholders to accept and thrive in an environment that has not settled quite yet."[3] *Sátántangó* produces a disruption in this process of change management; it deals with change badly. Without any return to its totalitarian past, this film critiques the adaptation process that looms in Hungary's future. The "desired state" that here is being acquired is, throughout this film, being put into question, but in such a way that figures no particular alternative.

Throughout its over seven-hour unfolding, *Sátántangó* follows, among other things, the progression of a group of roughly a dozen occupants of a rural Hungarian town. These people, members of something like a community farm, pool their money and give it to the mysterious Irimiás (Mihály Vig) in the hope that he will find them a new place to live and work. The film is often thought to serve as a thinly veiled allegory for the collapse of communism and the failed (or failing) promise of capitalism,[4] and Irimiás best embodies this reading: he disappears and reappears throughout the film, propelling the actions of (some of) the townspeople with what turn out to be false promises and corrupt negotiations. There are, of course, various asides—the all-too-authentic torturing of a cat at the hands of the child Estike (Erika Bók) serving as the most notorious—but the plot of the film moves in such delayed sputters that it very quickly becomes difficult to map any particular reading onto the characters' actions.

What is perhaps most often noted about *Sátántangó* is the length of its takes, which average out at about two and half minutes.[5] *Sátántangó* has become famous not only for its celebrated status in the history of the film festival circuit, but as something of an initiation or legitimization piece for cinephiles—surviving its length and difficulty signals a dedication to art cinema and serves as a kind of shorthand for a truly committed cineaste. Its long takes vary in their accompanying movements, some remaining absolutely still, others having elaborate crane and/or tracking shots that move the viewer through various spaces.

When asked about the reason behind the length of these takes, Tarr highlighted their status as different from the images to which viewers are habituated: "The people of this generation know information-cut, information-cut, information-cut. They can follow the logic of it, the logic of the story, but they don't follow the logic of life."[6] For Tarr, then, the habituated structures of film style have come to interfere with something that he calls "life." What constitutes "life" for Tarr is never made totally clear, but what is valuable about these takes, for Tarr, is their relationship to a kind of seeing less dominated by film tradition, a looking that allows for something other than what is generally made available. André Bazin was also rather fond of long takes shot in deep focus, and he spoke at times in terms similar to Tarr about them. Putting them in opposition to the "tricks" and "cheats" used by practitioners of montage, Bazin, in "The Evolution of the Language of Cinema," takes Erich von Stroheim as the ultimate filmmaker in terms of the unbroken long take. What these takes allow, for Bazin, is a "laying bare." To Bazin, "In these films reality lays itself bare like a suspect confessing under the relentless examination of the commissioner of police."[7] The "close look" that the unbroken take affords, then, allows a situation where the film offers up "reality" to the viewer, a system through which the film sacrifices its narrative hopes in the goal of letting the audience *see*.[8] But what is it that can be seen differently in the image for these two thinkers?

According to Bazin, shooting in depth and without cuts "brings the spectator into a relation with the image closer to that which he enjoys with reality. Therefore it is correct to say that, independently of the contents of the image, its structure is more realistic."[9] Reality is, according to Bazin's purview, purely achieved through aesthetic means. This is not to say that the narrative contained in the image is irrelevant, but that the audience's relationship to the image—their belief in it, so to speak—is derived through aesthetics; the actions of the characters are available for contemplation, but only as *content*—a set of qualities unattached to the presentation of reality.

Bazin addresses the value of this particular set of aesthetic characteristics by explaining the role that the viewer is encouraged to play in light of the persistence of the unbroken take: "While analytical montage only calls for him to follow his guide, to let his attention follow along smoothly with that of the director who will choose what he should see, here he is called upon to exercise at least a minimum of personal choice. It is from his attention and his will that the meaning of the image in part derives."[10] Herein lies the key to Bazin's supposed "ontology" (which is never quite that): the viewer of these films that he so treasures is called upon to make some amount of choice in these moments, asked to participate in what is to come. But this process is realized not through acting upon the literal unspooling of the film, but through deciding one's own relation to the images; examining them and writing, so to speak, an understanding of these moments. As Tarr put it in response to being asked about the reason for his extended takes: "Because I see the story as only just a dimension of life, because we have a lot of other things. We have time, we have landscapes, we have meta-communications, all of which are not verbal information."[11] For Tarr these shots open up a new space of some sort, a space for choice or change, a space that is unadorned with ready-to-hand knowledge and that the audience must therefore assimilate into their understanding of these images and events on their own.

Of course, this is nothing new. That Bazin and Tarr unite in something like an understanding of the long take is no surprise. What is valuable, though, is the political ramifications of these images given their particular historical moment. What these thinkers describe is an image of, or one that generates, a viewer free of the governing boundaries of habituation, a kind of ideal mode of total democracy—a freedom to choose that allows more choice even than the world itself, a democratic image alleviating the need for the authoritative figure (even that of the artist) to come forth and orient one's vision. But, of course, this ideal always vanishes. It does so with every cut, or with the raising of the lights, or when action occurs and a course is taken—either in us or in the film. To return to Iordanova, the disillusionments of the careful transition to democracy are, thanks to Tarr, becoming visible. Indeed, the easy, habituated choice that looms as inevitable is never here contradicted nor even exactly critiqued, but the time before it is extended. The return to the past of old Europe is pushed aside for just a second (or maybe a little over seven hours), and the viewing audience is left to linger, however briefly, with these images but without authority or habit to guide them.

A particular moment in *Sátántangó* helps to articulate this process. In the often discussed opening shot the credits relent to a slow fade from black revealing an incredibly muddy yard in front of a barn that looks very much like a rundown factory (see figure 5). The only movement, at first, is the rain failing into the muddy puddle in the foreground. Slowly, cows emerge from the building and meander around the yard. The camera tilts slightly, keeping the cows centered as they move. Suddenly, from inside the pack one cow mounts another, the two struggle and charge around the yard and then the cow dismounts, blending instantly back into the crowd. A single cow then re-emerges, walks toward the camera, and pauses at the side of the frame. The camera tilts slightly again as two more cows come forward, one stops and looks at the camera, and then rejoins the herd as the pack heads to the left of the frame (see figure 6). That camera tilts again and then begins to track with the herd, revealing that,

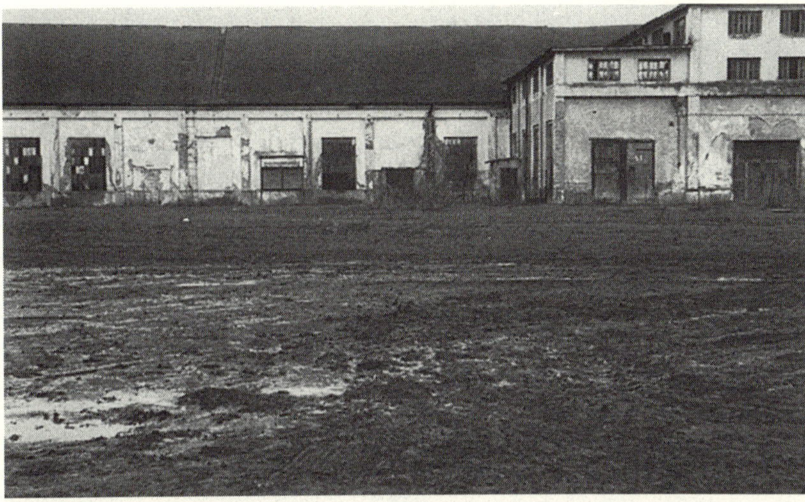

FIG. 5 Muddy yard from the opening of *Sátántangó*.

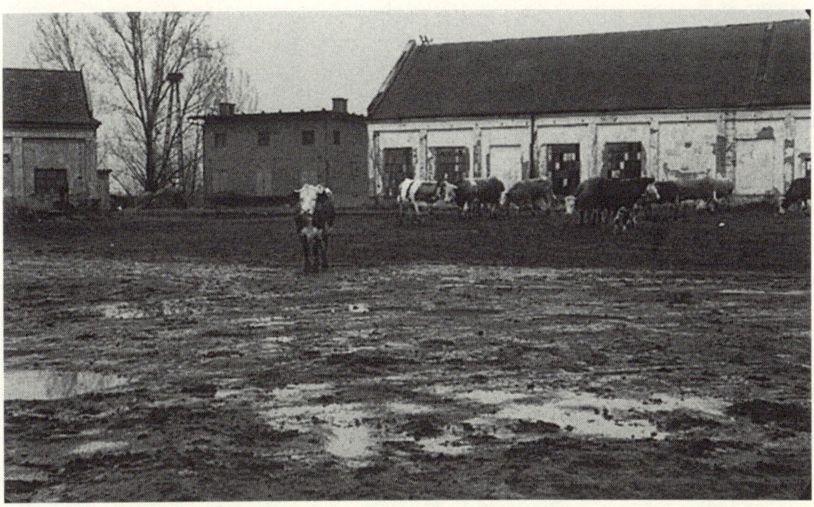

FIG. 6 Cows in the mud, from the opening of *Sátántangó*.

rather than a fenced area, this seems to be the town square. The camera continues to track, following the cows, but buildings slowly begin to separate the cows and the camera. At one point in its journey the camera displays nothing but a solid wall consisting of a mixture of brick and cracked concrete. But it continues on, and the cows return. The camera seems to totally lose track of the herd, though, as the number of buildings in the foreground increases, visiting with the cows only briefly in the spaces between structures. On the sides

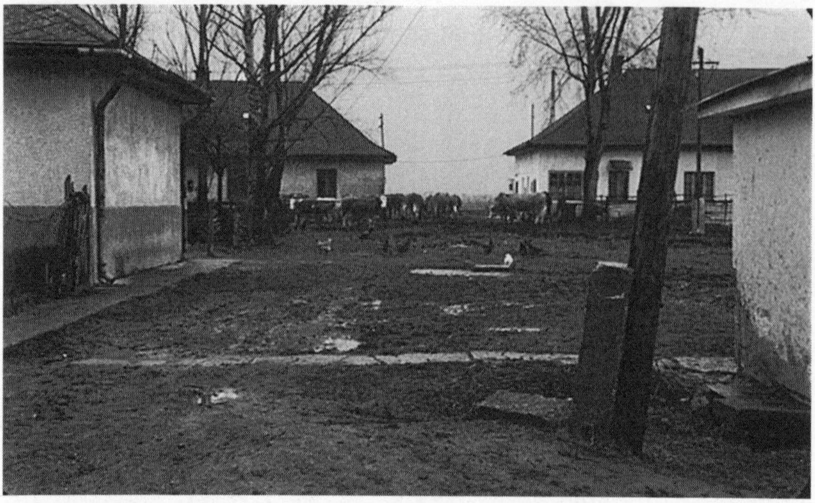

FIG. 7 The camera tracks to reveal more farm animals in *Sátántangó*.

of two buildings a pair of seemingly arbitrary gray numbers appear—sixty-three, seven—referencing some process or count the significance of which the audience is never alerted to. The camera finally finds some open space again and refinds its herd, now accompanied by some chickens (see figure 7). This position holds as the cows slowly exit through an opening between two buildings in the far background. One chicken is all that remains when the image finally fades back to black. This blackness holds and a narration begins that explains the layout of the town, now over the black screen.

This establishing shot of the town is presented in a seven-and-a-half-minute unbroken take. Given its position and its depiction of the town that occupies much of the film, this opening has come to serve for many critics as something of a primer for what is to come. According to David Bordwell, "The first shot, now famous, was a stunner. Cows wander through the churned mud of a village square, amble slowly to the camera and then drift to the left, the camera sliding along with them. Eventually they shamble into the distance. All the while, hollow, bell-like chords throb on. Great cow ensemble performance and a dawdling, slightly ominous introduction to a strange world: I was ready."[12] For Bordwell, then, this is an introduction to the style and the world of the film.

For Peter Hames, however, there is also something like an authorial purpose to this opening:

> The film begins with a much-quoted opening scene in which cows move from a shed towards the right of screen. The camera moves with them, tracking alongside to take in walls, outhouses and hens. The whole sequence is

> accompanied by haunting and reverberating sound. A narrative title informs us that the whole town has been cut off by the bog, mud and the incessant rain. "The news is that they are coming," announces a title. The narrative voice is that of the doctor, who watches events and records them from his desk at the window, the film returning to him at the end as the narrative begins again.[13]

For Hames there is an implied connection between the doctor's gaze and this shot. Furthermore, there is some conflation of the doctor with the director—his watching and recording of events coming to account for our view—and, given that much of this narration is from the novel on which the film is based, there is another connection between the story's respective authors.

For Manohla Dargis, finally, there is an additional link between this opening and a sardonic commentary about the film's characters that comes to inform a reading of the film as a whole. Dargis writes:

> The opening scene, which seems calculated to weed out fainthearted viewers, tracks a herd of cows as they meanderingly exit a barn and enter the muddy yard of the near-desolate village, with its cracked building walls and prodigiously strewn trash. As he does throughout the film, Mr. Tarr shoots this luxuriantly paced scene in long shot, using his beautiful framing and richly gradated black-and-white tones to find beauty in every miserable and mundane corner. In time, we meet the town's other slow-moving inhabitants—men, women and, notoriously, a young girl—none of whom appear more evolved than the wandering cows.[14]

To Dargis, then, this opening serves both as an establishment of directorial style and as a system to orient the audience to the forthcoming actions of the characters, particularly regarding their seeming resemblance to this group of cattle.

As this short sampling shows, the coherence of this scene in regard to any set of particular meanings is difficult to map across different viewers. Whether establishing a world to be occupied, declaring an authorial imprint, or orienting the viewer to the forthcoming narrative (or all, none, or something other than these things), this film is, from its very beginning, establishing some degree of ambiguity, as evidenced by these divergent readings. Ambiguity is, for Bazin, the major and most valuable result of the long-take, deep-focus style on display here. For Bazin, ambiguity is of importance because "the uncertainty in which we find ourselves as to the spiritual key or the interpretation we should put on the film is built into the very design of the image."[15] It is this design that gives the viewer the aforementioned ability to interpret, and subsequently some access to a democratic process, at least as it pertains to meaning.

## Hungary Year Zero

But the case of *Sátántangó* and its relationship to democracy far outstrips simply the discovery of the intended meanings of these images. It is its relationship to a particular moment in Hungarian politics that makes this film of particular value. As John Cunningham notes of the climate of post-Soviet Hungary, "Politically, Hungarians may have hoped for a period of steady acclimation to the process and practices of representative democracy. What they got instead, with the first decisions of 1990, was a right-wing government composed of an unstable coalition . . . which lurched from crisis to crisis."[16] This political turmoil is represented in the narrative of the film primarily through Irimiás's series of promises, lies, and persistent returns, but it is more significant in regard to the film's aesthetic approach. The lack of a clear purpose or governing principle paired with the extension of sight into an unfigured and nearly-but-never-quite-visible future positions the viewer in a unique mode of *waiting*. Indeed, the plethora of responses that *Sátántangó* offers but never endorses and its outright refusal to integrate its extended moments into an intelligible narrative produce a system that posits waiting as a coherent stance in relation to the peaks and valleys of the political transition that this film seems so intent on discussing *without ever discussing*. And by virtue of this waiting being woven into the very fabric of this exceptionally long film, the audience is asked solely and distinctly to sit and wait with it—free to interpret but with ideas never verified, wait never summarily ended.

As Cunningham makes clear, the period beginning in the 1960s and culminating in 1989 was far and away the most fertile in Hungarian cinema, but it was not altogether undone by the change in economic systems.[17] Much of the state apparatus responsible for funding filmmaking actually persisted into the late 1990s, and there was surprising continuity between the available forms of funding under both systems of governance.[18] There was, however, in the late 1980s serious anxiety about the availability of centralized film financing and the fact that the deeply challenging cinema of figures like Tarr would now be forced to more actively compete in the world of popular cinema.

Accompanying these anxieties was the much more widespread disillusionment with the transition to capitalism. Hungary had entered a recession that straddled the transition, and the lack of immediate economic renewal under capitalism led to a serious reduction in enthusiasm for a new market economy. This recession included "inflation standing at 23 per cent, about three million people living at or below the poverty line, the highest foreign debt of any Eastern European country and unemployment just below 400,000 and rising."[19] In addition, the newly held election, which people had hoped would help the nation transition into a stable market-based economy, resulted in a right-wing coalition of unstable allegiances.[20] Hungary, then, shifted from one unstable economic arrangement to another, gaining in the process deep debts, a very high rate of unemployment, and an increasing rate of inflation. The roots of this economic downturn are, of course, difficult to pin to a tidy source, but the steady decrease in quality of life that bridged communism and capitalism nonetheless helps to situate *Sátántangó*'s brutal pessimism, and its distrust of both economic systems.

This film's melancholy and general distrust, evidenced best perhaps by Irimiás's actions, demonstrates a particularly insightful example of what Alexei Yurchak, in *Everything Was Forever, until It Was No More*, describes as the unique blend of idealism and failure that carried the late Soviet moment into the transition to capitalism. For Yurchak, the moments before and during the transition carried with them what he calls a "curious paradox," which he says is characterized by the fact that "the system [communism] was always felt to be both stagnating and immutable, fragile and vigorous, bleak and full of promise."[21] It is this paradox that brings light to Irimiás's actions, and furthermore his readability as an allegory for disillusionment with both capitalism and communism. Irimiás's promise of a return to a community farm proposes exactly what the residents of the town know to be already failed, but it also provides the possibility for a return to a past that, if miserable, at least held with it the—perhaps illusory—ideals of community and equality. But Irimiás's capitalist leanings, his taking of their money and promising positive returns on their investments, proposes exactly the opposite: if capitalism here might produce a positive future of another sort—that of prosperity and abundance—it does so at the cost of any claim to community and collectivity.

Irimiás, then, stands at the crossroad between communism and capitalism. His is the vantage from which both systems become finally legible; their promises apparent, their failures palpable. It is this impasse that Tarr hopes to extend, and his system for completing this task is the extended take. The moment of decision is here extended to its limit. But, unlike in the case of *Germany Year Zero*, the availability of a positive future through a coherent path has all but vanished. Rossellini found a future predicated on a radical break from authority and Tarr here agrees, but where Tarr departs is in the limits of this break. Whereas for Rossellini communism was within the range of available futures, for Tarr it has been rejected, at least in any recognizable form. The horizon has shrunk, and with it the strange optimism that Rossellini produced. Tarr's openness, his spaces of contingency. and attempts to make available what is radically new are then both more devastating and more desperate than Rossellini's, for his wish seems all but unattainable. Under this unflinching and all-encompassing pessimism Tarr's *Sátántangó* finds itself in an inescapable bind and it is left only to wait, to wait for something to appear in the spaces of possibility it creates, to wait for something, finally, to arrive and produce some structure to carry us forth.

## Waiting (with Boredom)

Siegfried Kracauer explored the value of waiting by putting this concept in relation to his views on spirituality. For Kracauer the modern world is arranged in such a way as to make waiting an afterthought, a nonproductive and therefore obsolete state out of line with the world's emphasis on labor and productivity. His essay "Those Who Wait" thinks of the problems that a lack of waiting can cause in specifically religious terms. According to Kracauer, there are three available responses for the modern urban subject—the subject doomed to "linger in the void"[22] of urban anomie and metaphorical suffering[23]—when faced with the possibility of religion. First, there is skepticism "as a matter of principle," represented by the subject who turns his back almost arbitrarily from the matter at hand, taking as eternal truth their own status as skeptic.[24] Second is the subjects Kracauer dubs "the short-circuit people," those who dive headlong into the decisions that they face, short-circuiting what Kracauer finds to be the potential value of their choices by arriving too quickly and too easily at their spiritual conclusions.[25] For Kracauer, it is these short-circuit people who are prone to zealotry. Both halves of this pair of opposed responses produce extremism. The third response to the problem of the spiritual in the modern world, and the one that Kracauer finds to be of particular value, is that of waiting. For Kracauer waiting presents something of a state of productive indecision: "One waits, and one's waiting is a *hesitant openness*, albeit of a sort that is difficult to explain."[26] It is this "hesitant openness" that is of political value to the cinema of Tarr, and its accompanying status as being "difficult to explain" that accounts for the kind of deliberate ambiguity that is essential for Bazin. This difficulty of explanation is derived from the fact that waiting is always also a moment of indecision, a space where decision is halted, allowing potential to spread out in every direction.

This waiting is also necessarily durational. As Kracauer explains, when thinking of this waiting "one ought to think primarily of those people who have tarried and still do tarry in front of closed doors, and who thus, when they take it upon themselves to wait, are people who are waiting here and now."[27] This is to say that once a decision is rendered the waiting is ended, and its productive value becomes lost as it is placed in the past and figured, in retrospect, as just an intermediate state—an irrelevant interval. But it is when one is *in* "the waiting" that it is of value, when it pushes at the possible and before it is rendered knowable. Temporally, then, this waiting is never in the past or future: we never *did* wait and we never *will* wait. We only wait *while* waiting, and forget this waiting when it has passed.

Kracauer goes on to argue that "the actual metaphysical meaning of his [the one who waits'] attitude rests upon the fact that the irruption of the absolute can occur only once an individual has committed himself with his entire being to this relationship. Those who wait will thus be as hard as possible on themselves, so as not to be taken in by religious need."[28] This waiting, then, is also an avoidance. Those who wait must continue to wait until they can suffer no more, until the need to not wait has passed and something other than waiting finally arrives. Indeed Kracauer cautions against ending the wait too soon: "Maintaining the furthest possible distance, they [those who wait] almost make it their ambition to be pedantic and somehow cool, as a means of protecting themselves against flying embers."[29]

It is these "flying embers" that Tarr so carefully encourages his audience to avoid. The tangential and immediate turn to a decision too soon, the disruption of the wait that might prematurely end it before its advantages can arrive—these are what this film strives to avoid. The questions as to whether any particular reading of Tarr's cows can be settled upon or whether a return to old Europe or nostalgia for old communism can be found in these images—these are the burning embers that become available in the film's unfolding. But none of these burning embers ever fully ignite, and the audience is left only to wait. During this waiting, for Kracauer, the one who waits can never relax; she must maintain "tense activity and engaged self-perception."[30] Hence the absolute reduction of habitual ease in Tarr's takes. His cinema is never quite that of Andrei Tarkovsky, to whom he is so often compared,[31] because the beauty of his films never exactly carries the viewer away. Instead they are always left waiting, waiting for the next cut—an event which, despite all the waiting, so often arrives abruptly—or the next action.

But Kracauer ends his essay on a strange note, and in a way that addresses the difficult decisions as to when it is appropriate to stop the wait. His conclusion is presented as follows: "Must it be added that getting oneself ready is only a preparation for that which cannot be obtained by force, a preparation for transformation and for giving oneself over to it? Exactly when this transformation will come to pass and whether or not it will happen at all is not at issue here, and at any rate should not worry those who are exerting themselves."[32] For Kracauer, finally, the waiting is a preparation for something that is to come, but also an awareness that it might never arrive. The nature of the transformation offered always treats waiting as unfigured, and its point of arrival must always remain vague exactly until something comes, for once it takes form the wait is finished.

In *Sátántangó* there are, of course, disruptions that interrupt the wait, but they are always met with more waiting. Never does the transformation quite arrive—and never does the film offer the audience a course of action. What *Sátántangó* aspires to do is maintain a state of waiting, a perpetual asking of its audience to pause and think before the coming democracy can arrive. What helps Tarr's film stand out from the art house tradition that it so clearly claims is its unique position as an artifact of a transitional moment, a moment when waiting was of such great importance to Hungary's transformation. This film asks its viewers to think through this change; it signals toward it but never clearly articulates its concerns. But its length also asks that the audience "suffer," that they stare and wait as the cows meander, or worse still, as a cat is tortured in the name of nothing but a misguided claim to authority.[33]

But a film that deliberately demands to open up an expanse of waiting suggests a striking orientation of viewer to object. The viewer, suffering the demands of the wait, is left with a relatively slim scope of direct responses, leaving—or perhaps disregard or rejection—being of course the most available, and indeed it is this response that perhaps accounts for the relative disinterest from Tarr's domestic audience.[34] But the important question here is what does it mean to stay? To endure all seven-plus hours of Tarr's film and indeed to enjoy it, as many audiences claim to do. This sustained wait is best qualified under the term "boredom." That is, in order to wait, to truly wait in the sense that Kracauer and, I believe, Tarr demand is to be bored. To disjoin the positive outcome from the experience of stillness and to dwell in a state of total indirection—this is what it means to wait and its only coherent response must be boredom.

In her book *Experience without Qualities: Boredom and Modernity*—a masterful discussion of boredom's history and unsteady relationship with both philosophical and empirical methods of analysis—Elizabeth Goodstein summarizes boredom in the following way: "Boredom isolates, individuates, even as it blurs the world gray. A confrontation with nothing, then, or Nothing, or something like it. Perhaps just a name for what cannot be named, an encounter with the limits of language. An experience without qualities, with the deficits of the self masquerading as the poverty of the world."[35] For Goodstein boredom individuates and creates a limitless gray—a world perhaps found concretized in Tarr's films. But boredom also mistakes this grayness, or perhaps displaces it. In boredom the world outside appears gray and bland, but this blandness and indistinction expand past the boundaries of the image. They are also felt inside—to be bored is to feel that you are yourself as gray as the world that you see; one's self feels as tired as the object on display. In this way, boredom confuses the boundary between inside and outside. Goodstein continues: "In boredom there is no distinguishing in here form out there, for this world in its failure to engage collapses into an extension of the bored subject who empties out in the vain search for an interest, a pleasure, a meaning."[36] It is this emptying out that makes room for the wait, that produces the space for openness—true indifference and impartiality are boredom's qualities; it is constituted by absolute distance but also the failure to distinguish self from image.

For Goodstein, the rise of boredom is tightly tied to the effects of industrialization, and results from what she calls the "democratization of skepticism in modernity."[37] Boredom, then, results from a crisis of meaning brought on by the secularization of society and the constant appeal to the vagaries and vicissitudes of "progress" as the motor for modern urban experience. According to Goodstein, in boredom "the definitiveness of the loss of traditional frameworks of meaning registers in a hollow emptiness of self."[38] If it is in the absence of meaning where waiting finds its value, where politics opens up to possibility, and where change can find its most extreme forms, then boredom must be the state that characterizes this wait.

Another term, "patience," seems to be likewise valuable for approaching the wait, but what separates boredom from patience—and indeed renders boredom the more radical response—is to be found in the way that the subject is oriented. That is, whereas boredom confuses inside and outside and brings the object of boredom in close relation to the subject, indeed so close that the two become confused, patience maintains a distance and a direction in relation to the object. The difference here is that between waiting *with* and waiting *for*. Where boredom waits with the film, patience waits for it; for it to offer up its value, which is subsequently accepted or rejected by the viewer. Boredom must surely be considered the more messianic of the two, as in it the contract implied by patience is replaced with instability, and perhaps also the more idealistic.[39] But it also offers more—more options and, potentially, more and greater difference. In light of Tarr's context, his equating and confusing of both available economic options, and perhaps proposing that both seem to offer no promise other than misery, boredom becomes the far more alluring of these two responses. There is, for Tarr, nothing to patiently await. Only boredom offers the radical difference of completely unhabituated viewing that he demands.

Patrice Petro, in her book *Aftershocks of the New: Feminism and Film History*, also discusses the politics of boredom, and she does so by connecting boredom to the seemingly antithetical category of history. As Petro notes, boredom is typically thought of as inconsequential and therefore unassimilable to history. She summarizes this typical conception of boredom thus: "A time without event, when nothing happens, a seemingly endless flux without beginning or end."[40] History, on the other hand, typically categorizes and collects things of particular consequence. As Petro puts it, "History, by contrast [with boredom] is commonly understood to document that which happened—a series of events or, at least, moments thought to be eventful, which suggest that something occurred (rather than nothing at all)."[41] Petro's project, in contrast to these traditional conceptions of boredom and history, is to connect these seemingly incommensurate terms, and film and photography become the lever for this connection. That is, film and photography open up—in a particularly Kracaurian way—a space for reflecting on the industrialized spaces depicted precisely because they present boredom as a historically situated mode of experience. That is, boredom itself is the subject of the images that she finds to be of value. We have boredom now, the photographic arts seem to say, because of our current relationship to the industrialized world.

Boredom, for Petro, is the state of experience in which distraction—for her, as well as Kracauer and Walter Benjamin, the definitive state of experience for the industrialized urban subject—is reflected back through photography and turned into an object for scrutiny. Petro proposes this model as such: "The cultivation of boredom . . . discloses the logic of distraction, in which newness becomes a fetish, and shock itself a manifestation of the commodity form. To reverse the slogan of the Russian formalists, *boredom habitualizes renewed perception*, opening up the potential to see difference that make a difference, and to refuse the ceaseless repetition of the new as always-the-same."[42] For Petro, boredom, as cultivated through media, is a historically situated mode of experience that is valuable in its ability to make visible the repetitions of sameness and furthermore the possibility of difference.

If, as Benjamin posited in his *Arcades Project*, "boredom is the threshold of great deeds"[43] it is because, as Petro puts it, "hidden in the negativity of boredom and waiting . . . is the anticipation that something (different) might occur."[44] There are, I think, two particularly significant portions of this quote that are of supreme importance for understanding the political potentials of boredom. The first relates to "negativity," and it is indeed this quality that separates boredom from patience. For boredom to shatter the repetition of the new and the tyranny of sameness it must be felt as a negative quality, as a form of dissatisfaction with what is being observed. This negativity is of course also boredom's drawback, as it brings about the potential for dismissal. But boredom must push up against its own failure in order to propose the possibility of difference. This is why the indeterminate is of such value to boredom, and indeed the divide between nonevent and event (or boredom and history) becomes of such significance. In order to produce the possibility of difference, the barrier between event and nonevent must be dissolved, and it must become clear that any particular moment could be rendered eventful. Hence Tarr's emphasis on disrupting habituated viewing: what appears of little interest is exactly the thing that is capable of asking us to think again. Of course, in this total attempt at disrupting habituation, what events *are* valuable—and will subsequently be selected for history—also becomes indeterminate.

The other important portion of the Petro quote above is the placing of "different" inside parentheses. The problem that this parenthetical proposes is that the act of singling something out as different always necessitates a figuration. That something occurs is of course inevitable, but its labeling as different—unique and thus historical—is exactly the kind of selection and subsequent lionization that signifies the end of waiting, and therefore the arrival of something in particular. Greeting and verifying the moment of difference proposes an untenable juncture, as singling out and marking an event always functions to end the wait—and its accompanying subject position: boredom—too soon.

This is why I do not exactly think of *Sátántangó* as a pessimistic film. Surely it distrusts the two economic orders it mostly clearly figures—communism and capitalism—but it does so from the position of hope. This, like the other films I discuss here, is an optimistic film; it rejects meaning not in the name of pure distrust for the world, but in the hope that something better might arrive. This is the structure of messianism, and it is with a hopeful distrust that it absolutely dedicates itself to making us wait for that arrival.

*Sátántangó*, as previously discussed, runs up against the problem of how to end the wait, but it refigures this discussion of waiting and boredom by virtue of its historical orientation. Tarr's film, of course, has a remarkably complex relationship to change and the potentials of new political arrangements, as is most clearly evidenced in its distrust of the legacy of communism. If, for Kracauer, Goodstein, and Petro, the hope of boredom is to reveal the fissures and arbitrary arrangements of capitalism's complex and seemingly natural mechanizations, Tarr's film reactivates this wish, but without the cogent alternative that underwrites these other critiques. If indeed Benjamin's famous claim that "boredom is the threshold of great deeds" is the clearest summation of boredom's potential, Tarr's cinema is of particular value in highlighting the hidden assumptions of this quote. "Boredom is the threshold of great deeds" for sure, but it is always *just* that threshold, and never anything more. Through the semicoherent maneuverings, ramblings and dances of its characters, *Sátántangó* stands on this threshold, but never quite enters.

The aesthetic approach of Tarr—his tracking shots along with the overwhelming grayness of his photography—strive to produce boredom and waiting, but to do so in such a way as to reduce the distance between audience and image. As Goodstein notes, part of the structure of boredom is the confusion of inside and outside. What this confusion yields is a profound and total disenchantment with oneself and the world, the only available response to which is a call to reconfigure, to think anew about the world that has produced this disenchantment. This is Tarr's aim, and this is the potential of boredom. But, as will be explored shortly, the limits of this approach always and immediately haunt this film, for it becomes impossible in this waiting and its boredom to ever *do anything*—as any *thing* always ignites these flammable images, burning away all their potential at the very site of any particular arrival.

## Democracy and Contingency

What the viewers of *Sátántangó* await is not some religious awakening, but a forthcoming political change, a change that seems inevitable but that regardless must be thought, for thinking is the only way to attempt to determine and condition its arrival. But as the cows meander across the screen, what becomes available that has been otherwise withheld? Are the cows a communist collective or a cadre of capitalist consumers? Are they the characters that are to come or the vision of a world that has been left behind? And what of their exit? Is this emancipation or slaughter? And how can we ever tell? These are the questions that this film offers up but refuses ever to fully form, and is farther still from ever answering.

Two recent books on the work of Tarr expand on this waiting process by figuring, respectively, the end of waiting and its perpetuation. Their titles alone, when put in relation to each other, question after this process. The first, *The Cinema of Béla Tarr: The Circle Closes*, by András Bálint Kovács posits that politics are never the direct concern of Tarr, and that his films actually work to create a vaguely "Eastern European" space that is never particular to Hungary.[45] The second, *Béla Tarr: The Time After* by Jacques Rancière, argues that Tarr's films open up access to a new kind of temporality that allows for a new kind of relationship to the material world.

Part of Kovács's project is to show that Tarr's films are coherent across his directing career, and not easily sectioned into two periods, as other critics so often hold. He explains that Tarr's films "can in no way be regarded as political," but they do function in delivering a hopeless vision of small-town Hungary.[46] "The narration is slow; the environment represented is poor, shabby, dirty and run-down; and the stories' atmosphere is bleak. The characters are sad and frightened; they often suffer and often cause others to suffer; nobody in any of these films smiles or laughs; and nobody is cheerful. The visual atmosphere is dark, with no colours. The stories do not develop, just turn in circles, and there is no hope in them for anybody."[47] Given this attitude, Kovács—who in fact finds a lot of value in the films, if perhaps they are to him not upbeat or useful in terms of politics—spends the majority of his analyses arguing for the coherence of Tarr's oeuvre in terms of a particular style and categorizing Tarr, in particular his tracking shots and long takes, in relation to earlier European directors. For Kovács, Tarr's films function to generate something of a unified stance by virtue of their appearing historical without actually ever presenting anything particular. Due in large part to their strange relationship to location shooting (the exteriors often connect far disparate locations through cuts that appear to conjoin them into a coherent space), Kovács posits that what Tarr and his crew want to achieve is "the forming of this mixture of historical, social and political signs into a vision that shows neither national characteristics nor particular signs of a period of time any more specific than the end of the twentieth century."[48] Tarr ultimately does this through connecting far removed spaces and by depicting "a landscape which was very typical of a region, yet remained unspecific as regards concrete space and historical time."[49] Through this, Tarr is able to represent a generalized "Eastern Europe" that is knowable to a wider audience, a presentation that brings into view a kind of universal particular, a specific impression that accounts for the audience's understanding of these films, which takes the form of "the image of the underdog, the image of a helpless life."[50]

Whereas Kovács paints Tarr as a kind of sculptor of hopeless and disjointed spaces, for Rancière Tarr's cinema opens up new possibilities through access to a different kind of time. Like Kovács, Rancière pushes back against the idea of separating Tarr's work into two distinct periods. For Rancière, "From the first film to the last, it is always the story of a broken promise, of a voyage that returns to its point of departure."[51] What this circular structure allows for Rancière is remarkably different from Kovács' closed circle of coherent meaning rendered universal, however. For Rancière, what is key to Tarr and what he uses these films to set forth is a kind of essential grounding for his ideas on "realism": "The essence of realism—contrary to the program of edification known by the name of socialist realism—is the distance taken with regard to stories, to their temporal schemes and their sequences of causes and effects. Realism opposes situations that endure to stories that link together and pass from one to the next."[52] Rancière uses Tarr's films, then, to deploy a *logic* of realism, but Tarr's is a realism that pushes out narrative and instead asks that images be *felt*.

Some degree of narrative disruption—in Rancière through distance and in Kovács through spatial distortion—obviously connect the two thinkers, but Rancière's ideas are useful in describing how the pauses that these films present function to figure a politics. Where Kovács finds *Sátántangó*'s disjointed narratives and general incoherence disruptive to any political project, for Rancière it is exactly these qualities that allows for politics. According to Rancière, the disjuncture between narrative and form that Tarr provides generates a rupture that serves to produce a new style of seeing. "In order to exploit the breach [between narrative and reality] offered, it is already necessary to loosen the constraint that binds the arguments of stories to the exposition of 'problems,' the existence and domain of which are defined by the power of the planners."[53] While Rancière is referring explicitly to Tarr's work during the 1980s, this point still holds for Tarr's post-Soviet films. The emphasis on "problems," or what might also be called direct political issues, on which other films might rely is avoided here in favor of something else, something that disrupts the planning of a new (or old) society—a waiting that resists the reduction of these images to paths forward and instead exhibits what Rancière continually refers to as "reality." Rancière's term for what Kracauer might call waiting is "the time after." To Rancière, "The time after is not the morose, uniform time of those who no longer believe in anything. It is the time of pure, material events, against which belief will be measured for as long as life will sustain it."[54] This vague category resembles in many ways Kracauer's notion of waiting, but it elaborates on it by turning to *materiality*, to a connection between the spaces of the film and the characters who occupy them. Rancière titles his chapter on *Damnation* (1988)—Tarr's film previous to *Sátántangó* and which shares many of its characteristics, excepting of course its length—"The Empire of Rain," and in so doing highlights the connection between the characters and the world that they inhabit. For Rancière the long takes and general damp, muddy grayness on display work to disrupt narrative action and ask the audience to think about puddles and concrete in the same way that they do about the actors' repetitious movements. Rancière goes so far as to use this materiality and repetition to launch a kind of ontology of cinema. As he explains, "Cinema's proper task is that of constructing the movement according to which these affects are produced and circulated, the movement by which they are modulated according to the two fundamental sensible regimes, repetition and the leap into the unknown."[55] Given this ontology, Tarr serves for Rancière as von Stroheim did for Bazin, with Tarr's cinema affording exactly this process of repetition that is punctuated by a sudden leap.

For Rancière, the repetition and the possibility of the leap generates what he calls a "gap" between the actions that the narrative contains and the spaces of this world. According to Rancière, "It is in this gap that cinema constructs its intensities and makes them into a testimony or a tale about the state of the world that escapes from the dismal record of the equivalence of all things and the vanity of all action."[56] What is allowed to emerge through this gap is a moment where tale and testimony collide, where the direct evaluation of problems falls away and the potential for change opens up. When meanings melt and reform, and ultimately reassemble within and with time, material spaces—the mud puddles, the decayed buildings—allow for new connections to arise, but never to fully take form. This is finally the political potential for *Sátántangó*: what it does is melt solids into an unintelligible form—a puddle, a ruined building, a gray town square—and in so doing asks its audience to build from these forms—forms approaching formlessness—something that was not there before. Something new. We wait with this film, focused on repetitive actions and behaviors taking place in indistinct spaces, in the hopes of something new to arrive. Stuck in a position where the film's boredom becomes our own, *Sátántangó* asks for difference, and the longer it waits the more distant this arrival seems. From where it is to arise—from the audience or the film itself—also becomes muddled, muddied by our own gray confusion of our waiting and the film's. What it awaits is something new, something that will make sense of this world and return to it order, but it refuses to punctuate these claims.

## The Democracy to Come

What Tarr's cinema allows, finally, via Rancière, Kracauer, and Bazin, is a way to contemplate what Jacques Derrida calls *the democracy to come*. In discussing the idea of the "coming revolution," an impending but unfigured revolutionary change perpetually rising on the horizon but never quite arriving in any particular form, Derrida writes, "As paradoxical as it seems, it is in this unleashed overflowing, at the moment when all the joints give way between form and content, that the latter [the coming revolution] will be properly its 'own' and properly revolutionary. By all logic, one ought to recognize it by nothing other than the excess of this untimely dis-identification, therefore by nothing that is. *By nothing that is presently identifiable. As soon as one identifies a revolution, it begins to imitate, it enters into a death agony*."[57] For Derrida, then, this idea of the coming revolution proposes a particular model that figures radical change as always arising from nowhere, and which must immediately die once recognized. This is also the structure of the democracy to come. To quote again from Derrida: "The idea, if that is still what it is, of democracy to come, this 'idea' as event of pledged injunction that orders one to summon the very thing that will never present itself in the form of full presence, is the opening of this gap between an infinite promise . . . and the determined, necessary, but also necessarily inadequate forms of what has to be measured against this promise."[58] Derrida also locates a gap, but now it is between the infinite promise of a forthcoming democracy and the delimited now against which this future is weighed. Once this future has arrived, once the revolution is measured or the democracy has come, the future must escape and spread out again, not as utopia but as an infinite set of unfigured potentials: "The affectivity or actuality of the democratic promise, like that of the communist promise, will always keep within it, and it must do so, the absolutely undetermined messianic hope at its heart, this eschatological relation to the to-come of an event *and* of a singularity, of an alterity that cannot be anticipated."[59] It is my contention that this messianism describes the political hope at the core of *Sátántangó*.

The trouble, of course, with the messianism that unites Rancière, Kracauer, Derrida, and, for me, Tarr is its dedication to externality and its subsequent faith in the arrival of forces that will come to correct the suffering and chaos that Tarr so eloquently proposes. This messianism figures Tarr's film as hopeful; its gray, muddied streets glow with the availability of change. But messianism such as this also undermines the capacity for human action as a new, alternate outcome must always only be an external presence that looms just out of reach, promising the refiguration that these gray spaces demand through its own absence. If Rossellini wished for new modes of political action, Tarr's cinema distrusts any and all responses; it undermines collectivized as well as individualized responses to human misery and demands something so different that it finds itself incapable of depicting even a viable goal for what is to come.

Herein lies the tension at the heart of Tarr's film. The promise of political change persists, but it is accompanied by a total failure to render that change.

In fact, this failure is necessary for the potential to persist, as it is only in failure where messianism can find its full force. The messianic wish at the heart of Tarr's cinema requires misery and a refusal of positive outcomes, as it is in these conditions where hope can fully emerge. The goal is to deny figuration so as to maximize the role of the constitutive "outside" from which possibility can finally arrive. This presents an impossible bind, one even more restrictive than the one Rossellini found himself in, for whom collectivity sill loomed as a positive prospect.

The final shots of *Sátántangó* are of particular importance in this regard. The doctor, having arrived home, finally, after being awoken by the church bells, which he had thought dormant, and subsequently checking on them, shuffles through the papers on his desk, all the while muttering about how he has misrecognized the sound of the ringing bells. The rain batters the windows as he, increasingly agitated, digs through his belongings. The camera is placed at the rear of his small room, and a window at the front creates a strong silhouette, making his actions difficult to immediately decipher (see figure 8). It quickly becomes clear, however, that the doctor is removing the objects from in front of the window and placing them in a box, which he then places off to the side.

The doctor then walks to the right of the frame and opens a door. Located in the foreground, the door totally obscures the frame and blocks nearly all light from the window, leaving only an obscured image of the doctor's hand now very close to the camera. He proceeds to partially close the door, removing much of the obstruction and revealing half the frame, which is sporadically occupied

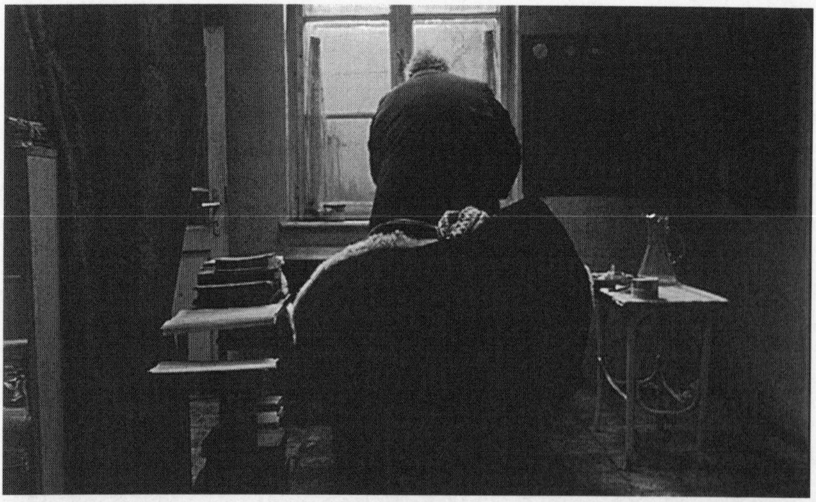

FIG. 8 The Doctor at his window in *Sátántangó*.

by his silhouette. The doctor, inexplicably frustrated, throws things from the closet through the frame, stopping only to place large boards—perhaps cupboard drawers—neatly against the chair that occupies much of the revealed frame.

Finally, satisfied with the amount of wood slats he has collected, the doctor moves the shelf pieces to the side of the chair and begins to clear the furniture from in front of the window. Gradually, it finally becomes clear what the doctor has been preparing. He places the first shelf board over the lower quarter of the window and nails it to the wall (see figure 9). He does the same with the second and, as the light from this single source begins to be extinguished, the third—meticulously nailing each board as he proceeds (see figure 10). Upon his placing of the fourth board the darkness overtakes the frame almost entirety, leaving only the sound of the doctor's hammer. As this hammering proceeds, a faint light directly in the center of the frame persists, the product of a slight gap in the boards. The covering and reopening of this slight opening indicates the doctor's movement. The sound of the rain persists over this nearly totally black image until, finally and without explanation, the tiny sliver of light is covered. Perhaps the film has faded to black or perhaps he has finished the task of boarding the window shut. The difference here is imperceptible. A heavy exhalation is heard. Exhausted, the doctor presents his monologue about the rains in October. The monologue is similar but not identical to the one presented at the start of the film, which followed the cows' exit and provided what little explanation we are given of the rain-beaten town. Then, finally, the credits appear over the blackness, with no system to distinguish their space from the blackness of the now totally dark interior of the house.

Through the figure of the doctor this film extends to the limit its attempt to keep the discussion at hand in the present tense, never producing a conclusion to the events depicted and the allegories they reach toward. For Pier Paolo Pasolini, the long take signified cinema's capacity to reproduce an open and endless present—an incomplete continuous mode that can only be synthesized after its completion. According to Pasolini, "The substance of cinema is . . . an endless long take, as is reality to our senses for as long as we are able to see and feel (a long take that ends with the end of our lives); and this long take is nothing but the reproduction of the language of reality, in other words it is the reproduction of the present."[60] This open-ended present is totally flexible and available for change, and it is only on the occasion of its ending—in cinema through the cut, in life through death—that this openness can be systematized and subsequently offered up for meaning. For Pasolini, these openings are valuable, but they also hinder expression. As he proposes, "As long as he has a future, that is, something unknown, a man does not express himself."[61] This is to say that one's life cannot be summarized and used to produce decipherable qualities until it has ceased, and for Pasolini this is likewise the case for

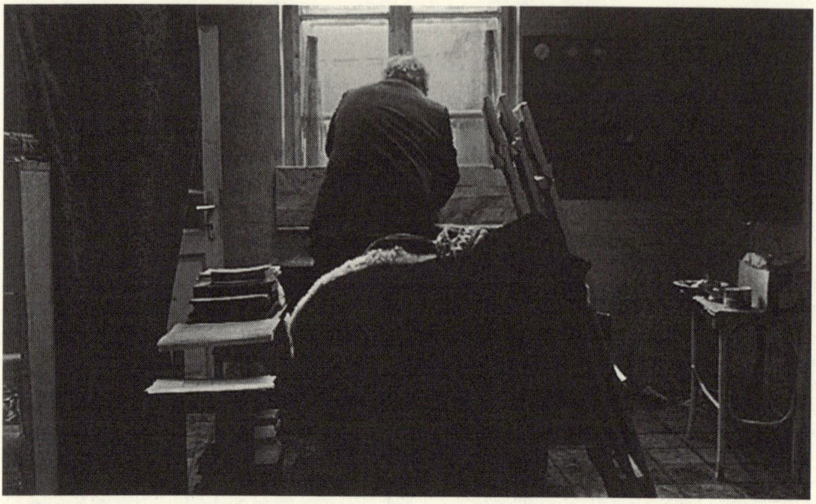

FIG. 9 The Doctor starts to board up his window in *Sátántangó*.

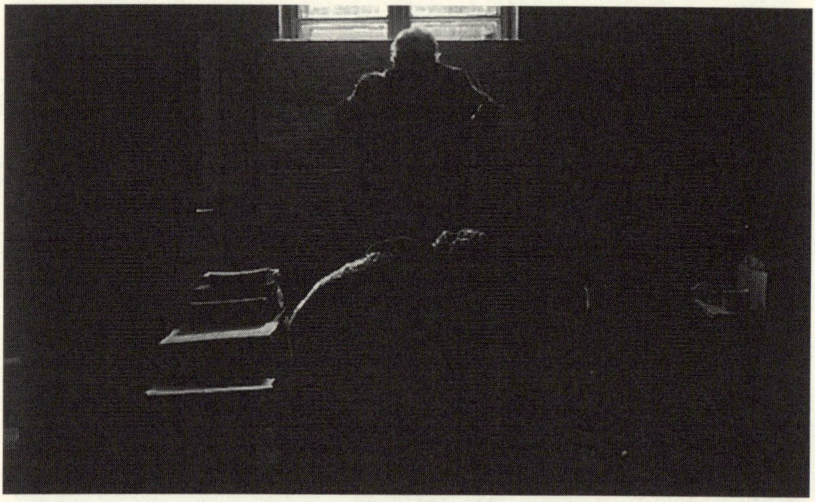

FIG. 10 The Doctor finishes boarding up his window in *Sátántangó*.

cinema. But in cinema this finality is—perhaps—less devastating: it arrives at the moment of every cut, at the always temporary severing from the current tense and the institution of a new stretch of time.

In light of Pasolini's claims, when the doctor shuts out the light and makes room for the credits, the cut is avoided or at least masked. Obviously, the film eventually ends, but this gesture serves as an attempt to perpetuate what Pasolini refers to as the substance of cinema, its ability to proceed without returning to reflect on the moments it has produced until everything has come to a conclusion.

Mary Ann Doane approaches this same relationship between take and cut, but she poses this dynamic as an "invitation" to change: "The long take is a gaze at an autonomous, unfolding scene whose duration is a function of the duration and potential waywardness of events themselves. Its length situates it as an invitation that is abruptly cancelled by the cut."[62] For Doane, what happens during a long take is a clearing of space for possibility to arrive, for change to accept the invitation and to attend. But this dynamic also creates a kind of paradox, a situation in which change is encouraged, but also in which it becomes impossible to tell if it has arrived. Indeed one can never say when the summons has been accepted and the cut can be enacted in order to make change legible.

For Doane, then, there is an "intolerable instability" at the heart of cinema's relationship with time and the present.[63] "The image is the imprint of a moment whose particularity becomes indeterminable precisely because the image does not speak its own relation to time."[64] In the case of *Sátántangó*'s conclusion, it is the unwillingness to cut, to stop and produce something, which accounts for and enacts this "intolerable instability." But this resistance to speaking for itself also serves as the mechanism for its rejection of authority. To stop, cut, and subsequently speak its own system and its own set of directives would amount to an authoritative gesture, and furthermore one that would dismiss the radical opening to change that this refusal of figuration presents. It is this termination that this film resists.

For Doane, this opening to changeability is most clearly evidenced in early cinema, and the objects that she highlights produce systems for rendering coherent this inchoate relationship to time. Her chosen objects in fact form a kind of dialectic between pure openness and its ordering, a conflictual relationship that she names "cinematic time." She explains: "The unreadability and uncertainty concerning the image's relation to temporality and to its origin are not problems that are resolved—they are, in fact, insoluble. But they are displaced through the elaborate development of structures that produce the image of a coherent and unified 'real time' that is much more 'real' than 'real time' itself. The resulting cinema delicately negotiates the contradiction between recording and signification."[65] In the cinema that Doane highlights there is a vacillation between rational and irrational modes, between openness to contingency and the production of structure. For Doane, as the history of cinema progressed, it was this contingency that was forced out by the increasingly structured and manageable systems of cinematic representation. Tarr's cinema—and in particular the ending of *Sátántangó*—attempts to negate this history and to produce a cinema even more extreme than that which Doane finds so valuable. This ending attempts, that is, to erase totally the systems of evaluation and meaning that elsewhere in the film tended to emerge. If, say, Irimiás's actions produced something of a cogent yet never quite fully locatable allegory, a return to an always-escaping-but-somehow-also-available meaning, this ending strives to eradicate those meanings entirely; to produce nothing but the wait, and indeed to turn that wait back onto its audience in the form of boredom. It asks those who watch to become those who wait, to occupy this now totally inchoate space that has finally severed the boundary between audience and image, placing both in the darkness, both inside, the window closed, the cut denied.

*Sátántangó* offers its audience a democracy to come. It waits, and with this waiting it keeps a messianic hope in its sight. The hope that a revolution will arrive, but the awareness that once it does it will already be compromised. When, in this final shot of the film, the doctor slowly boards up his windows—and with them the light that illuminates this scene—this wait is perpetually continued. Rather than summarily recap or finally provide a final rejoinder, the film ends with a waiting all its own. The doctor waits with us, in the dark and without hope for any particular outcome.[66] This is how this film, finally, presents a politics. Waiting here has become an imperative, a system for elongating the hope that transformation carries but always immediately extinguishes. It waits and so do we, for what none of us are sure, but with the unfigured spreading of potential before us. Rancière ends his chapter on *Sátántangó* and *Werckmeister Harmonies* (2001) with two short sentences: "They do not speak of hope. They are hope."[67] Waiting allows for the hope that politics requires, a messianic hope for something to come, but that always slips away at the moment of any arrival, a hope that we can wait for but that is never quite allowed. Its hiccups and disillusionments, to return to my beginning, are therefore also its promise.

It is this capacity for the simultaneous and contradictory deployment of both fear and hope that provides this film with its unique disposition. But these conflictual processes also map the film's politics, allowing it to serve as a beacon for change but also to immediately recede—a triumph of potential, but a failure of figuration. When the doctor summarily boards himself into his space and sits quietly as the credits role, this position of complete failure that creates complete hope is finally cemented.

The doctor has now lost his function as figure of surveillance and assumed the same position as the remainder of the characters in the film. By sitting in darkness he has finally and definitively acquiesced to messianism. He has revoked his own capacity for vision and retreated into a world of pure darkness. This position, and indeed that occupied by the characters that put such faith in Irimiás, is the pure position of hope—a hope unbridled from the actual and one that can only arrive in a moment of absolute misery. The trouble with this kind of hope is that its rejection of easily available outcomes in the name of a more radical alternative provides no system to ameliorate the misery that gave

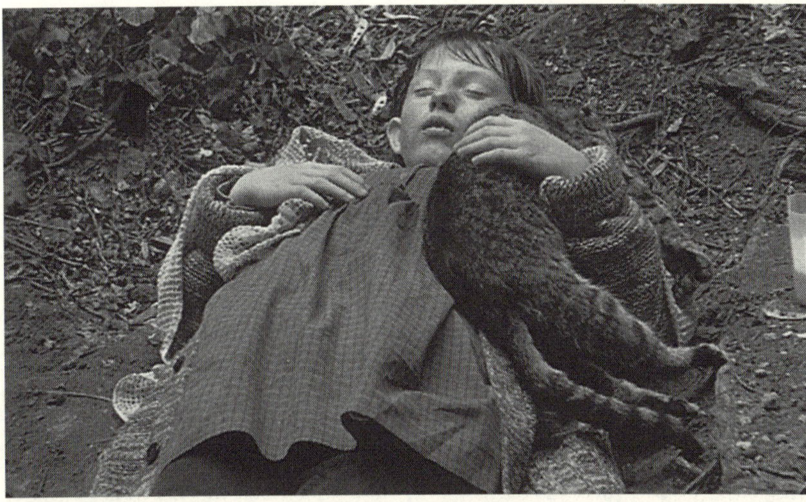

FIG. 11 Estike and her cat in *Sátántangó*.

rise to it in the first place. This is also the problem with the pure unhabituated sight that Tarr lionizes. Like the darkened house that the doctor occupies, aesthetic formations—ways of seeing or perhaps being seen—are essential to producing a unified and available politics. Without them hope may spring eternal, but not in a way that can directly produce the components needed for coherent change.

This dynamic is perhaps best exemplified by the infamous scene of Estike and her cat. After a seeming eternity of Estike torturing her cat—rolling onto it, striking it, repeating harmful names and phrases that she has heard from her family at it, and finally shoving its head into a bowl of milk laced with rat poison—she carries it, rigid in death, to a local ruin. Upon arriving, Estike also takes the rat poison and lays down to die with her stiffened pet. As the camera lingers, the narrator presents Estike's interiority, explaining that it is at this moment that she realizes the connection between all the events of the town: an "indescribably beautiful meaning" that bridges these characters (see figure 11).

Here death is figured as the extreme form of waiting, the ultimate way to escape the world and secure the expansion of external messianic forces. But it is also the moment of realization, the moment where meaning finally becomes available. Estike here goes too far; hers is the position that just surpasses the doctor's self-imprisonment. Estike crosses the threshold of waiting and extinguishes, finally, the capacity to react to the meaning that only now arrives. The wait has ended, and meaning has arrived, but not *in time*. Indeed, the waiting that this film produces must never lose track of time, of how long the wait has lasted and what it is that is being waited for. Waiting here is bound between two poles: the end signaled by action and the continued wait that crosses the threshold into death. Both of these extremes produce conclusions, but neither is capable of verifying with any certainty that the wait has succeeded. The rigidity of Estike's cat concretizes this example. Waiting refuses seeing and movement; it pushes against death. But death, despite its similarity to the wait, must never arrive, for once it does it creates form and rigidity, as it has with this cat's corpse. Rather than the openings and availabilities of the wait, Estike's death concludes and closes the state of possibility. The wait must remain on the precipice of this extreme; it must resemble death but never fully allow it.

For hope to burn its brightest it must come as close as possible to death without ever quite finding it.[68] It must retain some possibility to act but remain in a state of maximal delay. The doctor's darkened room is the place of possibility, but it must still keep time. Waiting then becomes a kind of activity all its own; it is conscious and alert but never quite fully articulated. Meaning never comes but in death, and so we cannot ever quite see it—and in the movie Estike's dying vision is of course never shown—until it is too late to be put to use. Meaning here is not available to Estike upon her death—it *is* her death. The rigidity and coherence that Estike and this film demand are only available after the cut, once things have ended and the world finally recedes into the past tense. What *Sátántangó* does is refuse us this closure, and so keeps alive its hope for a new way of ordering things.

Finally, to push forward upon this opening up to hope, my next chapter proposes still more refusal and rejection. Hong Sang-soo's *Woman on the Beach* (2006) relies on the traditions of ambiguity but in such a way as to level a critique at democracy, and in so doing jettisons the major bulwark against authoritarianism, with truly devastating results. In Tarr's cinema a hope remains that something will arrive to reunite the world, but for Hong that hope is dead.

# 3

# The End of Authority, the End of Democracy

## On *Woman on the Beach*

Béla Tarr's *Sátántangó* (1994) displays a distrust for communism while simultaneously rejecting its capitalist alternative. In so doing, it produces a profound ambiguity as to what economic system might alleviate the misery the film so clearly brings into view. Hong Sang-soo's *Woman on the Beach* (2006) furthers this distrust by adding to the list of rejected arrangements democracy itself, and it accomplishes this task by drawing and evaluating the kind of individual that the unique pairing of democracy and capitalism can produce. But this film levels its critique not with measured distance, but from within the boundaries of its own rejection. That is, *Woman on the Beach* delineates the kind of subject best suited for success under a neoliberal capitalist democracy and then proceeds to critique this figure, but it also refuses to remove itself from the scope of its criticism. The film's consistent equating of the main character with the writer/director and its opening to an autobiographical reading generate what can only be described as ambivalence—a kind of cold uncertainty regarding its major subjects that derives from a distrust of the filmmaker's own authorial perspective. This is complicated by the fact that ambivalence is perhaps also one of the qualities that this film seems to reject, creating a deadly circuit of rejection and return that rhymes with the characters' own actions.

Repetition here is key, as Hong seems to return to the same set of circumstances in many of his films. In *Woman on the Beach*, Hong attempts to perform the difficult task of diagnosing himself and his moment from within, but the film, like the others discussed thus far, never quite arrives at a coherent conclusion, remaining instead content to repeat its actions in a kind of endless loop of self-critique and self-recrimination. These repetitions are another characteristic of post-authoritarian cinema. South Korea's authoritarian past haunts this film, and its serving as a response to these conditions disallows this film from ever positing a coherent political alternative. All the while, however, the film helps to illuminate the ways that democracy and capitalism work together to reward individuals who understand that the openings in meaning produced by the conditions of democracy under capitalism provide opportunities to escape punishment for brutal and totally self-interested actions. This dynamic crystallizes the circumstances of this turn to ambivalence, for it is exactly the lack of alternatives that leads again and again to the reoccurrence of and reflection upon the same set of actions—a set of actions that, as I shall explore shortly, result in dissatisfaction but produce no coherent available alternative.[1]

In what follows, I first describe responses to the film and the literature that surrounds it, particularly as it pertains to the film's political appeals (or lack thereof). I then move into a discussion of the historical context of Hong's film, focusing on its relationship to the more overtly political films of the 1980s and early 1990s, commonly referred to as the "South Korean New Wave." Following this, I provide a formal analysis of *Woman on the Beach*, examining in detail its reflective qualities and its relationship to language and language's failings. I then move into a discussion of how the film critiques democracy, ultimately exploring how the unique combination of democracy and neoliberal capitalism combine to constitute a particular—and particularly destructive—subject. I next turn to the specific circumstances of South Korean capitalism in order to explore the relationship between contemporary economics and Hong's palpable ambivalence to it. Finally, I conclude by exploring how this film is positioned to critique neoliberalism broadly, and the role of ambivalence in leveling this critique. The discussion emphasizes how, in the South Korean context, post-authoritarian art cinema can function to reject *democracy* in addition to authoritarianism.

## Vantages

*Woman on the Beach*, Hong Sang-soo's seventh film, was released in 2006, the year after the economic peak of what has been dubbed the Hallyu, or Korean Cultural New Wave.[2] This year marked a significant downturn in what had been unprecedented export earnings for Korean cinema and is, in retrospect, commonly qualified as the first step in a dramatic decline in the economic health of South Korean film exports that has only recently been reversed.[3]

Hong's cinema, though, lies to a degree outside the economic peaks and valleys of South Korean mainstream cinema. Along with Lee Chang-dong's films, Hong's cinema maps what Kyung Hyun Kim calls a postpolitical moment in South Korean cultural production. This is evidenced by a move toward interiority and the crisis of meaning constituted by the "withering of political agency" after a period of intense political engagement.[4] This reading is corroborated by a number of critics and theorists who contend that Hong's cinema is concerned primarily with interiority rather than politics, as exemplified by critic/blogger Acquarello, who argues that "Hong exposes the subtly imperceptible (but revealing) acts of despair that momentarily betray the human soul in crisis," and further notes that it is questions of existence, not politics, that define Hong's cinema.[5]

Kim posits that pleasure—rather than the overt political concerns that occupied the directors of the late 1980s and 1990s—is what concerns Hong and some of his contemporaries and that breakdowns in communication are what primarily occupy Hong's films. He argues that his brand of cinema "strips away the thin veneer of reason and decency that covers every social network and shows, through his indignant, socially inept characters, that miscommunication is not the exception but the norm in everyday interactions between people."[6] According to Kim, this stripping away of reason and decency offers up the arbitrariness of language and in so doing disrupts the possibility for clear lines of communication. Likewise for David Scott Diffrient, "The slipperiness of selfhood and the ontological trickiness of naming" are "pivotal" for Hong's cinema.[7] The breaking apart of meaning and language that has come to define Hong's work, is, for these critics, not overtly political, but it nevertheless serves as a motif that, according to film theorist Akira Lippit, is political in that that it arrives "at the other end of politics."[8]

But, while Lippit also utilizes Kim's categorization of Hong as postpolitical to draw his point, his argument takes a distinct turn when it claims that Hong's cinema forms "lines of inquiry, communication, defense and escape."[9] These lines—lines of similarity from film to film, lines that take the form of questions posed between characters, lines of vision, and literal lines that appear in the film—produce, for Lippit, all kinds of connections but, as Lippit is careful to note, "The lines never seem to connect the point of origin with its intended destination."[10] For Lippit, this excess of lines creates chaos and pushes Hong's films always to the precipice of violence: "The questions that traverse Hong's films indicate a breakdown of the lines (through a proliferation of lines) that separate order from disorder; a collapse that leaves Hong's world rife with nervous disorders, failed personal relations, and an anxious democracy."[11]

For Lippit, these lines of communication that so often take the form of questions are also simultaneously lines of escape, systems that serve to evade blame, guilt and/or punishment by turning things around or reconstituting the situation.[12] But these escapes always return to haunt the characters, for these lines "never reach their destination; they disappear somewhere in route, only to reappear again elsewhere."[13] Rather than simple explorations of those who successfully depart and deceive, Hong's cinema, for Lippit, "is not one of limits and ends, but of repetitions, returns, and resumed lines."[14]

These lines thus serve to connect and separate the characters, always pushing outward with the possibility of unity but also, from the other side, separating them from each other.[15] Lippit, writing in 2004, explores Hong's first four films, but the trends that he locates continue, and in my view become crystallized in Hong's 2006 film *Woman on the Beach*. In a scene that I will discuss shortly, the lines of discussion here find their most literal form in a drawing by the main character that serves as both its own line of escape and, simultaneously, an attempt at an emancipatory ideal. The line that is drawn serves both to connect and to deceive and hence is the ultimate example of Lippit's proposed trope.

Where my argument departs from Lippit's, however, is in the degree to which politics plays a role in constituting the grounds of our understanding of Hong's cinema. Lippit is evasive when it comes to Hong's political position, but he does bookend his discussion by saying at the start that Hong's cinema occurs "at the end of and after politics. After the end of politics, at the end of the political lines that traverse and constitute Korean history, at the other end of politics."[16] And, at the end his analysis, Lippit states that "the 'postpolitical' nature of Hong's cinema and Hong's era comes not so much with the end of politics but with the unending nature of his politics, with the endless politics that continue to come after the end of politics."[17] Lippit's understanding of Hong's cinema seems to figure politics as a kind of structured absence, indirectly represented but immediately significant through its neglect. But this postpolitical-and-therefore-arriving-at-politics mode is troubled by the haunting and insightful claim quoted previously in which Lippit describes Hong's cinema as producing an "anxious democracy." Through this depiction of a troubled and troubling view of democracy, the film arrives at politics not through absence but directly, and indeed with vitriol. It is through a critique of democracy that this film creates a space for rethinking politics, but it does so in such a way that refuses a reinscription of the authoritarian logics that it wishes to leave behind. To develop this point, it is important to place Hong's film historically in a particular transitional moment.

## History

In 1987, after over twenty-five years of military rule, a wave of long-suppressed democratic enthusiasm swept through South Korea, leading to the first direct presidential election in years and ultimately—after the presidency of military figure Roh Tae-woo—to a civilian government beginning in 1993.[18] Pacing this politically spirited moment was an equally politically minded film movement: the Korean New Wave. Afforded a space to operate within the South Korean filmmaking landscape thanks to changes in the national censorship restrictions and the funding allowance to independent producers in 1988, this set of politically minded films arrived with the new democracy and were primarily produced by figures steeped in the activism of the 1980s.[19] Darcy Paquet describes the unifying principle of this film movement as "a commitment to using the medium of film to push for social change" and further argues that "the turbulent political events of the late 1980s called out for a cinema that engaged with the defining issues of the day, and shed new light on Korea's troubled past."[20] This New Wave movement is responsible to a large degree for building and otherwise expanding a cine-culture in South Korea, which eventually led to the boom of the 2000s; but as a politically minded and in many ways oppositional cinema, it started to decay in the mid-1990s.[21]

As Michael Robinson has argued, what concerned the films of the New Wave was the weight of history and politics in the democratizing moment: "For forty years cultural life and production had been weighed down by the heavy responsibilities of national cultural preservations, resistance to authoritarian politics, and the ambivalent discourse centered on the debate about a true Korean culture and the assault of Western popular mass culture."[22] Robinson goes so far as to say that in this politicized moment, by virtue of the ubiquity of political pressures, "there was little room not to be political."[23] Hong's cinema, of course, lies far outside this clearly historically bounded period and is instead found in a moment when the economic crisis had been beaten back—albeit at the cost of demanding labor and a decrease in access to full-time employment—and South Korea's status as economic and cultural power had been established. For Robinson, in Hong's contemporary moment the need to adhere to political "master narratives" had lessened and a new kind of cultural production emerged: "Something has clearly changed within the cultural industry in South Korea. The failing grip of the old master narratives has loosed new energies and made new synergies possible."[24] For Robinson, this lightness and newly allowed freedom grants the Korean films of the 2000s the ability to "laugh both with and at themselves," and to struggle with the past in new and dynamic ways.[25]

The directors who contributed to the boom of the early 2000s had a complicated relationship to contemporary politics. As Park Young-a explores through the example of the Korean Independent Filmmakers Association, the simultaneous transition to democracy and turn to an emphasis on cultural production led to a series of unstable alliances between filmmakers of the "democracy generation"—those whose politics were forged during the antiauthoritarian movement of the 1980s—and the seemingly contrary forces of a government committed to making South Korea into a more significant global economic presence.[26] For Park, much of the success of the South Korean cinema of the 2000s came about as a direct result of attempts by the governments of the late 1990s and early 2000s to mobilize the democratic generation and direct them toward the reconfiguration of the South Korean economy.[27] Referring to these newly minted alliances between the independent film world and the government, Park posits that "this emergent cultural field reflects a foundational shift in South Korean society, especially in its cultural production, in that the rigid boundaries that separated the state and political activism, corporate conglomerates and independent artists, filmic spaces of resistance and spaces of upwardly mobile, middle-class consumption, and local and global cultural realms have increasingly blurred."[28]

It is this turn that accounts in part for the apparent lack of politics in Hong's cinema. As these previously perceptible boundaries blur, so does the clean path toward political critique, making oppositional spaces difficult to discern. As a member of this democratic generation, Hong started to make films just at the moment of this absorption of the radical into the mainstream, and his critiques account for, and are in turn accounted for, by this transition. Without a clearly defined inside and outside—a stable authority and those excluded by its mandates—Hong's cinema finds itself unable to separate from the sphere of its own critique and as a result turns to ambiguity as the only available avenue for avoiding the total implication of its own creators.

Hye Seung Chung and David Scott Diffrient in fact place Hong and his close compatriot Lee Chang-dong as latecomers to the Korean New Wave.[29] But they are nonetheless reluctant to position Hong as a political filmmaker, instead reproducing the argument that Hong is "apolitical" because he is dedicated to the "social" and only arrives at politics obliquely.[30] Chung and Diffrient focus on narrative, in particular what they label the "cubist" process of Hong's cinema. The sputtering starts and stops, the repetitions, and the capacity to switch from the point of view of one character to another, according to Chung and Diffrient, "disables the fundamental impulse of narrative."[31] Politics, for Chung and Diffrient, is arrived at through the aporias made in this negative narrative trajectory. As they put it: "Because his films exude a textual instability based on narrative repetition, and disjunction, they force us to recognize the contradictions and nonconsensus of a society intent on denying its internal disintegration. In doing so, all three films show Seoul, its surrounding environs, and its inhabitants to be shattered remnants of their former selves."[32] Chung and Diffrient are speaking here of Hong's first three films, *The Day a Pig Fell into the Well* (1996), *The Power of Kangwon Province* (1998), and *Virgin Stripped Bare by Her Bachelors* (2000). But *Woman on the Beach* also shares much of this narrative paralysis. Where my analysis departs from Chung and Diffrient's is in the premise that what is revealed in these sputterings is urban inhabitants who are "shattered remnants of their former selves." Indeed central to my argument is the idea that a return to some great and powerful past or cogent unbroken self is haunted by the legacy of authoritarianism—a difference that reinforces the film's pessimism and the radicalness of its demand for change.[33]

For Chung and Diffrient, Hong's cinema serves as "an attempt to rescue 'meaning' from a modern milieu by way of repetition and variation," and these authors proceed to use this goal to link Hong's cinema to folkloric narratives—in particularly Korea's Pansori tradition.[34] What this reading neglects, however, is the possibility that revealing meaning in all its contingency is just as valuable as rescuing it, and it is the possibility of both reclaiming and destabilizing meaning in a single gesture that makes Hong's cinema unique, political, and always so obstinately ambivalent.

Moon Jae-cheol takes a more pessimistic stance in relation to the newness of contemporary South Korean cinema: "Today . . . social contradictions are no longer treated as the subject of film, and a director's historical consciousness or recognition of current social situations is no longer an important virtue."[35] Writing of this new attitude in 2006, Moon contends that "the self-identifying consciousness of history or reality is weaker for today's directors than for New Wave directors. Even the directors called auteurs show a different consciousness from that of the New Wave directors whose desire for newness originated from criticism of premodernity, ahistory, and commercialism."[36] To Moon, what compels these new filmmakers, of which Hong is explicitly included, is the search for newness—particularly as it pertains to technology—in the hopes of engaging their (in large part international) audiences.

Whether, then, a new lightness that allows new freedoms, as Robinson argues, or a thirst for technological novelty that effaces politics, as Moon implies, it is clear that what distinguishes the South Korean cinema of the 2000s from its 1980s and early 1990s antecedents is a distance that was previously unavailable. But counter to some claims as to the apolitical nature of 2000s cinema, I contend here that *Woman on the Beach* and the films of Hong Sang-soo more broadly engage in politics directly, in a way that might be more aptly described as working in line with the New Wave. What is different is that the political circumstances to which Hong wishes to respond are themselves more slippery and evasive than were those of the New Wave directors. His cinema, I propose, engages directly with its political moment in a way that critiques *democracy*, arguing, in effect, that democratic principles, when coupled with modern capitalist conditions, give rise to a particular subject that is unsustainable and, ultimately, deleterious. What complicates this critique, however, is the historical position of Hong's films; that is, he levels this critique of democracy knowing full well the dangers and damages of authoritarianism, and with the deliberate goal of avoiding the reinscription of these authoritarian logics.

An immediate difference between *Woman on the Beach* and the others previously discussed in this study is the distance between the film and the events that position it. Both *Sátántangó* and *Germany Year Zero* were made within a few years of their respective revolutionary moments and directly inhabit the transitional periods that spread out from the significant events that they refract. *Woman on the Beach*, however, arrives anywhere from fourteen to eighteen years after the end of authoritarianism in South Korean—depending on where one locates this ending—well after even a generous accounting for a transitional period.

This film is in fact far enough removed from the initial turn to democracy that it comes after a series of financial downturns and during a moment of relative prosperity—especially for the South Korean film industry. This distance is actually one of the primary factors governing this film, for it is what allows *Woman on the Beach* to expand its critique to include the democracy that has replaced South Korea's authoritarian past. If *Sátántangó* and *Germany Year Zero* still hold tight to the possibility that democracy might alleviate their concerns, *Woman on the Beach* turns its ire on democracy itself. It is this distance between event and critique that allows this film to widen its claims and to, finally, pull democracy into its list of failures. It is because of this distance, then, that this film finds the space to delimit and complicate the assumption that democracy will arrive and obviate the need for further inspection. As I will show, *Woman on the Beach*, without returning to authoritarianism, figures democracy as a potentially pernicious system whereby authority is reconfigured to serve the individualistic capitalist subject, who is intent on asserting its position as progenitor of meaning but with no particular project in mind beyond cultivating a new form of authority.

This chapter examines Hong's film through a series of ideas drawn from thinkers from Western Europe and the United States, but I think it is important to pause one last time to address the specific relationship to authoritarianism that makes the South Korean context unique and allows this film to make such a novel claim as to the limitations of democracy as well as authoritarianism. As Kim notes and as I have discussed, South Korea in the 1980s was torn between two poles: "It was a period of political inquietude when millions of people marched in the streets protesting the military rule and the complicit role of the United States in sustaining dictatorships in South Korea. It was also complicated by the fact that economic prosperity enabled millions to found their middle-class identities in the boulevards, shopping malls, and high-rise apartment buildings that mushroomed throughout Seoul."[37] In South Korea, authoritarianism and the comforts associated with a rapidly improving economy are uniquely linked, a pairing that persists and manifests itself in films that express nostalgia for authoritarianism.[38]

Unlike the cases of Italy or Hungary, South Korea's relationship to centralized authority is tinted by the possibility of authoritarianism being well suited for economic success. This linkage is tied closely to some of the economic decisions made by Chun Doo-hwan, president of South Korea during the 1980s and Park Chung-hee's successor as authoritarian leader of South Korea. As Kim notes of the differences between these figures, "Chun differed from his predecessor, Park, at least on one account by recognizing the importance of leisure and consumer spending as the crucial engine of capitalism and the comfort pill for the masses to temporarily forget the dispossession of their voting rights."[39] It is this difficult set of conditions that led, at least in part, to the specific ambiguities that concern Hong's film. Given this relationship between authority and prosperity, the paths for critique are complicated. Whereas, in the case of Béla Tarr the relationship to authority is linked to economic failure and, in the case of Rossellini, to national shame, the South Korean example of authoritarianism is linked to rapid and striking economic improvements.

The angry young men that Kim finds to be prevalent in 1990s South Korean cinema arise from these conditions. Having achieved their democratic goal but experiencing economic recession in the 1990s, the figures that Kim highlights lash out in response to a perceived state of powerlessness. For Kim, "Youth violence—sometimes explicit and disturbing—was surely redemptive and cathartic like those pictured in other emergent national cinemas of the West and Japan during the post–World War II era, and the compulsion towards inwardness and self-destruction tendered and imagined a pure form of male subjectivity."[40] Kim counts Hong's characters among these self-destructive males and notes that the director went to college and that his politics were largely formed in the conditions of the relatively prosperous and authoritarian 1980s.[41] Hong's turn to ambiguity and his extreme ambivalence as to the actions and abuses of his characters must be seen in light of this political trajectory, a path that greatly separates this film from the others discussed thus far. Authority here is suspect, but so are its alternatives, as it is authority that in the case of South Korean politics brought with it prosperity, and its absence economic failure.

## On the Beach

Near the beginning of the film, shortly after arriving at the off-season resort that contains the majority of the film's action, the film's protagonist Jung-rae (Kim Seung-woo), a successful film director suffering from writer's block, his colleague Chang-wook (Kim Tae-woo), and Mun-suk (Ko Hyeon-jeong), the woman Chang-wook has invited to the resort and later Jung-rae's love interest, begin a conversation that sets the tone for much of this film. After inquiring about the price of a room at the resort, the trio discuss their lodging options

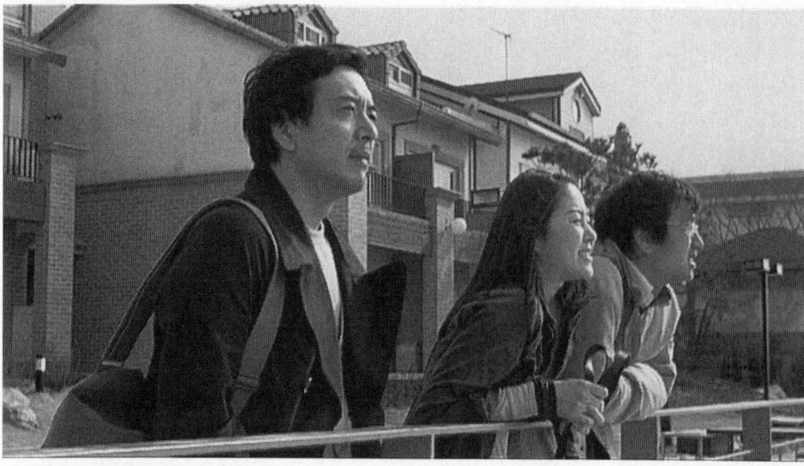

FIG. 12 Jung-rae, Chang-wook, and Mun-suk look at the ocean in *Woman on the Beach*.

as they stand looking at the sea (see figure 12). The topic quickly changes, however, as Jung-rae takes the opportunity to "compliment" his two companions on their actions thus far. Having heard her music in the car ride to the resort, Jung-rae explains that he really likes Mun-suk's musical style because it sounds like she is an ordinary person, and that he appreciates her music's amateur feel. He then moves to Chang-wook whom, he declares, he admires because he brought his girlfriend with him even though he is married, which he says indicates that Chang-wook really trusts him. Mun-suk responds by indicating that she is not Chang-wook's girlfriend, which Chang-wook bristles at. Chang-wook, offended, argues with Mun-suk as Jung-rae laughs, enjoying the spectacle.

Much of the film is built around this kind of sniping, generally coming from Jung-rae. In fact, Jung-rae's ability to use his position of power and the admiration of those around him to undermine and generally irritate his companions is the primary way that he achieves the romantic results that he seeks. But what is notable about his tactics is the way that they are depicted with a distanced tone of ambivalence; it is never made clear whether Jung-rae knows what he is doing. At times it seems that he is oblivious, at others he is clearly being devious, and at other moments still he seems to be a genuinely compelling figure who is simply speaking earnestly, and as the film proceeds all three of these different readings become increasingly confused. His seemingly accidental detonation of Mun-suk and Chang-wook's relationship surely pleases him, but it is never made clear the degree to which he can be thought of as orchestrating these events.

This uncertainty is heightened by moments where Jung-rae seems to be genuinely charming and thoughtful, many of which revolve around his ideas as a filmmaker. Immediately following this early exchange, for instance, Jung-rae makes the first substantive description of his idea for the film that he has come to this resort to write. The three, now standing on the beach, discuss Jung-rae's film idea, which he has titled *About Miracles*. As he mentions this title the camera pushes inward, tightly framing the three characters (see figure 13). After being prompted, Jung-rae explains the film:

> A man visits to a foreign beach and stays at a hotel, and in his room he plays Mozart on his CD player. Then he leaves his room and hears the same music on the elevator. He walks out of the hotel, than takes a turn at the corner, and on the street is a clown. He's doing his mime to the exact same music. It's an incredible coincidence, but this man doesn't think it's a mere coincidence. He wonders why he heard the same music three times, and he concludes that if he can find the reason why this happened, he can unravel a secret to the world, and he's obsessed with that thought. So he starts tracking hints. For ten years. First, he begins with info about the clown, the women he likes, his preferences, everything down to the brand of speakers in the hotel elevators.[42]

After being briefly interrupted, Jung-rae concludes: "In the end he finds this very thin string that links everything. I think that might be hard to get across, people only believe in things that are very sound. But that string, even if he finds it, well it's something like a soul. There is nothing bodily, it's very, very light." After a brief pause, Jung-rae asks if it is an interesting idea, and his small audience responds with silent bewilderment. Finally, Mun-suk, smiling, says that

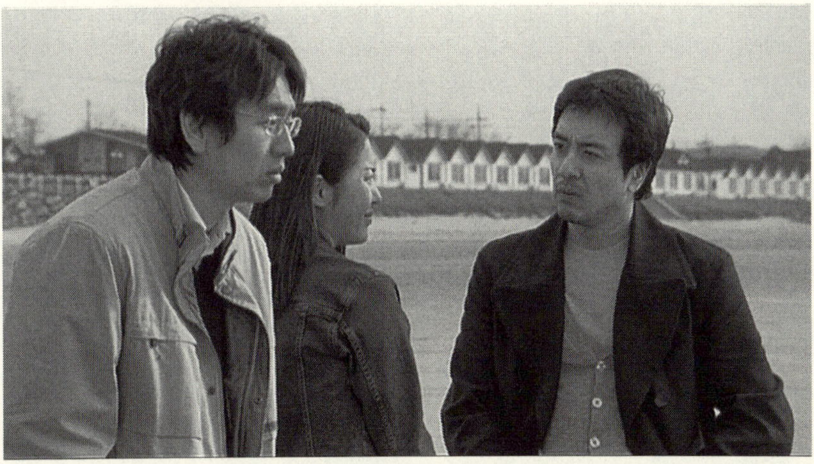

FIG. 13 Jung-rae explains his idea for a film in *Woman on the Beach*.

she doesn't quite get it, but that Jung-rae "has a way with words," and that she likes people who are eloquent.

Moments like these will be repeated throughout the film: Jung-rae renders a puzzling but nonetheless compelling thesis or idea, finds that his audience is confused but regardless impressed, and then uses this confusion to his advantage, here attempting (and as we learn succeeding) to entice Mun-suk through a display of his supposed genius. Whether this description was merely a lever in an elaborate plan or a sincere explanation of his idea for a film is never verified, but this same kind of performance by Jung-rae is seen over and over throughout the film. His goals always remain ambiguous, but as the film progresses he begins to use this same system to escape punishment for his actions. Indeed, he justifies whatever brutal decisions he makes through an explanation that is at once compelling and unique, but that always also allows him to escape blame and critique. Here, he has escaped being recognized for his backhanded compliments by moving the discussion to his idea for a film, and he repeats this pattern again and again, albeit in increasingly dire circumstances. It is in fact his capacity to render these ideas that justifies the perception of his artistic genius, and he uses this perception to achieve whatever selfish goal he has in mind and to subsequently evade any repercussions. His explanation that "people will only believe things that are sound" is largely his justification for much of his behavior: if the world only respected his genius and the difficulty of his claims, he seems to say, it would find his actions to be justified.

What causes this tone of ambivalence is that the arguments that Jung-rae makes, the justifications for his actions, are always convincing; there is always a possibility that he might be right. Coincidence has brought these three people together, and he seems to be indicating that further actions taken by them at this beach are merely a product of their following these mysterious threads that lead them from one place to another. This is at once a striking and compelling declaration, and also a validation for whatever actions he might take next. Given the reflective status of this film—it was made by a director and screenwriter (Hong) and is about a director and screenwriter (Jung-rae) who is visiting a beach and writing a film about a man who visits a beach—it becomes even more unclear how Jung-rae's ideas are to be received. Whether compelling explanations of difficult concepts or subtle tactics deployed to win the interests of those he addresses, these little asides are the fulcrum of this film and imbue it with its palpable ambivalence. *Woman on the Beach* refuses to indicate whether Jung-rae's actions are sincere or whether he is endeavoring on an elaborate scheme that is built on his perceived genius. The film is constantly caught between these two available passages, and refuses ever to resolve these contrary positions.

It is these asides and their constitutive uncertainty that mark this film as critique, as they reveal the ways that its characters, and in particular Jung-rae, are capable of escaping punishment by deploying an understanding of the world that is at once subtle and thoughtful, but also possibly illusory, just a sleight of hand that allows for escapes and further abuses. The conditions that allow for these evasions are constituted by democracy when paired with capitalism, a system that rewards those who champion uncertainty in the name of deception, those who claim genius but whose claims are always on unstable ground.

The plot of *Woman on the Beach* is surely recognizable to those familiar with Hong's work. The film is broken into two parts. In the first, Jung-rae, Mun-suk, and Chang-wook go to the aforementioned resort in the town of Shinduri. At the resort Mun-suk and Jung-rae begin an affair that leads to Jung-rae, the next day, acting aloof and backing away from their now pending relationship by escaping back to Seoul. In the second half of the film, however, Jung-rae begins to regret his actions in regard to their relationship and returns to the resort in the hope of rekindling their romance. Upon arriving and after attempting to contact Mun-suk, Jung-rae has a brief affair with another woman, Sun-hee (Song Seon-mi) to whom he is attracted because of her perceived resemblance to Mun-suk. Mun-suk arrives at the resort unannounced and discovers the affair, but Jung-rae firmly lies to her and, for the rest of the film, refuses to admit to the second relationship—a stance which becomes increasingly absurd as the film progresses. Finally, Jung-rae, having alienated both women, returns to Seoul with a completed treatment for his screenplay—a script presumably based on these same romantic entanglements and which is perhaps this movie that we are watching.

What this synopsis neglects, of course, is the style of the film. Consisting primarily of single-take sequences of characters speaking, this film consistently undermines its melodramatic thrust and instead allows its characters to relentlessly defend their actions. This can be seen in the scene discussed above when Chang-wook needlessly becomes frustrated with Mun-suk for explaining that they are not a couple. "Do we have to have sex to be boyfriend and girlfriend?" is his retort, providing further information for Jung-rae's potential plan to subvert their relationship and further alienating Mun-suk, who responds by saying that yes, they do, and then asking Jung-rae for confirmation. Shot in a single long take with an unmoving camera, this exchange illuminates how this film simply allows its characters to defend their actions endlessly, giving them enough rope, so to speak, to subvert each of their decisions. As a result, these characters become increasingly unsympathetic and at times outright intolerable.

Another moment exemplifies both Hong's style and his relationship to ambiguity and ambivalence. Late in the film Mun-suk asks Jung-rae outright if he has slept with Sun-hee. Persisting in his lie, Jung-rae argues that he interviewed her to get an understanding of the character he is writing based on his relationship with Mun-suk, but that nothing further happened. Attempting to change the subject, Jung-rae asks Mun-suk if she heard his earlier confession in which

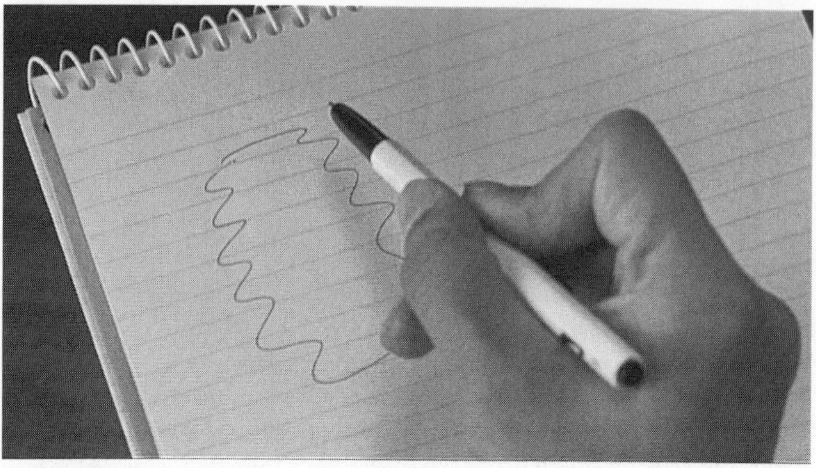

FIG. 14 Jung-rae's drawing of the "real thing" in *Woman on the Beach*.

he admitted he was deeply disturbed by her acknowledging that she slept with foreign men while abroad. While she had seemed to be passed out drunk during the confession, she here admits that she was in fact conscious. His semi-apologetic final response unfolds via a discussion of what he calls "images." According to Jung-rae, his obsession with purity and Mun-suk's refusal to accept his denial are merely "images" that were imprinted on them by others. In explicating this idea of images he draws a squiggly line on a pad of paper, a drawing that Hong emphasizes with one of the few inserts of the film (see figure 14). Jung-rae defines this squiggly line as the "real thing," what, for him, is constantly changing and infinitely curving. He then adds three points and connects them. Pointing to the resulting triangle, he argues that this is the "image that recurs." He then redraws the triangle and, isolating it on its own, emphasizes the three points to explain how they comprise an image via three distinct imaginary objects: the foreigner's face, the foreigner's penis, and their sexual position as suggested by his experience with porn (see figure 15). Once these three points are set, he explains, they come to correspond with the bad image that he cannot escape. This bad image, the triangle, then comes to overpower the original unknowable event (the squiggly line). Finally, adding some more image-dots to the original squiggle—these signifying fond moments—Jung-rae draws a new shape, one that might better represent his experience with Mun-suk (see figure 16). However, this image, he claims, is too unusual and, despite it being a better representation, is too hard to understand. He ends by saying that, despite the difficulty of this last shape, they must try their best to see it rather than default to the triangle. A cut back to Mun-suk reveals that she is impressed and that his attempts to dig himself out of trouble have for the time being succeeded.

Referring to this sequence, critic J. Hoberman notes, "At one point, the irate Joong-rae [*sic*] draws Moon-sook [*sic*] a diagram to illustrate his convoluted mental processes. The joke is that it's the most baffling image in this immaculately constructed movie."[43] This is to say that, for Hoberman, this sequence generates a variety of problems that trouble its interpretation. What Jung-rae calls for, at first, is a model whereby images come to form new shapes and subsequently new perceptions. The problem with Jung-rae's model is that these shapes remain shapes and thus will always fail to account for the potentials of the things they claim to represent. For Jung-rae, there is no way out of this bind,

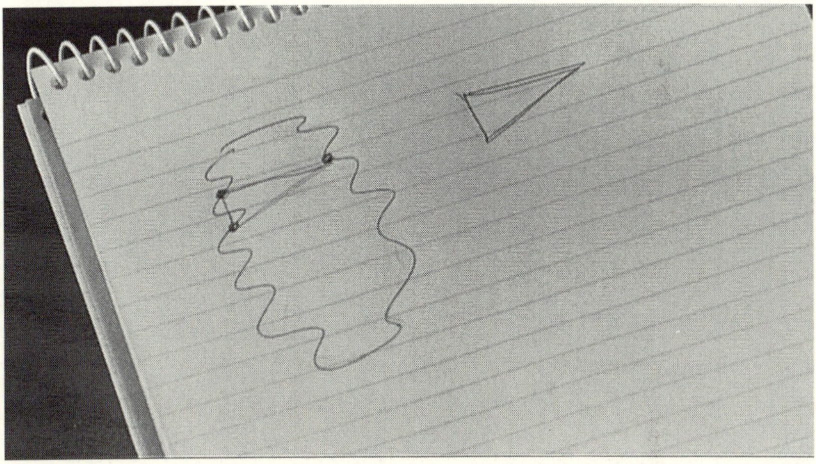

FIG. 15 Jung-rae's drawing of the "image that recurs" in *Woman on the Beach.*

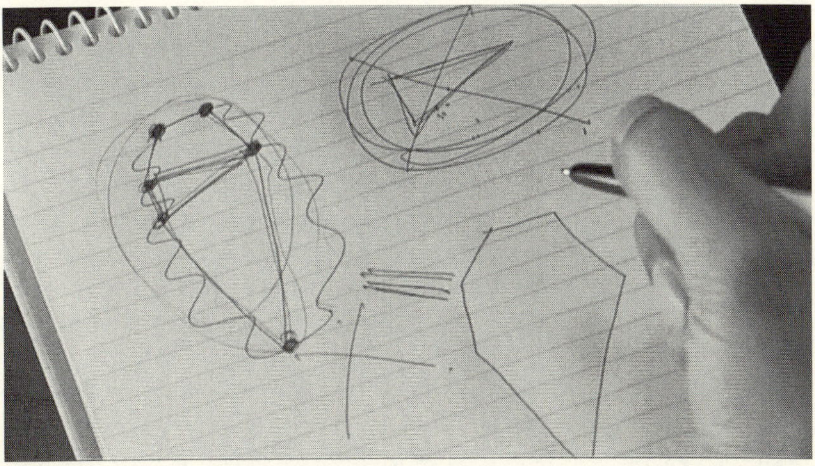

FIG. 16 Jung-rae's new shape in *Woman on the Beach.*

only the softening of some of its jagged edges via the introduction of new shapes—themselves, of course, full of jagged edges of their own.

The other problem that haunts this scene is the question of its sincerity. Jung-rae has utilized this explanation as a system for escaping Mun-suk's questioning. She has here confronted him directly with the question of his sexual tryst and this explanation is to some degree an attempt—and ultimately for the time being a successful one—to avoid her accusations. To be clear, Jung-rae has developed, or at least outlined, this system as a way to convince Mun-suk that she has been overcome by previous images, but she is *correct*, and her easily deduced conclusion is actually on the mark—a fact of which Jung-rae is, of course, well aware. This model then holds a double meaning: it is the outlining of a system to escape ready-made meanings and to confront the boundaries of the perceptual system, but it is also in this context a way to avoid confrontation and to escape the implications of one's actions. The question that this scene suggests is this: How can one determine whether Jung-rae is sincere about his model or if the system for coming to knowledge that he outlines is merely a ruse? And, furthermore, how and why does this distinction matter?

The dynamic that Jung-rae activates is best phrased as the interaction between the power and potential of a productive openness and the avenues for retreat and deception that this openness makes room for. In *A Thousand Plateaus: Capitalism and Schizophrenia*, Gilles Deleuze and Félix Guattari produce an explanation of openness and its potentials, but they are also careful to note the violence that this process can entail. In discussing the topic of "the smooth and the striated," Deleuze and Guattari propose that the act of bringing contours and form to any indeterminate or "smooth" operation (an idea, image, memory, or piece of knowledge) inevitably brings about a brutal process whereby certain ways of interacting with the operation are excluded. As Deleuze and Guattari posit, this process of "striating," or realizing concrete form, "is an operation that undoubtedly consists of subjugating, overcoding, metricizing smooth space, in neutralizing it, but also in giving it a milieu of propagation, extension, refraction, renewal, and impulse without which it would perhaps die of its own accord: like a mask without which it could neither breathe nor find a general form of expression."[44] The content of this claim is that any particular arrangement—of politics, of aesthetics, of thinking—always produces an outside, an exclusion that, through the repetition of this striating process, can be corrected over and over, always creating new exclusions but moving, however slowly, toward inclusion. It is the procedure that they call "deterritorialization" that governs this process, pushing on these recently erected barriers between inside and outside and asking what can kinds of reconfigurations are necessary and available. The space between coherent modes, or what Deleuze and Guattari call a smooth or indeterminate state, is the space of pure potential, but this smooth state is not actualizable. While full of promise, it has no structure of its own to make it material or coherent. The smoothness, then, must always call forth a particular configuration—a reterritorialization—that produces another set of contours, a knowable arrangement that can be acted upon or in relation to. The trouble with this new arrangement is that it must be restrictive, delimited, and cogent, and it must therefore produce an outside, a negated section that will in turn make new demands on the inside.

For Deleuze and Guattari this back-and-forth is a cruel process that always leaves something out. But it is also a model for change and creation. That is, through this slow process something like a gradual but substantive change is constantly underway, and throughout these developments new exclusions can constantly find their voice and make demands on the reconstituted whole.

Jung-rae's doodles gesture toward this same model. His attention to shapes and the need to rearrange them so as to account for difference and divergence adheres closely to Deleuze and Guattari's ideas. The ideal Jung-rae procures—new shapes that are less familiar but that better account for his experience—matches Deleuze and Guattari's model for change and the way that habituated formations must be pulled apart and reconstituted. But Jung-rae's actions also serve to illuminate the dark side that underwrites this system: the possibility that this model for openness and reconfiguration also proposes an available out, a mechanism to obscure one's true intentions and/or circumvent processes and arrangements that might condemn or otherwise punish, or at least make one be held accountable for, a set of actions.

Jung-rae's actions, then, enable two perspectives that point in totally opposite directions: They at once serve as a sincere attempt to break apart regressive or restrictive modes of seeing, but also renounce nothing in particular and propose the possibility of new understandings of the world in order only to provide avenues for escape. That is, Jung-rae reserves for himself openings to back out through and denies to others the path to pursue him. This is the dark brilliance of Jung-rae's actions throughout the film. He critiques society but never quite verifies the critique that he renders. Never gives specific structure to his concerns nor indicates how they might be leveraged to bring about any particular change. His critiques only serve to mystify his actions, and, given the particular moments when he voices these claims, their major function seems to be misdirection. His arguments serve the purpose of providing an avenue for escape, an escape that winds a path through the language of inclusion and acknowledgment. *Woman on the Beach* itself occupies much this same position. This is a film capable of acknowledging both Jung-rae's accuracy and his capacity to propose substantive arguments for change, but it also and ultimately eviscerates him for using his intelligence in the name of deception. Like Jung-rae himself, this film does not altogether trust the system for slow and incremental change that it supplies. Or it trusts it and it does not. It sees Deleuze and Guattari's model for change as available but also lacking—as a conditioning mechanism that produces a deceptive subject as much as a useful model for politics. It is this tension, the thinking of this model for change as both productive and deceptive, that yields the ambivalence that structures this film.

## Critiquing Democracy

*Woman on the Beach* affords a view of the modern, upper-class subject as constituted by the transition from authoritarianism to democracy. In order to support this proposition, it is necessary to bring into this discussion how democracy, despite its myriad clear advantages, when coupled with capitalism in its modern mode serves to constitute a particular, and particularly troubled, subject position.

In "The Eros and Ambitions of Psychological Man," Stephen Gardner articulates a critique of democracy that is based on the particular tensions it produces. For Gardner, the key to this critique is his locating of the "psychological man," a particular subject constituted by the circumstances of democracy. Gardner argues, "By removing or crippling the old formalities and conventions of social life, democracy creates a culture in which individuals are supposedly free to relate to each other simply as such—pure individuals or pure "natural" beings, as it were. This idea of nature evidently presupposed the total socialization of man, but in a way unlike any other society. Believing that they are children of Eden, these "emancipated" democrats act out the latest script written for them by popular culture."[45] For Gardner, then, the separation of authority from its hierarchical structure and any claim to a greater outside knowledge produces a desiring figure convinced of its own genius, but that is in fact no less guided by the circumstances of its political and economic position.

This figure is what Gardner locates in his psychological man, which he defines as "an individual who is morally detached from communal order and rendered, at least in his own psyche, the free agent of his desires, the demigod of his Eros and ambitions."[46] Gardner defines this subject by asking us to "imagine a character who is neither outside nor above the social order (like a mystic or a monk) yet not at home within it, a social yet a-social individual, able neither to transcend society nor to identify with it."[47] Gardner's psychological man maintains a distance form society, not in the name of some ascetic principle, not because of a wholesale dismissal of any particular quality of the modern world, but because this subject perceives the social as having nothing to offer. But this subject is unable to fully disconnect; instead, the psychological man is stuck in a middle space, neither all in nor all out, bound by social restrictions but not believing in them, trying to shirk authority but unable to muster a coherent alternative (or even a critique).

Gardner's model for the psychological man is based upon an understanding of the capitalist subject under democracy being guided by the desire to emulate the positions and actions of those that they feel are successful. Indeed, for what Gardner terms "democratic desire" mimesis is key, as this mode of desire is based "in the cultural exigencies of democracy."[48] This is to say that the central ideals of democracy, when combined with capitalism, beget a kind of competitive desire as a result of the mimetic process of seeing and emulating one's fellow free beings in a kind of endless loop of self-fulfillment that refuses any external claims to authoritative boundaries or any set of goals that pertain to anything other than one's self. Desire in this scenario is unfettered by any claim to hierarchical order and is therefore composed solely from the perceived successes of those that one encounters—there is no governing claim that functions to justify any set of actions, and the result is intense avarice.

For Jung-rae, this relationship to one's image of other people finds its logical conclusion in the figure of repetition. Jung-rae's rejection of Mun-suk and his subsequent replacement of her with a woman he finds reminiscent of her figures his desire as the attempt to replace some perceived absence with the very object that he himself rejected. Jung-rae's seeming understanding of the "images" that force him to repeat his own actions reveals his status as to some degree aware of his own psychological dynamics. But his initial and obvious locating of his desire in his friend's romantic interest and, in the second half of the film, his perception of having lost a potential wholeness, locates his actions squarely in the cycle of endless repetition of desire and rejection. Jung-rae's desire carries no justifying claim or coherent set of goals and, what is more, *he knows it*. What eludes him, as Gardner might say, is the degree to which democratic capitalism, and the qualities that it engenders, are responsible for this knowledge.

In the moment when he draws the shapes and escapes, for a time, his punishment, he is not merely presenting a viable alternative to seeing the world; he is also (or perhaps only) finding a way to justify a set of behaviors. But it is important to note that these behaviors are not what he necessarily condones, for there is no coherent argument on his part that serves to defend them. What is most striking about this moment, and this film in general, is that Jung-rae has no particular interest in reconstituting society in a new direction, no particular moral position or any emancipatory spirit. He is incapable, it seems, of identifying with the figure, Mun-suk, that he mistreats, but he holds no particular belief system that is any different from that figure's. The only thing that makes Jung-rae unique among the characters in this film is an unwavering confidence in the persistence of his own genius, which, for him, justifies any decision he makes to deceive and abuse others.

Whereas the malaise of, say, Michelangelo Antonioni's protagonists or Marcello in Federico Fellini's *La Dolce Vita* seems motivated by an attempt—however unsympathetic—to find an understanding of their place in the world, Jung-rae seems engaged in no such search. His is not a quest for the finding of meaning but is instead an attempt to shirk the burden of meaning altogether. He holds no particular point of view, but he rejects wholesale the world with which he interacts. His attempt to constitute something new—what is here the expansion of shapes and the subsequent expansion of images—connects Jung-rae, to return to chapter 1, to the ideas outlined by Zygmunt Bauman in *Liquid Modernity*, particularly by way of this character's ability to recede into the fractures of meaning that poststructuralist thought offers in an attempt to navigate one's surroundings. For Bauman, "The present-day situation emerged out of the radical melting of the fetters and manacles rightly or wrongly suspected of limiting the individual freedom to choose and to act. *Rigidity of order is the artifact and sediment of the human agents' freedom.*"[49] The attempt to expand shapes is accounted for in the case of Jung-rae's by a kind of thoughtless pursuit of freedom for freedom's sake, an empty revolution that holds no particular wish for change.

Speaking of the absence of revolutions in the contemporary moment, Bauman states: "If the time of systemic revolutions has passed, it is because there are no buildings where the control desks of the system are lodged and which could be stormed and captured by the revolutionaries; and also because it is excruciatingly difficult, nay impossible, to imagine what the victors, once inside the building (if they found them first), could do to turn the tables and put paid to the misery that prompted them to rebel."[50] When, to return to his explanation of shapes and their limitations, Jung-rae presents his explanation of freedom and habituated ways of seeing the world, he is doing exactly what Bauman presents as pernicious. He plans here to remove the control desks and hide the buildings that constitute his treachery, and in so doing to remove any system whereby Mun-suk might level a counterargument. His argument is about freedom and how it can be achieved via a rethinking of the things we frequently encounter, but he uses this explanation also as a way to justify his own destructive behavior. If we would only rethink our understanding of *him*, he seems to say, we would be able to think differently about his actions. This is the dark truth of claims to freedom and potential: they allow us to think about things in new ways, but provide no avenue for organizing critique. To speak of this project directly, Jung-rae therefore at once proposes an eloquent explanation of the gains of ambiguity—its allowing us to rethink our habituated understandings of the world and, hopefully, arrive at a new politics—but also, through his actions, makes clear how these ambiguities can serve as lines of escape for those who might take advantage of the world's new freedoms.

The South Korean context strongly encourages this reading. The intense modernization that South Korean underwent in the 1970s and 1980s was overseen by violent authoritarian rule, but unlike in the case of the authoritarian

Italian or totalitarian German governments of the 1940s, the arrival of democracy in South Korea was not punctuated by intense destruction. As a result, authoritarianism in South Korea avoided a connection with the depths of depravity and guilt that are associated with the revelations of the conclusions of World War II. There is then an available nostalgia for authoritarianism that is unique to these conditions. The possibility that a centralized and hierarchical authority could alleviate some of the insecurities and destructive tendencies that compel Jung-rae contributes to the ambivalence on display here, but it is tempered by the memories of violence that accompany these hierarchies. This is to say that the competition, doubt, insecurity, and self-obsession of Jung-rae bring to mind the failings of democratic capitalism, but the authoritarian alternative that this critique brings to mind is in this case blocked by the violence that marked authoritarian South Korea. Without either authoritarianism or democracy offering any respite from crisis, then, what can be done in light of the critique that Hong has offered? Jung-rae never attempts to assert his own response to the gaps in certainty that he locates and takes advantage of. *He just wants to get away with things*, and he is happy to use the openings in meaning inherent to democracy to achieve this goal. He is the figure of ambivalence that only South Korea's context can provide: he mistrusts democracy as much as authoritarianism. One offers brutal hierarchies, the other brutal horizons, and neither is particularly strongly linked to well-being.

Jung-rae's actions propose a critique of the openings provided by certain avenues of critical theory as readily as they lionize these same openings. That is, Jung-rae recognizes the contours—or perhaps the potential negative outcomes—of calls to openness like those voiced by Deleuze and Guattari. But he also recognizes that, in the milieu that he occupies, this emphasis on inclusion also provides a series of outs that he is happy to take advantage of. This film, given my reading, stands as both a celebration of openness while also acknowledging the paths for escape that this same celebration always—and in this case quite literally—draws. The question remains though: Can *Woman on the Beach* do both of these things at once? Can it celebrate and critique the same set of availabilities simultaneously?

For Bauman, the history of critical theory was predicated on the coherence of a centralized authority to push against, and the modern crisis of critical thought has arisen in response to the absence of this authority.[51] But this is not the same as saying that the antiauthoritarian methods of old are no longer valuable. It simply means that their effectiveness—which itself was always in question in the first place—has diminished. This is exactly the problem that *Woman on the Beach* strives to illuminate. Its purpose is not the rejection of Deleuze and Guattari's project, but instead to offer a rejoinder that recognizes its failures and difficulties when it comes to contemporary capitalist democracy. And it is its relationship to authority that concretizes this film's line of critique. For

Hong, authority would provide the cogent inside that an outside could then push against, but that inside has disappeared and with it the availability of leveling a call for a new reconfiguration. What is there to reconfigure, this film seems to ask, if all the methods for locating and constituting an authority have been rejected in the name of democratic capitalism?

*Woman on the Beach* illustrates how critical thought in the Deleuzian mode is not an unassailable methodology. In fact, this film shows how its methods can and have been assimilated into neoliberal capitalism, and how market logics have incorporated fluidity, inclusivity, and openness into their own systems of self-justification.

The self-reflection implied in Jung-rae's shapes is indicative of the transition to democracy that haunts this film. Jung-rae's actions conflate reflection with defense. The borders that outline the self are the focus of his theory of the world; his goal is to expand them, and to allow others to expand theirs, but his purpose remains veiled and, perhaps, incoherent by virtue of his ulterior motives. According to Gardner, the psychological man "entered into the twilight zone of modernity, the realm of ambivalence and ambiguities that ensue when every fixed point of reference is dissolved into the sheer interplay of individuals in a culture that can no longer sustain its origins."[52] For Jung-rae, the fixed points that might account for the shapes that he draws are what need to be liquefied, a point that he explicitly makes in his drawing and redrawing.

The capacity to create and represent this explanation for ideas and memories and their becoming calcified is surely a democratic gesture and a repudiation of a centralized authority, as it was for Deleuze and Guattari. But the available interpretation of Jung-rae's actions as the justification for an elaborate lie, with only escape and further deception as its ideal outcome, dissipates the clarity of his actions and brings into view the way that democracy can be reduced to a tool to justify unethical behavior. Democracy, for Hong, cuts both ways; it allows for both liberation and manipulation by destructive forces, hence his ambivalence.

This ambivalence also extends to the precarious position of the women in this film. For Freudian theorist Juliet Flower MacCannell, democracy has positioned its subject in remarkably new and different ways. For MacCannell, "Our 'collective' logic—our naïve belief—is that we no longer have a superego, that *It* wants nothing. If we look more deeply, however, we find that, in the wake of the democratic revolution in governance, what has been done away with is only the recognizable parental function of the super ego, and its best part."[53] According to MacCannell, the *It*, the superego or big Other that constitutes social standards and judges our actions, has not been erased in modern democratic society; it has been refigured. Where the symbolic figure of the father had traditionally held this position, he has been supplanted in the modern world by the figure of the brother. In what MacCannell calls "post-Oedipal society," this figure of the brother assumes this position in the name of a democratic and equal world. This regime of the brother, rather than actually diffusing meaning, creates a range of problems. Speaking of this figure of the brother, MacCannell says, "Agent and sole heir of patriarchy's most negative features, he creates as many false leads and artificial ties as he needs to cover his destruction of his real familial roots and relations. And he thus absolves himself of any obligation toward them. He does not have to fill the father's role any more responsibly and positively than the tyrant had: he is only acting, after all. It is he who is a pro forma father, without a communal or global species-saving goal, a despot, a mute sovereign, the (only) one who really enjoys."[54] That is, in modern democracy the superego has not been deposed of and remains the center of orientation for the rules and values in place. But the form of this superego has been transferred from the figure of the father, the violent but obsessively protective tyrant, to that of the brother, a figure that makes claims to freedom even as it institutes brutal rules. The brother, unlike the father, enacts controls in the name of equality and self-governance, and has therefore shirked much of the protective principle that constituted the father in the first place. In this new order, the brother has supplanted the father as the organizing principle for our social order, but this figure is no less destructive. Its major difference is that it is justified by the rules and values of democracy rather than those of traditional society; that is, it asserts its position by virtue of its relationship to freedom and self-governance, not hierarchical control.

The regime of the brother is therefore much more deceptive than that of the father, as it occupies a position that modern society pretends does not exist—self-governance, after all, supposedly subverts the need for this figure. As MacCannell outlines, women in this new regime, those who had the most to gain in the deposing of the patriarchal order, actually find themselves in a heightened position of precarity. "The thought that he [the brother] becomes a man only by comparison with and difference from his equal but different 'other' is never admitted. He suppresses his sister's specific desire—for equal access to identity—making it the basis for his law, his rule. The brother seizes the sexual 'symbol' in a power grab rooted in his own inability to accept a mere genital difference as the foundation of his 'identity'—and of hers."[55] In this way the woman in the regime of the brother must bear the brunt of the brother's insecurity, his need to justify his position of power by something other than simply his similarity to the father. Deep down, the male in this arrangement knows that he has no particular reason for his power, but he must overcome this insecurity by virtue of his differences, of which gender becomes paramount. Under the logic of the regime of the brother, male domination is reinstituted, now with a heightened animosity for women that results from the knowledge that the power granted to men is arbitrary and constituted only by the fact of their wielding it.

MacCannell's description of the status of authority in modern democratic society goes a long way in explaining the otherwise incoherent actions of Jung-rae in his treatment of Mun-suk. By demanding her approval and, after securing it, rejecting her, Jung-rae uses Mun-suk's feelings toward him as the measure of his self-worth, and his ability to reject them as the means by which he proves his genius and therefore his central position as master of meaning. Mun-suk, who is at times no less manipulative than Jung-rae, is admonished and ultimately rejected for acquiescing to Jung-rae's demands. She is unable, it seems, to make the right move, for any position she takes will feed back into Jung-rae's game of acceptance and rejection. This film's distrust of democracy and its depiction of the damage caused by a society dedicated to the fiction of self-governance is helpful, then, in revealing the way that the supposedly self-made genius capable of organizing the world is constituted mainly by sexual difference. This construction necessitates gendered exclusion and violence in order to reaffirm these positions of power.

MacCannell's take on the structure of power in democratic society is valuable for again critiquing democratic capitalism, but like this film in general it cannot help but produce ambivalence because, much like in the case of *Woman on the Beach*, the traditional society that this new regime has arisen from, the regime of the father, is no better. This ambivalence refuses outright dismissal, as democracy in even this representation holds within it the positive potential to be evaluated and hopefully changed. The shapes that Jung-rae previously outlined and their ability to be rewritten represent just this kind of democratic potential, and *Woman on the Beach* does not wish to replace it outright. What confounds this position is the question of what is to be done with distrust, with the possibility that the malleability of ideas that democracy engenders can be abused and destroyed, and furthermore that capitalism encourages and rewards those who wish to escape through democracy's gaps. As in the case of Jung-rae's explanation of memories and ideas, democracy is at once a valuable and coherent arrangement that takes into account the capacity for humans to differ and diverge. But in its horizontality democracy also produces the room for deception, the opportunity to disrupt, overrun, and, most importantly, to take advantage of the decentralization of meaning and authority that it demands.

## The Market

The topic of the capacity for market logics to undermine the Deleuzian deterritorialization process is perhaps best addressed by putting it in relation to critiques of neoliberalism. Such critiques have grown in strength and precision as the forces of market capitalism have continued to ascend in recent years. As David Harvey puts it, "Neoliberalism is in the first instance a theory of political economic practices that proposes that human well-being can best be advanced by liberating individual entrepreneurial freedoms and skills within an institutional framework characterized by strong private property rights, free markets, and free trade."[56] This simple definition illuminates some of the issues that haunt Jung-rae. The capacity of individual entrepreneurs totally unfettered by regulation and free to pursue any new system for increasing gain is figured in terms of relationships in *Woman on the Beach*. But what becomes clear thanks to Jung-rae's maneuverings is the degree to which this logic of "free" entrepreneurship that neoliberal capitalism demands can devastate human interactions when translated from its original context as a market principle.[57] The ways in which neoliberalism has moved from the market and into other contexts has produced much—but certainly not all—of its devastating effect. As Harvey posits, neoliberalism "has pervasive effects on ways of thought to the point where it has become incorporated into the common-sense way many of us interpret, live in, and understand the world."[58]

The damages of neoliberalism and its failure to account for those on the wrong end of its ever-widening income divide are well documented.[59] The damage unleashed on those who stand to benefit from neoliberal logics is less often discussed, however. As Harvey effectively notes, "Those thoroughly incorporated within the inexorable logic of the markets and its demands find that there is little time or space in which to explore emancipatory potentialities outside what is marketed as 'creative' adventure, leisure and spectacle. Obliged to live as appendages of the market and of capital accumulation rather than expressive beings, the realm of freedom shrinks before the awful logic and the hollow intensity of market involvements."[60] It is this "hollow intensity" that best describes Jung-rae's actions. Left to pursue some vague "freedoms" that yield only incoherent and irrelevant gains in his quest for proof of his genius, Jung-rae approaches each human encounter with intense aggression, as though each is a potential financial victory.

Through the character of Jung-rae, Hong strives to address neoliberalism from the angle of those who might favor it. His film denounces neoliberalism's failings not just for the damage that it does to those who might suffer as a result of the services it cuts and the income gaps that it creates, but also because of the demands it makes on those who might stand to benefit financially from its principles. Jung-rae's actions are severely limited by the corrupt and incoherent "freedoms" neoliberalism creates—the freedom to get ahead and conquer at all costs, the freedom to proceed without regard for the ramifications of one's actions, the freedom to constitute one's own authority and to proceed with no regard for providing any justification other than the (supposed) absolute truths of action, genius, and individuality. This is so say that this film is at its core suffused with the logics of neoliberalism, but its reflective and ambivalent depiction of these events also creates the distance needed to evaluate these logics. *Woman on the Beach*, then, is a bit like Jung-rae's own explanations of his actions: it at once levels, by virtue of its disdain for its characters, a critique, but also benefits from its own claims to ambiguity and genius.

The specifics of South Korean neoliberalism help to account for the particularities of Hong's critiques. As Jesook Song notes, the neoliberal practices of flexible labor have disturbingly combined in the South Korean context with the claims and wishes of the leftist movements of the 1980s. According to Song, "Radical socialist movements that led to the end of the South Korean fascist capitalist state (1960–87) not only promoted the emancipation of the suppressed working class, but paved the way for the liberalization of the economy and the emergence of individual rights discourse. This transition to liberalization ushered in the neoliberal capitalist logic of individual responsibility and flexibility after the Asian debt crisis."[61] In South Korea the initial leftist conception of labor rights was predicated, as elsewhere, on the emancipation of workers from the brutal and exploitative conditions of the workplace, in particular factories, but was quickly co-opted by the market-minded government of postoppositional South Korea. For Song, in the wake of an oppositional politics, a harmonious relationship between the state and the citizens was presented as viable, and the mass demonstrations of the past were presented as harmful to regular and reliable business practices.[62] "The flexible and self-sufficient labor subjectivity that South Korean leftist intellectuals devised to counter the late-developing authoritarian state and Fordist capitalist production is not effective in defying neoliberal governmentality and post-Fordist capitalist production. Unwittingly, the flexible subjectivity has become subsumed in the new system of capitalist production and the state control of labor."[63] Song's discussion serves here not only to lay out the neoliberal practices of flexible labor that seem to factor into Hong's films, but also to explain how these qualities are uniquely grounded in the change from an oppositional politics to a postpolitical moment, exactly the same moment that ended the run of the Korean New Wave film movement.

*Woman on the Beach* presents, in the character of Jung-rae, an individual positioned by the South Korean neoliberal transition. Jung-rae is a figure whose labor and leisure time are inextricably linked, indeed to such a degree that his leisure activities are not only subject to marketization but have become indistinguishable from his labor. In fact, the justification of his actions as contributing to his screenplay-writing process—the system by which he helps himself and others to make money—is what allows him to act so brutally toward the other characters in the film. As long as it is in the name of genius, Jung-rae's maneuverings seem to assert, any set of actions is allowable—particularly if these actions might result in the breaking of his writer's block and the subsequent completion of a new screenplay.

Hong's film illuminates the way that flexible labor and the disintegration of a labor/leisure divide encourages any set of actions that might generate economic success. This is exactly the process by which neoliberalism begins to absorb aspects of life outside the narrowly defined category of "the workplace." The question of how to overcome this set of pressures, however, is much more difficult to answer. If Hong implicates Jung-rae then he also must be implicating the South Korean film industry in which the genius and flexibility of a figure like Jung-rae are so richly rewarded. And, to widen the purview of this indictment, Hong himself, as the figure to which Jung-rae is so obviously related, must also fall within this critique. How then does one escape this loop of increased monetization, and furthermore how does one render a critique from the position of being rewarded by this very process? Its being so clearly imbricated within the system it wishes to denounce leaves this film at an impossible juncture. How, it asks, are we to proceed?

Take, for instance, the final scene of the film. After Jung-rae departs—admitting in the car ride home that he has written his script (presumably based on these events) during his short stay at the resort—the film leaves him on his drive back and returns to Mun-suk, still at the resort. She wakes up in the room where she has just had her most recent, and most destructive, row with Jung-rae and walks, slowly, to the hotel's front porch. Surprisingly, she receives a call from Jung-rae, who coyly asks her again if she is still interested in him. She responds by jokingly asking if she should find a new man that resembles him and then firmly explains that she does not repeat mistakes. They agree not to meet and she hangs up. She next sees Sun-hee, hands her a wallet that she had found under the bed in Jung-rae's room, and departs, joyfully. In a mysterious final scene, Mun-suk drives away from the resort across a beach. But, as she finally leaves the location, her car gets stuck in the sand. Two men arrive from off-screen and offer to help her by pushing her car free of the sand. They push,

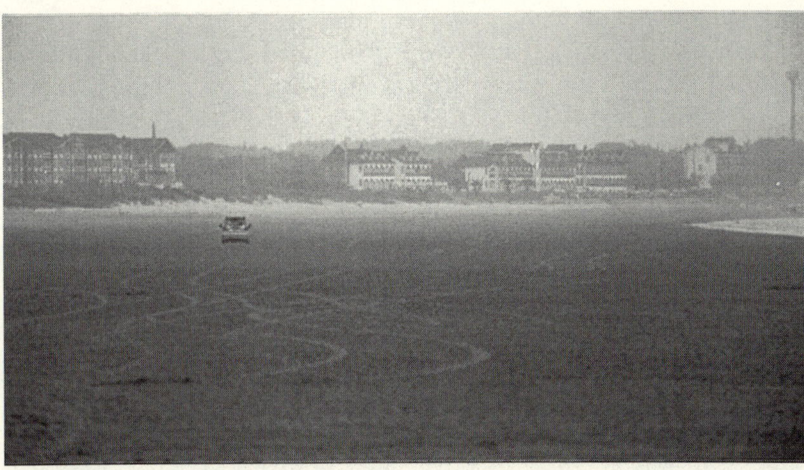

FIG. 17 Mun-suk departs in *Woman on the Beach*.

briefly, and ultimately succeed in freeing the car. She thanks them and they leave, and so does she, in her car, smiling; and so ends the film (see figure 17).

This final sequence refocuses the dramatic direction of the narrative. Whereas Jung-rae, with his call, continues in his unceasing repetition of his self-destructive and oddly competitive actions, Mun-suk clearly indicates that she will take a new direction, as she does not repeat mistakes, or so she claims. Whereas Jung-rae has reasserted his genius and succeeded in what he needed to do in order to continue in his repetitions, Mun-suk ultimately drives off into an uncertain future, thanks to the help of a pair of men that seemingly expect no compensation. I would hesitate to call this ending hopeful, as it provides no particular solution to the problems that the film has unearthed nor any positive horizon that might alleviate the concerns that haunt it. This point is solidified by the fact that, after being helped free of the sand, Mun-suk's car makes a subtle but clear 180-degree turn and ends up heading in the direction from which she initially departed. This character's perspective, as a result of this turn, is left ambiguous, as is the perspective the audience is to have in relation to her. Throughout the film her outbursts and general pettiness mirrored Jung-rae's, but her ability to overcome these concerns is *at least* left open, if never in any way verified.

It is this reluctance to clarify that anchors this film's critique. Whereas for Rossellini and Tarr ambiguity served as the opening necessary to produce a perhaps individuated but nonetheless radical difference, in the case of *Woman on the Beach* ambiguity is valuable in its capacity to undermine the film's own meanings. Ambiguity here is paired with ambivalence—a system through which the authorial perspective refuses to render apparent its own understanding of what is on display—in order to undermine authority altogether. In this way, this film generates a unique perspective whereby ideas are deployed but never verified; they seem to bounce freely but are never arranged into a coherent whole.

This nonconfirmation is key for this film. If *Woman on the Beach* seems a little freer to produce meaning than did, for instance *Sátántangó*—as is evidenced by the former's willingness to reject certain decisions and actions—its rejoinders are not any more structured or clear as a result. This is because each point it deploys—the possible efficacy of authoritarianism as well as that of a radically open democracy—remains unconfirmed. However, thanks to this nonconfirmation, the film also renders perhaps the most eloquent critique of authority of all the films discussed in this study: a mystifying negation of its own authority, and subsequently of authority at large. What results, however, is a crushing ambivalence, a total dedication to indecision figured as a final and total rejection of a variety of political possibilities. Through this system this most damning critique of authority also manifests as a rejection of its own ideas. A gap opens here: How can one say anything, do anything, without some turn to authority?

In a particularly revealing moment in *Woman on the Beach*, the crisis of authority that the characters are undergoing is shown with striking clarity. About halfway through the film, after the characters have left the resort and returned to Seoul, an intertitle declares that two days have passed. After the intertitle, Jung-rae is shown climbing on some dunes near a beach that, we learn shortly, is back at the resort in Shinduri. He stops abruptly as he sees three trees, his back to the camera as he seemingly studies them (see figure 18). After a few seconds he kneels and bows in front of the trees three times in what appears to be a prayer (see figure 19). After the third bow the camera pushes in on him,

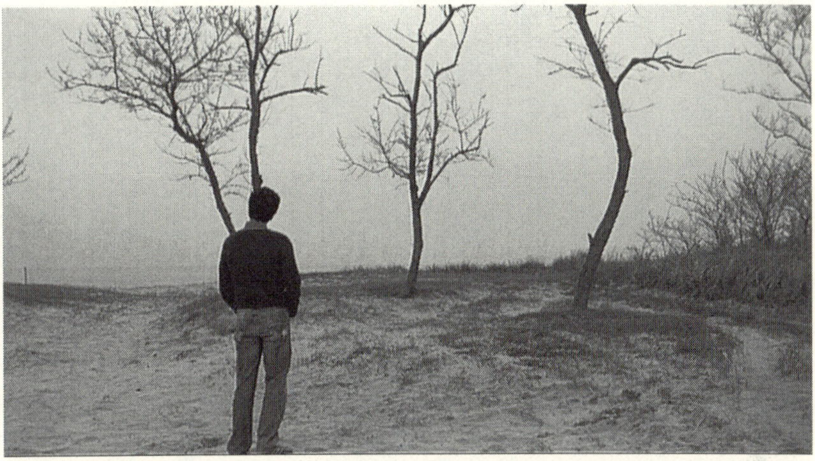

FIG. 18 Jung-rae ponders three trees in *Woman on the Beach*.

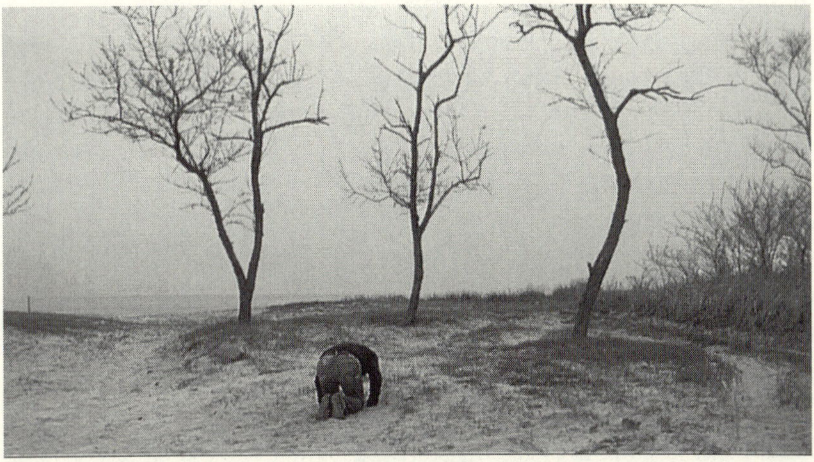

FIG. 19 Jung-rae kneels before three trees in *Woman on the Beach*.

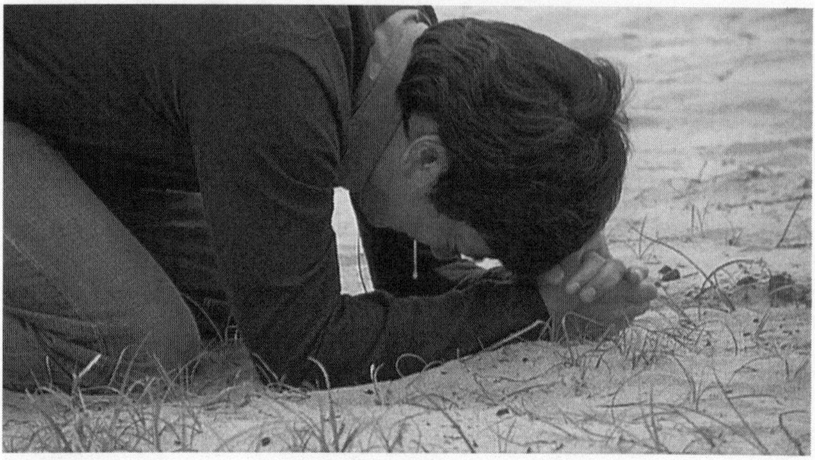

FIG. 20 Jung-rae cries in *Woman on the Beach*.

cuts to a shot of the trees, and then back to Jung-rae, now in close profile, his head resting on his hands. "Please help me," he whispers, as he drools and clenches his face, crying (see figure 20). A cut back to the dunes reveals Jung-rae, now walking leisurely and leaving a voicemail on Mun-suk's phone as though the sequence of his prayer before the trees never happened.

What has happened here? This sequence stands out in that it shows Jung-rae in what has to be taken as deep introspection and regret, but once it is over he returns to his regular abuses in the second half of the film. This sequence is the only one that indicates any guilt or indecision on the part of Jung-rae, and the film refuses any return to this kind of display of emotion. Jung-rae's later actions are in no way disrupted by this brief interlude. The appeal to some religious order or structure of authority is hinted at here, but Jung-rae, and Hong, seemingly dismiss this brief episode. Is religion an authority that is capable of ordering these events and providing Jung-rae with a hierarchy that can offer some solution to the lack of authority in his life? The distanced camera and abrupt cut away from this sequence refuses to substantiate this reading, and the sequence is swept away as the film moves back into a close analysis of Jung-rae's maneuverings.

This short scene is valuable in that it seems to push hard on the problems that haunt the actions of its characters, but also because it produces no answer to them. It proposes the possibility of solution—something like a traditional authority—but refuses to articulate it fully. And how could it? What amounts to a solution here must also always simultaneously register as a failure—as must be the case when authority is negated, for with it departs the capacity to verify.

This pulling away from a straightforward critique is also embodied in Jung-rae's status as the director's surrogate. At the end of the film his completed script is based, we can fairly surmise, on the very experiences we have witnessed, and it is therefore fair to assume that his film will look something like *Woman on the Beach*. Are we to think, then, that his will be a film that critiques these characters, as did Hong's? Is Jung-rae also planning an evisceration of the subject under democratic conditions? And, conversely, can we then assume that Hong's life bespeaks some experience similar to this new script? Does Hong himself evidence some of these same qualities?

This film is historically situated in such a position as to require the kinds of problems that this ending produces. Located in a moment free from the "weight" of politics, and maintaining the distance it requires to toy with the past, this film presents its critique of the modern democratic subject always with an eye turned backward to a moment when authoritarianism was the arrangement, and with an understanding of the damage that this configuration of governance brings. Hong's ending, coupled with the confusion as to the viability of Jung-rae's expansion of shapes, performs its critique of democracy in such a way that brings into question a particular moment without implying the converse (in this case, authoritarianism). What this gesture supplies, then, is an argument that refuses to figure a viable alternative, and in so doing simultaneously refuses its own status as master of meaning; it denies its own position as authoritarian figure capable of presenting something new.

Hong's is an antiauthoritarian cinema; it refuses even its own expertise and leaves the audience stranded in its ideas with no recourse to any kind of closure. This film critiques democracy but brings into question its own critique, and in the process forces its audience to struggle with these ideas. The demolition here finally pertains as much to authoritarianism as it does to democracy, for, while it shows the terror at meaning that democracy might create, it does so with a view of a violent authoritarian past only recently deposed.

Hence the impossible aporia with which the film ends. Mun-suk's driving away serves as a cogent, if clichéd, attempt to forge ahead toward an unpaved, open horizon—a path that, given her smile, we are led to believe she is happy to be on. But what can we make of this smile? Particularly given the film's ambivalence, this smile as readily suggests irony as it does hope. Perhaps the future she heads toward is no less devastating than the past, or the present—she has, after all, headed back the way she came. Perhaps Mun-suk's hopes are naïve, and the film is articulating that the kind of optimistic openness that she embraces will only lead again to one of the subject positions that the film so vehemently rejects. *Woman on the Beach* takes advantage of its unique historical position and declares as its project an exploration of how ambiguity and ambivalence erode meaning. But it also notes that this erosion is both a good and a bad thing. Whether the openings declared by this film's conclusion amount to hope or failure likewise becomes undecipherable. The answer as to whether Mun-suk's journey into the horizon is rendered here as viable or rather dismissed as too inarticulate and uncertain to resist co-optation by contemporary capitalism is offered up to ambivalence, another meaning overwhelmed by its shattering gaze.

If *Germany Year Zero* held firm to the availability of a positive but as yet unfigured future, and *Sátántangó* disintegrated the readily available options for change while holding on to hope as a fulcrum from which change could arise, *Woman on the Beach* tests these assumptions, particularly with respect to the possibility of hope. Hope, here, is brought into question as the film turns on itself and seems to eradicate the possibility for a positive future altogether.

To put this another way: by constantly undermining its own authorial voice, this film renders readability impossible, but it also overturns the Deleuzian dynamic whereby instruction falls away in favor of pure potential, and as a result critiques the capacity for creation rather than simply reproducing attempts at creating openings to it. What remains after all this turning is a series of negations, a crashing of meanings that points away from possibility and toward what must be described as a kind of negative dialectic. Every position that is proposed in this film is turned on its end, the weaknesses of each exposed. But this is not to say that each proposal for a positive future is rejected outright—each is negated as a singular trajectory, but this turning always leaves behind some residue, the salient markings remaining in a kind of reduction that indexes some qualities of what has been reduced. This is a process that, as is discussed in the coda to this book, is best named "thought." Thanks to this structure, Hong's cinema offers up a kind of methodology—a posing and positioning that generates argument but that never totally adheres to a cogent project. What is left of each coherent point—whether it is illuminated by Deleuze and Guattari's views on creativity; Gardner's on democracy, capitalism, and authority; MacCannell's on patriarchy; Bauman's on liquidity; or the critics of neoliberalism's take on contemporary capitalism—after each has been turned and dismantled is the germ of an idea that still holds the spirit of each approach.

These negations and diminishments do not amount to a coherent political agenda, but they do allow the particularities of this case to speak back to each of the ideas under discussion. This is, perhaps, an ineffective approach to political realities—and it is no doubt rather cynical—but it does digest a range of availabilities while holding tight to the necessity for change, change that can hopefully be realized thanks to the model for thought on display here. What arises thanks to this constant turning is a kind of detritus of ideas, a series of detonations that leaves behind the ruins of a cogent response. Whether these ruins amount to a productive approach remains unclear, but the project of cobbling together something—anything—coherent from this rubble remains available. What would happen, this film seems to ask, if we were to build upward from these oppositional and irreconcilable groundings? Could a politics be built that unifies these approaches? These questions are what this film proposes, but in the spirit of antiauthoritarianism it refuses to produce any answers.

*Woman on the Beach* finally finds itself in the same impossible position as the other films I discuss in this study. It stands among ruins but finds itself incapable of proceeding. Haskell Wexler's *Medium Cool* (1969) also locates this juncture, but in the context of a remarkably different series of events, and furthermore in direct relation to the violence that these aporias can produce. It is to this film that I turn in my final chapter.

# 4

# Force, Hope, and Death

## On *Medium Cool*

Haskell Wexler's *Medium Cool* (1969) is the clear outlier in the group of films I am analyzing. Made in 1968 and shot in large part at or around the 1968 Democratic National Convention in Chicago and its surrounding political demonstrations, *Medium Cool* was *not* made under or after authoritarian rule. It is not my intention here to denounce the United States as authoritarian, nor to indicate that authoritarianism can exist in some kind of covert form. This might very well be the case, but it is not my focus. Instead, I examine the approaches employed by a filmmaker who *perceived* the infiltration and reproduction of an authoritarian presence. This topic is of particular importance since it allows a glimpse of how a film might rush to a cause early in its development, and how in so doing it might differ from, or connect to, the other films included in this book. *Medium Cool*, then, shares with my other examples a preoccupation with authority—both the ways that it spreads and the ways that it can be resisted—but it differs in that the presence of the authority it distrusts is only just taking hold.

Another of the primary differences that separates this film from the others I have discussed is its profound distrust of media. Rather than the clear-cut instance of an oppressive authoritarian force that my other examples offer, *Medium Cool* rejects a perceived beginning, focusing on a different set of mechanisms; and so a distrust of the media and its perceived proclivity for rendering world-changing events coherent and knowable—and perhaps as a result powerless—is one of the major concerns of this film. The way that this film renders its critique of media representation while also attempting to produce something like an antiauthoritarian stance itself is central to this examination.

In this chapter, I begin by contextualizing *Medium Cool* historically and philosophically. I then explore the aesthetic philosophy of force as proposed by Christoph Menke, and in so doing examine how this film's connection to force, its unique relationship to and understanding of a kind of unordered but nonetheless palpable power, works to render an antiauthoritarian politics. I then turn to the topic of death, discussing how death and hope interact and how the unique dynamic between them provides this film with a system to render an argument that finally and fully rejects systems of authority that might otherwise command meaning. Finally, I examine the context of politics in 1968, positioning *Medium Cool* within its contemporary political movements and exploring the role that art and art films play in regard to the political conditions of massive youth-based demonstrations and strikes. Ultimately, my goal here is to explore how film interacts with governance, and how authoritarianism can be met, comprehended, avoided, and perhaps reaffirmed through rejections of authority and the ambiguities that arise in its absence.

This chapter is largely concerned with distrust: distrust of government and distrust of the capacity of mediation to evaluate the failings of a centralized ruling force. Through its unique aesthetic approach, *Medium Cool* reveals a palpable suspicion of the events and figures that it examines, but it does so with equal doubt as to its own capacity to give form to meaning. This film, like my other examples, pushes back against authority via the path of ambiguity, but it does so from another vantage point: that of fear of a developing authoritarian presence. How to simultaneously reveal and reject authority, and how to do so through a medium that the film explicitly rejects, are the questions that *Medium Cool* provokes.

## Contexts

*Medium Cool* follows photographer John Cassellis (Robert Forster) in his personal life, in particular his exploits at upper-crust parties and subsequent romantic affairs. Intertwined with these activities, though, is John's increasing awareness and interactions with the social movements of the late 1960s, particularly by way of his role as a news photographer. At the start John remains more or less indifferent to the issues and events that he is asked to record on assignment. But when his reporting takes him to the neighborhood and eventually to the home of Eileen (Verna Bloom) and her son Harold (Harold Blankenship), John begins to take an interest in the events that he had previously ignored. He pursues Eileen romantically and this leads to him gaining a much stronger connection to the political demonstrations of 1968 in Chicago. It is important to note, however, that neither John nor Eileen become significantly involved in these demonstrations; instead they seem to mainly distrust them, despite the role these events increasingly play in their lives.

The year 1968, of course, contained a number of worldwide political movements, particularly the May 1968 strikes and revolts that shut down France for weeks in protest at the conservative politics of Charles de Gaulle. The events in France reverberated globally, instigating and escalating social movements around the world. Of these, the antiwar political movements of the United States in the 1960s are paramount. Sharing many of the characteristics of their French equivalents, the U.S. political movements were likewise largely associated with a youth culture concerned with what appeared to be a principally and increasingly authoritarian government hell-bent on deflecting communism globally at all costs, as evidenced most directly by the conflict in Vietnam. Of course, principal among the costs to the United States in the fight against communism were the very young people so opposed to this war, as the universal draft demanded that many of those who rejected the conflict fight and die in it. As in France, the antiwar American movements of the 1960s were predicated on disrupting the affairs of a government that seemed to care little for those whom it was willing to demand so much of.

The demonstrations at the 1968 Democratic Convention in Chicago were one of the culminating activities of these antiauthoritarian youth events. Robert Kennedy's assassination, which happened less than three months before the convention, left the Democratic Party in disarray; these circumstances led to the primary being contested, with the antiwar Eugene McCarthy and the hawkish vice president Hubert Humphrey as the leading candidates. Despite antiwar candidates McCarthy and Kennedy receiving 80 percent of the primary vote, Humphrey, the more conservative and supposedly responsible and "tested" of the remaining candidates—and the contender who maintained lineage with Lyndon B. Johnson's wartime presidency—received the nomination thanks to his performance in caucusing states, even though he did not enter any primaries.

This result was not totally unexpected, but the nomination of the prowar candidate inflamed the antiwar movement's fears and increased the disenfranchisement of antiwar activists that had escalated throughout the decade. This was a nation, it might have seemed then, dedicated to war more than it was dedicated to democracy, an authoritarian system predicated on violence, the certainty of its economic system, and securing a global marketplace at all costs. The idea of democracy, that citizens of the country had the right to choose between a range of candidates in the name of having their interests represented, seemed to dissolve with the decision to nominate Humphrey, as the role of the United States in Vietnam, and indeed in other anticommunist wars, seemed to be, thanks to both presidential nominees being for the conflict, no longer under debate.

*Medium Cool* culminates, famously, in documentary footage shot around and inside this convention, but it narrativizes this footage by placing Eileen at the center of the protests in search of her son. During Eileen's search, John, having lost his job after losing his temper upon hearing the news that his footage had been repeatedly provided to the FBI in advance of its broadcast, meanwhile navigates the inside of the convention as a freelancer. The film's final sequence is generally the focus of most analyses, and this discussion will focus on it as well. What remains striking about this scene is how harrowing it appears; police violence is quite literally on display in this film, as is the striking size and military might of Chicago mayor Richard Daley's police force. But what is similarly striking here is the strange novelty of the narrative properties of this footage. Eileen's navigations of the crowds and the extended takes of her interacting with both demonstrators and police remains unique, and indeed seemed to have baffled both parties at the time—particularly the police, who, oddly, allow her to cross barriers and otherwise disrupt their attempts to enclose and later abuse the demonstrators.

Ethan Mordden places *Medium Cool* at the center of the poststudio era of the 1960s. According to Mordden, "By the late 1960s, movies spoke intimately yet pedantically to their various publics. Film no longer regarded itself as a church, an enforcer of the received social values, normative above all, but as an agent of transformation, often defiant of the ruling interests."[1] *Medium Cool*, for Mordden, fits this defiant mold: "The film is made of antagonisms—generation war, class war, race war, the Vietnam war, even the war of the moral free-lancer against the reckless Corporation, and of course the war of the camera with its subject."[2] But all of this warring and aggression met—for Mordden productively—with the fragmentation and disorder that arrived with the end of a coherent authority. Continuing with the church analogy, Mordden contends, "This marked not merely a separation of church and state, but a reformation that broke the church up into many sects, each free to challenge or support the relevant wisdoms."[3] He continues by presenting a list of films that map to different views on the generational conflict, but he carefully leaves *Medium Cool* off these lists. And he does so rightly as this film's politics are difficult to decipher. That is, it wears its distrust openly, but it is hard to gather exactly what it says outside of its myriad rejections and refusals. This difficulty poses a number of questions: What is to be made of a film so deeply invested in politics but that refuses to render a coherent platform? That is, why not make John and Eileen political activists? Why, instead, is this film careful to delineate their distance from, and inability to identify with, the demonstrations and protests that it depicts? What good is a film about politics but seemingly without political opinion?

The complications of aligning this film clearly with the politics of the youth culture that it depicts are posed most clearly toward the end of the film when

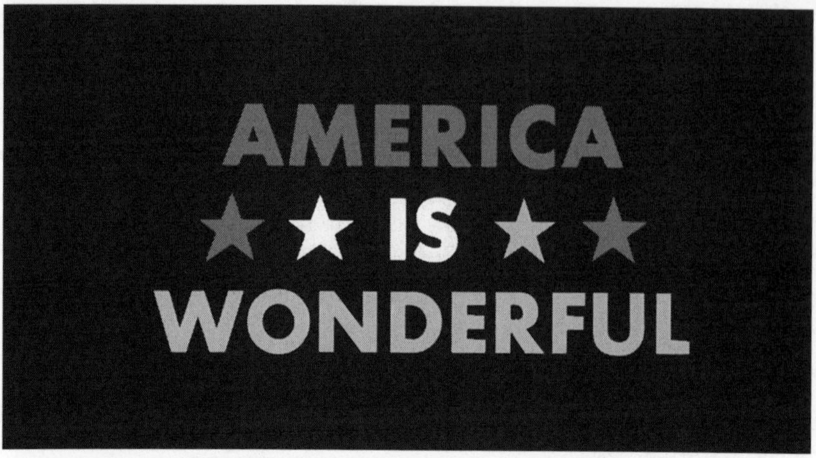


FIG. 21 Abrupt intertitle in *Medium Cool.*

John and Eileen, at this stage a couple, briefly attend a nightclub. Suddenly departing from preparations at the convention center, this sequence begins with an abrupt intertitle that reads, mysteriously, "AMERICA IS WONDERFUL" in bold, red, white, and blue capital letters (see figure 21).

But this text is promptly replaced with a dissolve in which the letters and the blackness that surrounds them are supplanted with footage of people dancing at the nightclub. Abstract images of the nightclub attendees turn out to be a result of strangely placed mirrors, which shortly reflect the arrival of John and Eileen. The pair walk through cavernous hallways illuminated in different colors as snippets of dialogue are overheard from the oblique figures whom they pass. Finally, they arrive at the dance floor. The band on stage, clad in flower-patterned fabric and with psychedelic images projected behind them, plays as strobe lights provide glimpses of the violently dancing crowd. John and Eileen navigate this crowd, walking through without taking part. A previous romantic partner approaches John on the dance floor, says something we cannot hear, and then John and Eileen leave abruptly, ending their short appearance at the club.

In a film full of odd and awkward sequences this one stands out as perhaps the strangest of all, and serves well to illustrate the barriers to analysis that this film presents. John and Eileen's motivation for coming to this club remains as indecipherable as their total unwillingness to interact with those in attendance. What is communicated, though, is a clear ambivalence in regard to the other people at the club. It remains unclear whether this sequence was presented to set up—perhaps critique?—1960s youth culture, to show the shallow underside of the youth movement's political edge, or simply to indicate how John and Eileen are unaccustomed to interacting with people younger than themselves. All that is made clear in this sequence is John and Eileen's awkwardness and unease. They are surely not the kind of people who would have fun at this club, we can gather once the sequence has concluded, but it is never revealed why they had decided to attend in the first place. The irony of the title card loses its teeth in light of this ambiguity. "AMERICA IS WONDERFUL" is the bridge between an empty convention center, which will soon be full of high-minded presidential rhetoric that will subsequently be dwarfed in importance by the police/protestor clashes happening outside, and a full nightclub where people dance to songs—perhaps themselves ironic—about smoking weed in San Francisco. If the initial available reading leads us toward an account of the vapid self-indulgence of 1960s youth, this is perhaps corroborated by the expressions on John and Eileen's faces. But what generates this ire and what role does it play in the subsequent police violence? These dancers are not figures deeply engaged in radical change, but John's life is indeed not any more purposeful. The meaning of this sequence, like the title card itself, hangs in the air, somewhere between unearned cynicism and under-thought sincerity, and this is indeed largely the tone of this film. It distrusts what it depicts, but it conversely feels something of great power and sincerity spilling from the very thing it distrusts. This is how this film depicts these political actions, and, as we shall see, how it views the media more broadly.

It is suspensions of judgment like these that this film strives to create. What separates *Medium Cool* from films like *Z* (Costa-Gavras, 1969) or *The Battle of Algiers* (Gillo Pontecorvo, 1966)—contemporary films also about significant political events—is the incoherence of its politics, and its ambivalence about political currents. On the other hand, what separates it from *La Dolce Vita* (Federico Fellini, 1960) or *Darling* (John Schlesinger, 1965)—contemporary films about wealthy socialites and their melancholic escapades—is the film's direct association with political events. Herein lies the unique quality of *Medium Cool*. It is a political film without politics and, conversely, it is a film about melancholy and celebrity, but one that explodes with direct images of political violence, images that indeed render its critique of success insignificant. To take the opening of *La Dolce Vita* as example, *Medium Cool* is like if Marcello Rubini (Marcello Mastroianni) were to pilot his helicopter into 1968 Paris, or 1968 Chicago. It is a film that aims to use the tools of art cinema in pursuit of political commentary, but at the same time veers from this goal just before attaining it, content instead to simply extend forward, incapable of producing the distance required for mannered critique but likewise unable to produce the direction needed for a more direct politics. This unique configuration, I contend, is exactly what allows this film to reject authority as efficiently as it does. To further support this point it is necessary to look at the contemporary responses the film engendered.

For Roger Ebert, writing in 1969, *Medium Cool* signified a radical shift in the way that American films interacted with their audience. Aligning the film with *The Rain People* (Francis Ford Coppola, 1969), *Easy Rider* (Dennis Hopper, 1969), *Alice's Restaurant* (Arthur Penn, 1969), *Midnight Cowboy* (John Schlesinger, 1969), and, particularly, *The Graduate* (Mike Nichols, 1967), Ebert explains that the significance of *Medium Cool* lies precisely in its refusal to separate documentary from fiction. He contends of the various events of the film that "they are all significant in exactly the same way. The National Guard trips are no more real than the love scene. . . . All the images have meaning because of the way they are associated with each other."[4] Wexler, for Ebert, looks closely at the characters and arrangements and "sees not the symbols but their function."[5] For Ebert, this associative vision is totally novel for American cinema. Whereas previous films presented narratives that developed characters and foreshadowed their eventual actions, *Medium Cool*, for Ebert, skips the foreshadowing and explains how the immediate presence of people and events interact, and indeed does so on a massive scale. The freedom of Wexler and his contemporaries to do this was predicated on their audience's familiarity with cinema, with our ability to "understand cinematic shorthand," as Ebert puts it.[6]

The cognitive process outlined by Ebert is striking for its teleological assumptions. Because we have seen John Wayne, he contends, we can imagine the narrative gaps that this film inevitably opens and closes thanks to a series of tested assumptions, a procedure that brings to mind the gestalt process. This process lessens the need for a coherent narrative flow by relying on the audience, already familiar with the traits and tropes of, in this case Hollywood cinema, to draw the missing connections and in so doing proceed as though the narrative were more traditionally arranged. For Ebert, the entire plot of *Medium Cool* relies upon these tested assumptions, and what this approach creates is a cinematic shorthand that allows the director to focus on images that surprise or shake us. What I see in this film is precisely the opposite. What is valuable about *Medium Cool* is its ability to disrupt this associative process, or at the very least its ability to ask us to re-evaluate it. When John and Eileen enter and leave the club we can intuit some of their motivations, but the film's reluctance to fill in these gaps is precisely what is useful—it asks its viewers not to reproduce the meaning they have seen established elsewhere at the risk of not understanding at all. Rather than functionalize the narrative, *Medium Cool* makes it dysfunctional; things break apart, they fail to work, and they leave us with no explanation as to why. This is a film, then, in a state of disrepair. The gears of the industry to which it belongs have ground to a halt, and like this film Hollywood filmmaking lingers in a state of suspension. Characters do things, but why is never made clear. This, too, is the attitude this film takes toward the police and, to a degree, the protestors. Rather than outline either side's concerns and then weigh in on them, it shows these events as though no explanation is available.

Wexler, of course, was no nihilist, and his political concerns are well outlined by his later films.[7] But what he chooses to address in *Medium Cool* is not the contours of an argument about America's authoritarian turn. Instead, he leaves this meaning open without verifying it. In what serves as a truly antiauthoritarian gesture—in the sense that it rejects authority more directly by denying its own—Wexler refuses to establish narrative coherence for the events he depicts, and in so doing he largely disables his own capacity for routing a path through these turbulent images. This is evident in the previously discussed scene set in the nightclub. The reasons for John and Eileen's abrupt arrival and departure and the function of this sequence in terms of its narrative contribution are met with an ambiguity that is mirrored in the depiction of the space of this disorienting club. What Wexler proposes here is an explanation of the capacity of cinema to escape meaning, rather than its ability to contain it.

In his review of the film, Vincent Canby touched upon some of the issues outlined so far, but for Canby these conflicts amount to negative qualities. "The story of the gradual emotional and political awakening of John Cassellis," he writes, "is somehow dwarfed by the emotional and political meaning of the events themselves, which we, in the audience, experience first-hand, rather than through the movie protagonist."[8] Indeed, where this move appears abnormal, as Canby posits, is in the way that the experience of the lead characters does little to illuminate the deeply disturbing events that surround them. This disjunction, however, creates a novel viewing experience, one in which the viewer is asked not to come to understand events through the perspective of a coherent narrative, but to reject that narrative in the name of an extended relationship to disorder. Canby continues, "This is a fundamental problem in the kind of movie-making that attempts to homogenize fact and fiction, particularly when the fiction has the oversimplified shape of nineteen-thirties social protest drama and the fact is so obviously of a later, more complicated world."[9] Canby's claims as to the qualities and complexities of both fiction and fact in the 1960s versus the 1930s ring rather hollow, but his concerns about the homogenization of fact and fiction remain valuable. He continues this line of thought: "The shock of *Medium Cool* comes not from the fiction, but from the facts provided Wexler by mayor Daley, the Illinois national guard and the Chicago police."[10] For Canby there is a sense of the force of this film being unearned, the sense that its power is derived not from working the characters through something in any recognizable fashion, but from the impact of the real events that provide the setting.

Judgments of quality aside, for this book Canby's observations provide a significant example of a film engaging with politics in a novel way. Rather than interjecting a narrative perspective into some issue or event, as the aforementioned *Z* and *The Battle of Algiers* might be said to, *Medium Cool* does the opposite, interjecting a significant event into its, admittedly slight, narrative perspective. The footage of 1968 Chicago, then, serves as a kind of disruption, a rupture that renders a relatively inconsequential narrative powerful, but provides no direction for this power to take. Indeed Canby, despite his distaste for the film, is careful to recognize this power: "The result is a film of tremendous visual impact, a kind of cinematic 'Guernica,' a picture of America in the process of exploding into fragmented bits of hostility, suspicion, fear and violence."[11] Canby here compares *Medium Cool* to Picasso's famous painting that, it is often contended, serves as a response to the bombings of the village of Guernica by the Axis-backed nationalists during the Spanish Civil War of the 1930s, connecting these two as pieces of art that are both said to digest political turmoil. Finally, Canby ends on a particularly mysterious note: "*Medium Cool* is an awkward and even pretentious movie, but, like the report of the President's National Advisory Commission on Civil Disorders, it has an importance that has nothing to do with literature."[12] The report referenced here was a large-scale explanation of civil disobedience, particularly as it pertained to African Americans, commissioned in the 1960s by Lyndon B. Johnson's administration. This report advocated for the improvement of social services, particularly housing, as a solution to the demands of civil rights and the unrest that accompanied those demands. The report serves as an interesting comparison for *Medium Cool*, which is by no means strapped with the responsibility of producing solutions to the problems it depicts. But the comparison is telling in that it signals to a form of political importance based on something other than representation, a power not usually attributed to the arts and that complements the mysterious assertion that this film has nothing to do with literature.

What Canby seems to be suggesting is a relationship to nonrepresentative power, some ability to produce unmediated access to these events. This film, Canby seems to say, arrives and announces itself like a document that purports to measure and propose a solution to a particular problem. It serves as a *report* on the events that it depicts. Whereas narrative, in this analogy, is indirect, this film—despite its refusing to produce a coherent object or solution—*is* direct. It works, he implies, like a kind of commission designed to reproduce and distill the variables of an issue. I am not sure that I agree with Canby's claim that *Medium Cool* can have no relationship to literature, but the judgment that he offers—that this film is a narrative disaster but that it is nonetheless powerful—is exactly the reason that I too find the film of interest. To address the strange power it holds—a power that seems to stand between artifact and report—I transition now to a discussion of the images here, and indeed the mysterious hold, of unmitigated force.

## Force

At a pivotal moment in *Medium Cool,* John and Eileen stand watching a television show. The show, a special on the lives of John F. Kennedy, Martin Luther King, and Robert Kennedy, is never shown, and is represented here only in light cast on the characters' faces. "Jesus, I love to shoot film," John interjects as the two stare at the television. "Do you feel it?" he asks Eileen, holding his hands toward the out-of-frame television set (see figure 22). "X-rays, is that what it is? Does it grow hair? Is it vitamins? Can you feel violence?" "I don't know what to think," Eileen responds, "It seems like no man's life is worth anything anymore." On this point John turns to Eileen and says, "You see, the media's got a script now, by the numbers. Flags at half-mast. Trips canceled. Ball games called off. Schools closed. Memorial meetings. Memorial marches. Moments of silence. A widow cries, and then she says brave words. More moments of silence, then the funeral procession." Dripping with disdain, John smirks and adds, "A lot of experts saying how sick our society is, how sick we all are. The script is a national drain-off. People say, 'Yeah, yeah, we're guilty. We're bad.' 'Cause a lot of people are afraid. They're afraid. The Negroes are coming to tear up their stores, burn neighborhoods, so they have this nationwide, coast-to-coast network serial called 'Mourn the Martyr.' Nobody's really on the hook, you see?" John approaches a nearby window, now looking out. "When the script is finished and Tuesday comes around or Saturday and national drain-off week is over, everybody goes pretty much back to normal. Normal this, normal that. You know, normal." In the background as the two stare, confounded—Eileen at John, John out the window—the television continues, now emitting the

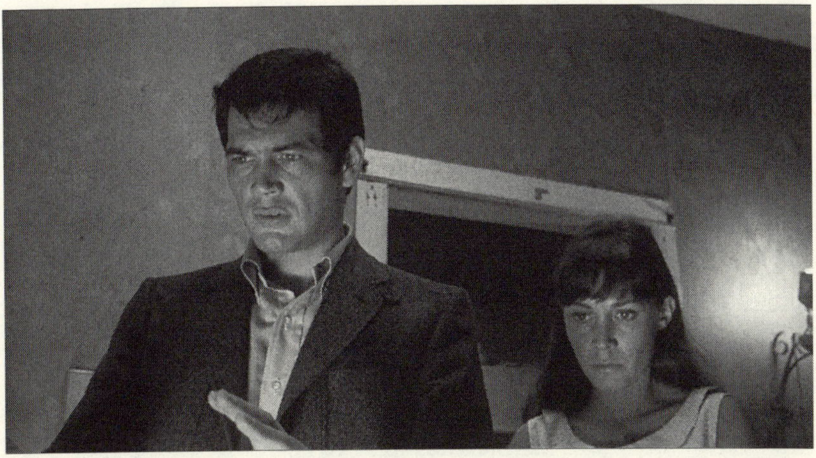

FIG. 22 John and Eileen entranced by the television in *Medium Cool.*

monumental, "Free at last! Free at last! Thank God Almighty, we are free at last!"

What is striking about this brief scene, and what is corroborated by John and Eileen's anguish, is the degree and object of this pair's frustration: frustration at the media's proclivity in, in John's opinion, rendering clear and normal the world-shattering events that had become so routine by 1968; but also frustration at the undeniable power of the images that the television provides. It is in fact this very dynamic that is the source for John and Eileen's turmoil. The trajectory of this film serves as an attempt to explore and perhaps alleviate this conflict. How, *Medium Cool*, asks, is a film to use and extend the power of the image without simultaneously reducing the events it depicts to easily understood platitudes? How is it able to show anything without rendering into knowable terms the effects and circumstances that it reveals? And how is it to deliver information and ideas without suturing the wound that events like this create? This film strives to answer the question of how cinema can produce politics that serve as a radical break from the normalcy and restrictions of the world that we occupy.

The system by which this film pursues these questions is through its use of documentary footage at the 1968 Democratic National Convention, an event during which an estimated 25,000 police clashed with the 10,000 demonstrators. The primary frame this film uses to present these events is Eileen's search for her lost son. Shown navigating increasingly violent and inchoate spaces, Eileen, dressed in bright yellow, walks in and out of protestor and police activities (see figures 23 and 24). But what renders these images most striking is her seeming disinterest. Eileen, dressed and framed so as to contrast with both protestors and police, navigates these conditions as a kind of outsider, unconcerned with the actual demonstrators and cops except insofar as they divide her from her son. In one striking moment she even crosses a police line; for some reason the cops assume her to be different from the crowd and allow her passage. The effect of this framing mechanism is to create a kind of ambiguity as to the actions being depicted. It is through this ambiguity that *Medium Cool* positions its attempt to render this significant course of events. What this ambiguity provides is a kind of distance, but also its opposite—an undeniable power and immediacy. It is the power felt by John in the light of the TV, and it is the force of these images.

In *Force: A Fundamental Concept of Aesthetic Anthropology*, Christoph Menke pursues what he feels is the central question of philosophical aesthetics: "How to conceive of the indeterminacy of the beautiful, as an effect of the imagination, in view of its overwhelming power."[13] *Medium Cool* connects with Menke's project through the way that both are centrally concerned with this "overwhelming power," but the film joins this energy to the specifics of the protests in 1968 Chicago, and furthermore to the perceived authoritarian

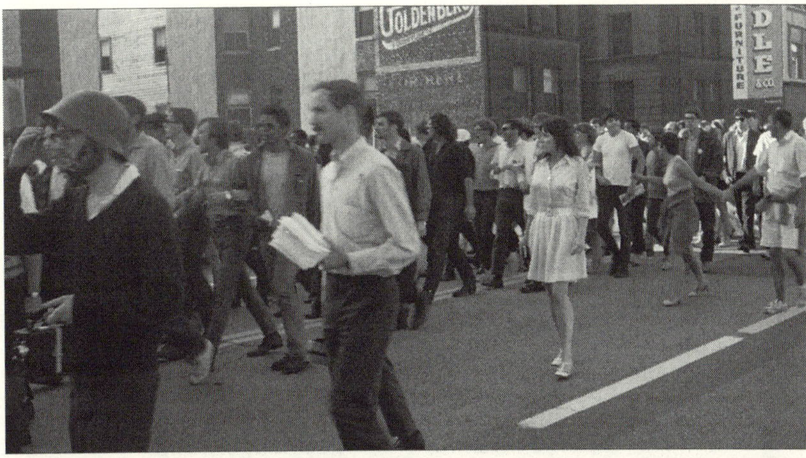

FIG. 23 Eileen among activists in *Medium Cool.*

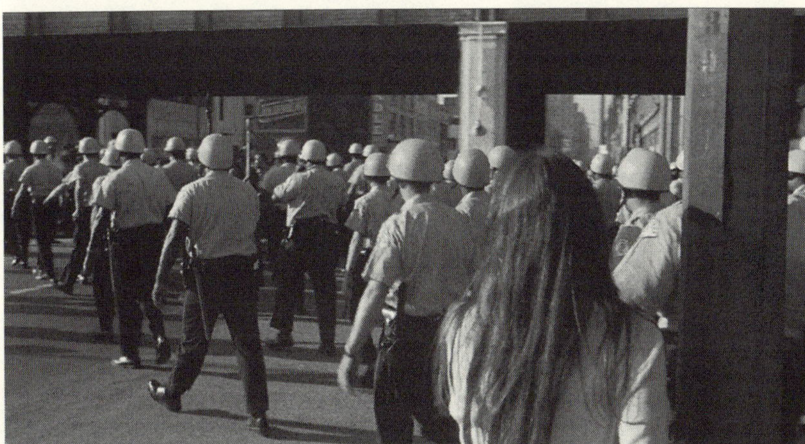

FIG. 24 Eileen among police in *Medium Cool.*

response that they engendered. To be clear, what Menke provides for this discussion of *Medium Cool* is the language and ideas for how to conceive of the film's relationship to radical politics, but this is not to say that I believe that these texts engage in an exploration of the same project—far from it. *Medium Cool* is deeply concerned with the power of images, but is confounded by the constant countertendency of that power to be reabsorbed into knowable forms for viewing the world, forms that this film indeed finds to be venal and destructive.

Menke uses the concept of imagination to push upon the boundaries of the parent category to which it belongs: the sensible. For Menke, "The imagination belongs to the domain of sensibility, for it is incapable of endowing its idea with any representational capacity or its images with any cognitive capacity."[14] According to Menke, who draws upon Descartes, "sensibility" is defined in part by its relationship to imagination and indeterminacy, but also by its difference from "intellect"—the domain of rational thought and activity. But Menke presses upon this divide, ultimately contending that "the intellect requires the resources of the imagination . . . yet for this to happen, imagination must be brought under the guidance of the intellect. The intellect must have command over the imagination."[15] Menke has thus far examined and clarified the frequently discussed dynamic between intelligence and imagination, but he begins to trouble Descartes's claims when he writes: "The imagination is anarchic and undisciplined, and that is why it not only must be—but also can be—subject to the guidance of the intellect in its methodical progression. *But why is external regulation necessary*? On its own, the imagination is always unpredictable; it does not pursue its own direction; thus it can be directed at will."[16] This is the conflict that haunts *Medium Cool*: How can imagination—an unrationalized and indeterminate movement that still holds within it some connection to thought—persist without always surrendering its power to the rationalized and "active" realm of the intellect, a realm that in this example is perceived to be bankrupt and shot through with a growing authoritarian strain?

The specifics of this problem are realized through *aesthetics*. For Menke, "Aesthetics is a different way of *conceiving* sensibility. It is not merely a reevaluation of sensibility, although it is that, too, because it involves a redescription of sensibility. Aesthetics is a way of thinking that conceives the indissoluble indeterminacy of sensibility in conjunction with its internally guided, principled activity."[17] For Menke, aesthetics takes from the imagination the inchoate madness of the sensible world, but orders it in some kind of way that follows a semisystematic guide, allowing it to function autonomous of the intellect. He continues: "The sensible is radically indeterminate because its generation of ideas cannot be reduced to self-conscious and self-controlled acts, performances of methodical operations of the intellect. At the same time, the ideas generated by the senses are neither a mere confluence of causal effects nor a haphazard and arbitrary play *but an internal, though unconscious, operation belonging to the imagination*."[18] Aesthetics is capable of eliding the rational world while still maintaining the capacity to produce ideas and coherence. As Menke puts it, "The program of aesthetics aims to think about sensibility as a phenomenon beyond the Cartesian alternatives of self-conscious actions and causal mechanism, of self-guidance and haphazard projection. Indeed it must reconsider these very alternatives and reconceptualize our ideas of knowledge and action, of play and imagination."[19]

In order to further explore this problem of aesthetic experience's relationship to any concretized form of knowledge, Menke reactivates Leibniz's bifurcation of aesthetics into two primary "aspects": faculty and force. The first of these aspects, faculty, allows us to "grasp the things around us adequately, although not consciously and methodically."[20] This first aspect is defined by Menke as "the faculty of engendering sensible cognitions that are as indeterminate as they are adequate."[21] Never quite rational, the functions of aesthetic experience defined by faculty nevertheless have some organizational drive, which is governed by an "internal principle" whereby things are ordered and rendered coherent, even if never quite fully readable. The second aspect of aesthetic experience is the drive that pushes in the opposite direction: "The force propelling an ongoing transformation of the unconscious ideas that constitute us."[22] According to Menke, what provides a glimpse of force at work is the sensation that "there is an efficacy or power to these perceptions that far exceeds that exercised by the judgments of the intellect, a power that draws us into an infinite 'sequence' of images engendered by and transforming into one another that confounds the intellect."[23]

The idea of force as described by Menke brings cinema into view. The sequence of images that constantly melt into one and another and seem to link in a way that surprises and confounds the capacities of cognition is perhaps best modeled by the incoherence of cinema experienced as a kind of reverie. But cinema always reproduces and relies upon the functions of faculty too—the capacity for experience to be contextualized and accounted for as a reproduction of coherence, what brings to mind the logic of continuity. Never fully organizable into a coherent set of repeatable principles, continuity takes up some kind of generalizable logic, some kind of "internal principle" that is never exactly fully available but always familiar. This is the way that cinema reproduces meaning or, at least, presents itself as readable. There is the constant puncturing of force with faculty, and this is the model for experience that cinema reproduces.

In *Medium Cool*, what confounds John about these images is whether force can be maintained without its descending back into faculty. He is haunted by the "efficacy or power" of the recorded image and the way that it "far exceeds that executed by the judgments of the intellect."[24] He loves shooting film, but can never exactly explain why, and indeed any explanation would always fail to account for the force of the images, or worse yet work to defuse it. The distrust that this sequence finds in faculty has for John two aspects of its own. First, faculty is feared to reduce the power of the image in that it might function to transform force back into practical material, to reduce the capacity to shake and disturb, to nullify the image's relationship to raw, inchoate, indeterminate power. But what frightens John more about faculty is the way that its organizing tendencies reinstitute the corrupt and antidemocratic principles that governed these events. He agrees, of course, in the tragedy of the deaths shown in the television special titled *Mourn the Martyr*, but it is when these events are rendered *meaningful* that he comes to distrust them. John's response is then one of profound disillusionment. His wish, it seems, is to relegate everything to force, a state "without normative substance"[25] where faculty is avoided altogether. This is the wish of true disillusionment, of one who is truly disenchanted, of one who wishes for something radically different, anything that might fundamentally upset how we organize the world. But what this wish betrays is also hope, and indeed hope in its most potent form—a radical hope dedicated to absolute difference.

This radical hope is also deeply messianic; it provides no outlet for activity, but it holds within it absolute potential.[26] The sequence of Eileen navigating the protests of 1968 Chicago now takes on a new form. Where these images identify with the political agenda of the protestors is not in the particular platforms of the antiwar movement—although they do of course to some degree identify with these—but in the very incoherence that these images and events offer.

Of course, much background information that might serve to order these images is perhaps already provided by the promptness of this film's release; it was initially distributed on the one-year anniversary of the events it depicts. However, while obviously focusing on the overwhelming police presence and, ultimately, police violence that took place, this film nonetheless refuses to align itself with the protestors. Indeed *Medium Cool* is unwilling even to explore the platform of these demonstrators. What the lack of clear allegiance in this semidocumentary footage produces is a kind of unpatterned depiction of these brutal proceedings. Indeed, even continuity is tested, as most of the sequence is shown through the use of full shots or unestablished close-ups of Eileen walking through the protest activities, and what cuts it does contain appear as irrational glimpses of other spaces or related events. This refusal of a clear perspective results in horror at the police violence against the demonstrators, but the film deliberately leaves any avenues for making sense of this intense sensation unexplored.

What this footage strives to produce is force, the unmanaged flow of material that withstands order and reproduces the power that John felt emanating from the television. For Menke, "The aesthetic force . . . turns against its own expression, transforming it into another. The aesthetic expression is, therefore, as initially antagonistic as the aesthetic force itself."[27] This internal antagonism is on display in *Medium Cool*, for it wishes to reproduce force as force without betraying any recognizable standards or norms. But this is an impossible task, as the systems of organization always reassert themselves—they must for any footage to "travel" and "arrive" at any destination, both figuratively and materially. This pushing toward its impossible task is also an emblem of the film's extremism. It holds tight to the hope that whatever form aesthetic experience does take will be strikingly new—somehow organized in such a way as to overcome the brutal reductions that John attempts to reject.

Force, then, is here figured as the hope for radical politics. This footage attempts to propose that new arrangements for politics must always arrive in the form of total departure from the expected and available outcomes. As Menke contends, "In the operations of aesthetic force *nothing* realizes itself."[28] And it is exactly this nothing that yields ambiguity. Given the circumstances of the time, including the increasing police violence and what appeared to be the systematic elimination of those that opposed it, absolute aesthetic force remains perhaps the best available response; a wish made when there is no hope, which is exactly when hope is most available. But what this solution faces is the specter of absolute inaction; such is the bind of messianism, which holds that most opportunity for change is totally unverifiable, indeed totally incoherent and totally impossible to generalize, and the only way to usher it in is to hope for it in the abstract and never to encourage its arrival.[29] What is lost in this case, then, is the play between force and faculty that constitutes, for Menke, the aesthetic process. Indeed *Medium Cool* ultimately runs up against the problem with imagination: it has no outlet toward reflection, no system by which order might be generated and allow something like cognition or change to arrive. The film, in this way, meets its goal, it persists in its messianic wish, but this wish must always be *just* a wish.

A final quote from Menke is instructive, here, on innovation: "It [innovation] does not happen as a consequence of reasons, as a realization of purposes I already have, but because my forces are alive in an unknown situation, before an unknown object."[30] This is the gift that art can provide, the vantage from which it can look back at us. What John finds in these images—in the colors they cast toward him, the force with which they press upon him—is the possibility of the unknown, the hope with which they irradiate us. But this hope must find its way back into faculty, for the only alternative is an inactionable and incoherent eternity or, worse yet, the possibility for the arrival of something far more devastating than what we have. John's dream—and what too must be the dream of this film—is also a nightmare, force without faculty, unknowability that uproots order, a kind of hope asymptotic to death.

## Accidents

At the end of the *Medium Cool*, John and Eileen, having finally found each other in the crowd, escape downtown Chicago in a station wagon belonging to a news channel. Shown riding home and listening to the escalating protests at the convention site on the radio, they exchange troubled glances as the radio

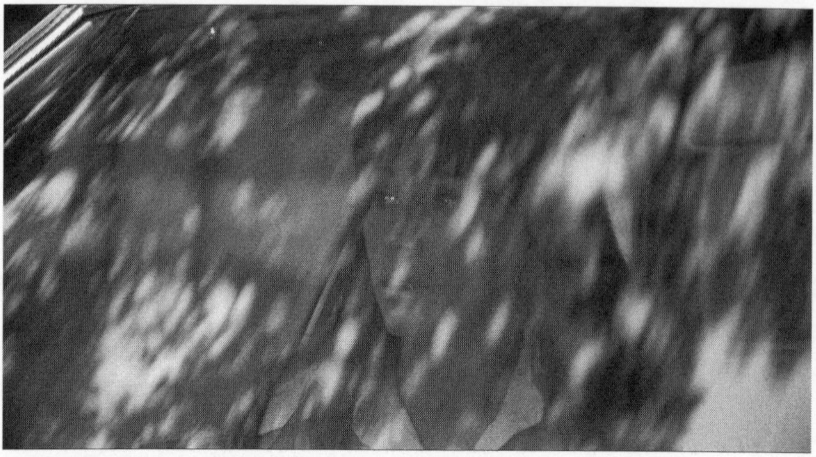

FIG. 25 Eileen through a glary windshield in *Medium Cool.*

report declares the accelerating police violence. Finally the radio report evolves from the chaos of the convention coverage into a clearer report, more likely recorded in a studio. "The victim was identified as former Channel 8 news cameraman John Cassellis," the report explains. "Cassellis was taken to Michael Reese Hospital where he is reported to be in critical condition. Cause of the accident is under investigation. A woman companion, not yet identified, was dead on arrival," it continues. During this report the exterior of John and Eileen's car is shown. Upon cutting back inside, however, the radio report returns to the erratic coverage of the protest. The report elucidates the bloodshed caused by the police response to the demonstrations, and all the while the camera pushes forward, toward Eileen's shocked face (see figure 25).

As the camera zooms, the intermittent glare reflected on the windshield caused by the breaks in the tree cover begins to increase. Using the overexposed, almost white image as a kind of fade, the film cuts on the white to show John, himself totally blown out by the glare, in a matching close-up. The film continues to cut between the two as the amount of glare likewise escalates. The image is increasingly obscured as the white intervals overtake the characters' close-ups.

Abruptly, the sound of tires squealing breaks their concerned gazes. The camera wheels wildly, then cuts between an approaching tree, close-ups of John and Eileen, and a broken car window until a crash and then a scream are heard, followed by darkness. The radio report covering the protest continues over the black. Finally, another car is shown driving by, its driver leaning out the window (see figure 26). The camera pans with this car and reveals the news station wagon that John and Eileen had been driving, smashed into a tree. The other car continues to slowly drive by as a child in the back seat leans out and takes a photo. An abrupt cut—the last of this film—shows another angle of the wreck (see figure 27). The onlookers gone, John and Eileen's car is shown now in a wide shot, aflame. The camera zooms slowly out, the soundtrack still consisting of radio coverage of the demonstrations at the convention. The camera begins to pan; as it does other voices—presumably demonstrators—begin to overtake the radio broadcast. "The whole world is watching," they chant as the camera pans left. The chant increases in volume as a new subject is revealed: another camera with its own operator. The new camera pans, slightly behind the pan of our view, and points directly into this frame (see figure 28). A zoom takes us into the lens of this new subject, pushing forward into the black square of this new

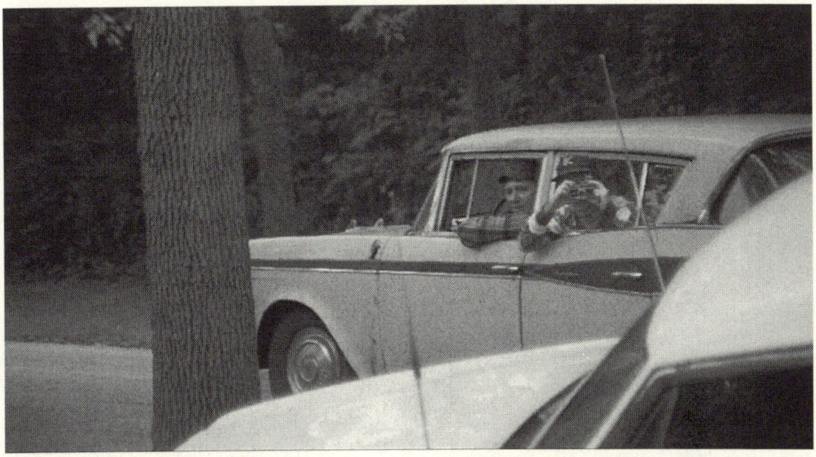

FIG. 26 Onlookers in *Medium Cool.*

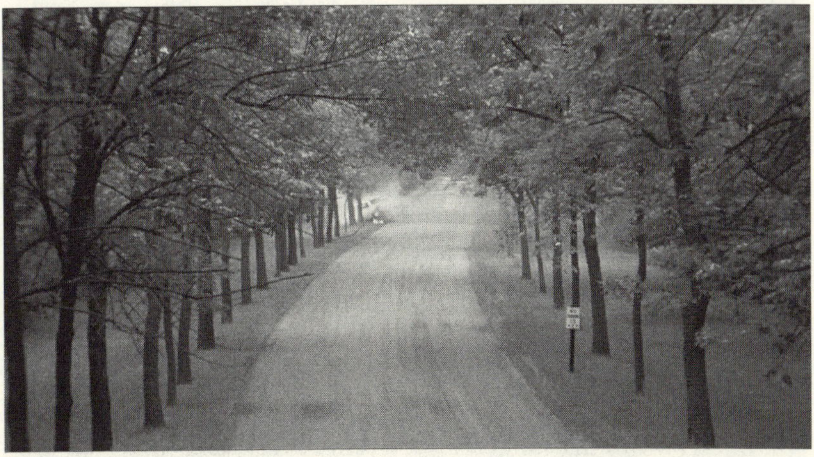

FIG. 27 The accident in *Medium Cool.*

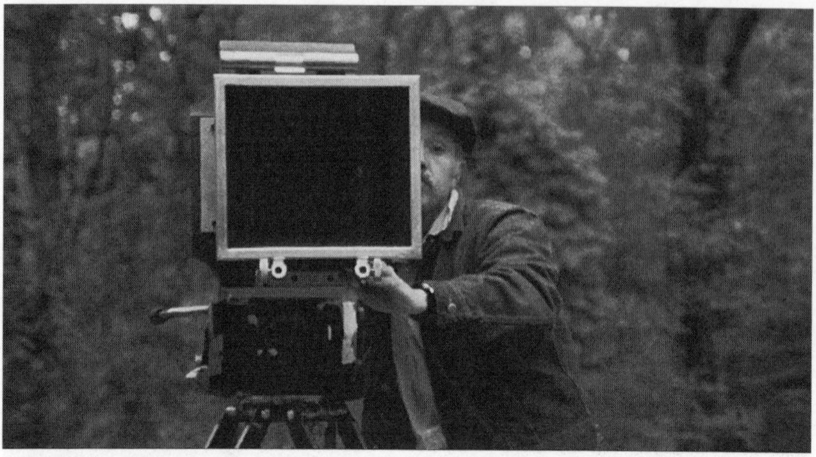

FIG. 28 Dueling cameras in *Medium Cool*.

camera's lens, presumably returning the gaze that has produced this image. As this black square overtakes the frame, serving as a kind of fade to black, the credits appear.

This final sequence is notable for many reasons. Its abrupt and overwhelming cynicism helps to situate the film clearly within the New American Cinema of the late 1960s and early 1970s—*Easy Rider*, another significant early entry in this cycle, had been released roughly a month before *Medium Cool*, and shares with it an ending in which the main characters are abruptly killed, with the camera lingering on automotive wreckage. But the final sequence of *Medium Cool* is also striking formally. The use of glare to interrupt the close-ups of the characters before the crash mimics the effect of a camera running out of film, and prefigures the conclusion of the subsequent New American film *Two-Lane Blacktop* (Monte Hellman, 1971), in which the film stops and then appears to burn in front of the projector. This appearance of a "roll out," as it is called, strives to reveal the film to be artifice, a series of fictions set to a documentary score. The chant of "The whole world is watching," however, complicates this analysis.

As was established in John's monologue about television reporting, *Medium Cool* distrusts, or at least attempts to complicate, the rhetoric that reproduces the idea that the media has the capacity to represent the world-rending events of the 1960s without reducing them to repetitions of already known, and necessarily conservative, truths—events that include the demonstrations at the Democratic National Convention in Chicago. Its previously declared distrust of images makes this final sequence significantly more difficult to interpret. "The whole world is watching" chant, often met the appearance of news cameras at demonstrations of the time, and the repetition of this phrase in

Chicago is clearly the product of the prominent news coverage of these demonstrations. Protestors chanted this particularly often in moments of police aggression and/or violence, indicating to the police officers that they could be held accountable for their violent actions as a result of there being recorded proof of their activities. *Medium Cool* is not so sure about this possibility, however. The film here indicates that the qualities of the moving image do not so clearly map to accountability. As this sequence demonstrates, images are in fact quite malleable. The fast and aggressive editing of the crash in particular notes the capacity of cinema to clearly present an event without ever directly showing it. There is no doubt about the occurrence of the accident (in a narrative sense), despite direct evidence being totally absent. Fiction, in *Medium Cool*, is absolutely available—what the film finds more difficult to produce is fact. Indeed, the juxtaposition of "The whole world is watching" with images of a camera itself presents a puzzling series of connections: on the one hand this sequence reaffirms the capacity of the camera to record—the second camera serving as a kind of reminder of the presence and proliferation of images; on the other hand, however, it seems to be questioning the role the camera plays in events such as these.

The two cameras—the one recording and the one that is being recorded—reproduce the at once hopeful and disillusioned dynamic that John had previously declared and that this film in general posits. The reproduction of images is, hopefully, capable of redistributing truth and accountability, but it is this same reproduction that haunts the capacity of these images to *do* anything. When the cameras face each other, it brings to mind a kind of hall of mirrors, indeed a cascade of reproducible images that all seem to undermine each other are, this film contends, the only kind of images that cameras can produce. This sequence and its culmination with the other camera poses a long and increasingly complex series of questions: What can we say about this final sequence? And what do the images that this second camera presumably records say about us? Is this a call for an audience to interact and ultimately take action in response to what they have just seen? If so, what does it ask us to do with regard to this film, and what part of the film does it have in mind? Are we here looking at ourselves? Or are we looking at the media that would record and witness, rather than act upon, tragedies such as these? Are we perhaps outside the media? Is this camera recording us? The other camera? Nothing at all? And are all these things the same?

These kinds of questions about media and action and images reflect John's monologue back on the viewer, but *Medium Cool* never quite verifies what it has established. It values images for their force but distrusts their faculty. What it grants, then, is the annihilation of meaning that accompanies the utter confusion of the film's ending. When the camera looks into the lens of its compatriot/competitor, it registers nothing. In response it zooms, looking closer and closer, indeed as closely as it can. But it finds only blackness. The closer it looks, the more the blackness increases, a blackness that can only consume the film as it has the frame in a kind of total irresolution. Like Béla Tarr's *Sátántangó* (1994), *Medium Cool* concludes with the obliteration of visibility, and in this obliteration it finds again its capacity for force or, as John might put it, its capacity for love. But, again, what of the other camera, the one that turns to, at once, this film and its audience? What does it see? When it zooms into our lens, what does it find? Blackness? But blackness is something: it is, at the least, the image unexposed, the possibility for a new image, the possibility that John and Eileen might return—*Medium Cool 2*—or that there is something important still to be found within, and by way of, the lens of the camera.

## Death

Writing in a moment not at all far removed from the production of *Medium Cool* and the events that it depicts, philosopher Jean Baudrillard identifies a similar set of difficulties when it comes to reproducing, articulating, and critiquing the culture of late capitalism. For Baudrillard, the fight against the oppressive forces of capitalism had met a series of dead ends because many of the approaches of 1960s radical politics had misidentified the nature of their target. According to Baudrillard, "You can't fight the aleatory by imposing finalities, you can't fight against programmed and molecular dispersion with *prises de conscience* and dialectical sublation, you can't fight the code with political economy, nor with 'revolution.' All the outdated weapons . . . are gradually neutralized by a higher-order general system. Everything that filters into the non-finality of the space-time of the code, or that attempts to intervene in it, is disconnected from its own ends, disintegrated and absorbed."[31]

For Baudrillard, the order of late capitalism has developed a relationship to the symbolic in which the lines between signifier and signified have been drawn and redrawn so often that the signifier prefigures the supposed connection it is said to have to reality. This creates a network of empty linkages that claim to present reality but in actuality constitute it, pointing always to its own hollow linkages as proof of its grounds. This unmoored, free-floating scaffolding creates a system whereby traditional methods of resistance are from their inception incapable of reconstituting a new order; they are incapable of contributing or signaling to another order of things because they no longer have any ground that can escape the destructive forces of late capitalism. To this situation Baudrillard poses a question: "Is there a theory or practice which is subversive because it is more aleatory than the system itself, an indeterminate subversion which would be to the order of the code what the revolution was to the order of political economy?"[32] To this Baudrillard posits his own tentative response: "Perhaps death and death alone . . . belongs to a higher order than the code. Only symbolic disorder can bring about an interruption in the code."[33]

Given John's previously stated interest in taking on and subverting the "code" though which images and events are reconstituted and absorbed by a knowable system—the system, for him, of hegemonic order and sanctioned grief reproduced through funeral footage—*Medium Cool*'s closing sequence, its turn to death as the final rejoinder, is of major significance. Death serves as the only outside to the code of continuity that covers over the reception of events. Death as the experience of utter rupture in the order of things. This is a kind of death that can arrive and interrupt the codes. It is not JFK's death or RFK's or MLK's, but death as experienced by John and Eileen. This ending is then an attempt to stave off the absorption of its images back into a knowable a system, an attempt to keep open its forceful qualities without their being taken up by a rational code. Hence the significance of the radio broadcast that prefigures this accident: via this broadcast we hear how the random tragedy that has befallen these two is already being rendered in coherent terms. And indeed the specifics of this broadcast are valuable: John, of relative fame and notoriety around the city, is recognized, but Eileen, who remains anonymous to the broadcasters, remains unidentified. The forces of power, through John, are already at work reproducing how we should feel about this accident—"Womanizing wealthy cameraman in deadly wreck after convention"—without, of course, mention of his turn to a more radical politics and a more critical attitude toward current events finding its way into his eulogy. Eileen, with less financial and social capital, falls totally out of view.

Baudrillard elaborates on the function of death by remarking that "every closed or metastable, functional or cybernetic system is shadowed by mockery and instantaneous subversion (which no longer takes the detour through long dialectical labour), because all the system's inertia acts against it."[34] This is to say that a system designed to be totalizing and entirely available for inspection, one that is insulated from its outside by efficiency and certainty, is overturned most easily by its disavowed outside, what is always its failure: death. "This is the fatality of every system committed by its own logic to total perfection and therefore to a total defectiveness, to absolute infallibility and therefore irrevocable breakdown: the aim of all bound energies is their own death."[35] For Baudrillard, systems that present themselves as total inevitably fail because of the vehemence with which they deny the very possibility of that failing, of an outside that they absolutely disavow. The refusal of this outside means that it will only return with greater precision, at some point undermining the system's functioning. And, for Baudrillard, this undermining must present itself as death, as the radical disruption that totally subverts a principle, turning over its functions and proving its inadequacy. Death opens up a fissure in the otherwise stable façade of modern rationality, and in so doing points always to its limits. It is impossible to account for and it alone can rupture assimilation, at least for a little while. This, for Baudrillard, is why "the ever increasing fascination with the catastrophic, the accident and the assassination attempt: reason itself as pursued by the hope of a universal revolt against its own norms and principles."[36] Indeed death is the one subject that reason cannot strive to address. Fascination with catastrophe, for Baudrillard, is evidence of a society's reversibility; death is not a subject that can be investigated, and that is what makes it so fascinating.

Baudrillard's major intervention here is not the deployment of the way that death haunts and undermines total systems—this is no doubt a significant topic, but it is not his emphasis. His intention is instead to focus on the ways to combat these total systems, and death is simply one way of doing this. According to Baudrillard, "Things must be pushed to the limit, where quite naturally they collapse and are inverted. At the peak of value we are closest to ambivalence, at the pinnacle of coherence we are closest to the abyss of corruption which haunts the reproduction of signs of the code."[37] Hence the impossible bind that John recounts: all his systems for defense and critique are reduced to the code for understanding and evaluating media images. And hence *Medium Cool*'s abrupt ending, where any system for making meaning clearly fails, and where two cameras turn to look at each other only to be met with emptiness in return, an utter blankness that refuses to tell us anything more.

Baudrillard contends that "simulation must go further than the system. Death must be played against death: a radical tautology that makes the system's own logic the ultimate weapon."[38] Rather than deploying a cogent critique or a constructive retort to a system's qualities, the most effective response to the total system is to push it toward its own extremes. The approach whereby *Medium Cool* mounts its attack on a government that it depicts as increasingly violent and threatening is not to point outs its flaws, but to escalate them. The shallow, image-obsessed John does not find a solution in the radical politics of the 1960s; he finds that as unwelcoming as the world he fights against. Instead of building a system to identify with the demonstrators, *Medium Cool* further distances itself from the world, content to observe this seeming disintegration of order and to reproduce it through images, which can be loved, as by John, but which should also be distrusted. The film's solution, then, is neither to point out the order whereby images find meaning nor to attempt to present images unavailable to that order. Instead, *Medium Cool* responds by reproducing the system over again. Hence again the radio broadcast that prefigures the crash—these images will be rendered knowable. In this way a random event will become meaningful, but the function of the code is to render these meanings in a very strict way; it will absorb them into its system. The film tries to represent this process before it has even taken place, speeding the very procedure of absorption up to help its audience see it happening.

Baudrillard labels one way to disrupt this system of absorption "pataphysics," what he defines as "a science of imaginary solutions."[39] It is through the process of producing "the extreme limit of simulation" whereby the boundaries of a system can finally be viewed, and perhaps reversed.[40] This film presents the absolute limit of the violence on which the system relies—for Wexler a major marker of growing authoritarianism in the United States. This is a system of pure media reproduction that locks in an ideology simply through the multitudes of mirror-like reproductions that contain it, a media environment with total control and centralization but almost no platform. When, earlier in the film, John loses his job, it is because of his refusal to authorize his footage for government inspection. This moment crystallized John's project: his simultaneous love and distrust for images is finally placed explicitly against its use as a tool for stabilizing and reproducing power. This is the pataphysics of *Medium Cool*: that the moving image holds within it some mystical power that exceeds its ideological potential, a kind of asignifying thrust whereby images can amount to something that overwrites ready-to-hand knowledge and captures something new. And it is the reproduction of images—highlighted by the dueling cameras at the end but also by the protest footage itself—that troubles this project, that reveals it to be just an imaginary solution, one with no substance or coherence but that nonetheless contains something of significance, a solution that, even in its own failure, helps us see something of the boundaries of the system. This is the appeal of pataphysics; it reveals something in its own inadequacy and, in so doing, hopefully points to its own reversibility and, finally, to the reversibility of what it critiques.

For Wexler, the kind of death that Baudrillard describes is literalized. John and Eileen's abstract collision—the cause of which is never presented to us—arrives and punctuates the narrative of the film, breaking apart its already disruptive order and offering up the possibility of its own failing, the possibility that it also only locates the same order that it tries to disrupt, the order that puts tragedy in its place and denies the possibility for something new. But, to be clear, it is its doubt that allows *Medium Cool* to critique these totalizing systems. Wexler's film can be said to align with Baudrillard's ideas concerning a disavowed outside providing the only solution for undoing contemporary forces of power, and the system that it wishes to dismantle is indeed American democracy threatened by authoritarianism, an American democracy in particular predicated on order and economic prosperity. This is not, as is Hong Sang-soo's *Woman on the Beach* (2006), a total rejection of the concept of democracy, but a rejection of a democracy that seems to be trending toward authoritarianism, for it is authoritarianism—its mixture of violence and certainty—that is total and self-justifying and that most clearly pushes against the invisible boundaries that Baudrillard discusses. *Medium Cool* tries to photograph its own death, tries to figure an outside to the systems of organization that it is itself trapped within. Its solution, though, can only ever be blackness.

## A Global 1968

The perception that a new era of authoritarianism was on the rise was of global concern in 1968. In May that year there were riots and strikes on a massive scale in France. Starting in the universities and spreading eventually though much of the country, in the range of nine million workers across all fields of employment took part in the strikes, bringing France to a halt for weeks. As Kristin Ross explains, "May '68 was the largest mass movement in French history, the biggest strike in the history of the French workers' movement and the only 'general' insurrection the overdeveloped world has known since World War II. It was the first general strike that extended beyond the traditional centers of industrial production to include workers in the service industries, the communication and culture industries—the whole sphere of social reproduction. No professional sector, no category of worker was unaffected by the strike; no region, city, or village in France was untouched."[41]

Largely a response to the conservative government of Charles de Gaulle, May 1968 has become famous as a beacon of both the possibility of radical change and its failings. The latter because, according to many accounts, the French 1968 movement failed to bring about major political reforms, and conservative forces managed to further consolidate their power in its wake. Regardless of its effects, the modern conception of May 1968 in France, as Ross argues, is that of a nonviolent and relatively benign series of events that have merely mapped the transition "form an authoritarian bourgeois state to a new, liberal, modern financier bourgeoisie."[42] Ostensibly muting its political aspirations, Ross contends that May 1968 now serves as a kind of mere teleological transition from a predemocratic moment to a modern capitalist democracy, an essentially toothless undertaking that simply prefigured modern France. Ross, of course, pushes back against this trajectory, and instead focuses on an attempt to question the official story of May 1968 in the hopes of refinding some of its radical potential. She introduces her project as follows—I shall here quote it at length because I think it resonates well with *Medium Cool*:

> The paradox of May's memory can be simply stated. How does a mass movement that sought above all, in my view, to contest the domain of the expert, to disrupt the system of naturalized spheres of competence (especially the sphere of specialized politics), become translated in the years that followed into little more than a "knowledge" of '68, on the basis of which a whole generation of self-proclaimed experts and authorities could then assert their expertise? This

> moment swept away categorical territories and social definitions, and achieved unforeseen alliances and synchronicities *between* social sectors and between very diverse people working together to conduct their affairs collectively. How did such a movement get relocated into defined "sociological" residences: the "student milieu" or "the generation"?[43]

These are the same questions that confound *Medium Cool.* In response to the world-changing events that took place in the United States throughout the 1960s, the film asks how the protests that it records are to avoid the reduction that Ross attributes to 1968 in France; that is, how are they to avoid being taken up by the forces that might solidify and stultify their effects? How can they do what John hopes moving images can do, present something new, without falling again into a teleological account that reinforces the system in place?

Ross's solutions to this problem follow two trajectories, on the one hand tracing the legacy of May 1968 in France through the actions and ideas of philosophers and activists that it helped to inspire, and on the other hand directly examining the practices of those who participated in these events. Her main assertion is that the events of May 1968 represent "above all else a massive refusal on the part of thousands, even millions, of people to see in the social what we usually see."[44] *Medium Cool* is of value in its striking degree of *refusal.* John's distrust of the ways that images are ordered, and the open and ambiguous ending refuse the status of this film as progenitor of meaning or prominent talking piece. Instead, the camera turns itself on itself, turns itself inside out, and refuses such a status. The film thus stands with the movement it depicts, resoundingly refusing to see the social in the rigid, predetermined ways that might deploy a cogent rejoinder, renunciation, or clear rendering of the events it depicts.

Ross uses the example of the art students who occupied their university in order to address the function of the arts during the May events themselves. For Ross, the incommensurability between politics—defined broadly as the contestation of some order—and culture was essential to the movement. "The failure of cultural solutions to provide an answer, the invention and deployment of political forms in direct contestation with existing cultural forms, the exigency of political practices over cultural ones" is, for Ross, definitive of the 1968 student movement.[45] Hence, for Ross, these students, who produced signage and slogans usable to the movement only in regard to *continuing*, without attempting to orchestrate any direction. Speed became the mode of artistic critique here, not articulation. This idea is of particular importance in understand the conclusion of *Medium Cool*, as it maps a way of thinking about the political function of art. Politics in this view functions as the name for a contestation against a calcified order, and the function of political art therefore becomes either engendering or spurring on this contestation. What art cannot do is bridge the fissure that this contestation creates, for if it were to do so it would then take the form of governance, and would abdicate its role as site of rupture. This reconfiguration of the role of art in regard to politics then favors openings over closings, and engagement over resolution. For this model of art to function it must always push against the principle of meaninglessness; it must strive to make us see *something* but never tell us *how* to see it. This is a very difficult dynamic to maneuver, as it demands that art never function as example *or* authority. Art must remain between; it must ask us to rethink the social, but never quite tell us how or why. It must refuse, and in this refusal renounce also its own form.

This category of art then becomes very difficult to locate, and furthermore generates a strange set of questions: Can a political artwork in this mold exist outside its context? Can it be made to deliberately *do* anything? Can it account for its own outcomes? Ultimately, what can political art *say* in contexts like these? For Ross, and perhaps also for Wexler, the answer must be *nothing*, for to speak a meaning is to redact its use as object calling only for something new. *Medium Cool* attempts to enact this problem in its conclusion. It keeps at bay the forces that might render the political events it depicts meaningful and understandable; but this keeping at bay is always also its failure, as a refusal of meaning is also a refusal of coherence, understanding, and autonomy. Art is always just supplement here, helping us to look but never telling us what to look for. Like the ending of *Sátántangó* or Jung-rae's escapes in *Woman on the Beach*, *Medium Cool* pushes up against the void of its own meaninglessness, but its direct presentation of political violence highlights the stakes of this dynamic. What are we to do now? Having seen this film and understood, perhaps, what it has shown us, what available avenues for response does it engender?

Alain Touraine likewise discusses the student movements of May 1968 in France, albeit from a different perspective. For Touraine, the movement had two distinct sources from which it drew its strength, and these generally stood opposed to one another. The first of these is encapsulated by the ideas of Claude Lefort and Edgar Morin, who lionized the disruptive and anarchic elements of the movement. Touraine represents these views by saying that for these thinkers "the movement is defined by the capacity to transcend its own objectives" and "is defined less by its objectives than by the type of community that it creates."[46] Touraine associates these types of thinkers with the university, and I think this is how we can define *Medium Cool*. For this film, the value of the political movement that it depicts is not to be located in its adherence to a particular set of principles; its value can instead be found in the simple perpetuation of its position of rejection—it seeks only to maintain an opposition to authority. In Touraine's words, *Medium Cool* strives to locate an "antisociety" defined by its opposition to a dominant order, not through any allegiance to a particular set of goals or principles.

But, as Touraine notes, this antisociety also produces its own set of problems. For Touraine, the rejection that propels this kind of movement "either leads to marginality or ends by overturning the social order, but it is impotent in the face of the political problems of governing and directing society."[47] This is to say that this kind of anarchic social movement constantly butts against the inability of an agenda-less arrangement to present a coherent response to the problems that they have joined together to solve. This is also a criticism of *Medium Cool*, for, as we have seen, its turn to disruption over and above coherent critique is productive, in a sense, for the project of depicting the effects of a violent government. But where it stumbles is in its capacity to produce a unifying alternative to the problems it identifies.

Pushing against the antisociety mode is what I shall call the *definitional* aspect of these movements. Less aligned with the universities—about which Touraine has many reservations—the definitional pull strives to clearly articulate its oppositional points and produce an alternative. As Touraine observes, "In the United States, the movement at Berkeley and Columbia cannot be separated from the struggle against the Vietnam War and the black revolt; in the socialist countries, the student action was part of the struggle against Stalinist or post-Stalinist techno-bureaucracy; so, almost immediately, the major concern in France was the union of students and workers against the Gaullist regime and capitalist society. . . . The struggle constantly moved out of the university faculties and developed in the streets, led by students and young workers who were more and more at one with each other."[48] For Touraine, it is when these definitional and antisociety drives meet that a movement can begin to be broadly effective. *Medium Cool*, however, refuses the second half of this equation—it demands openness but provides no recourse for the reconstitution of society, and in this regard nobly fails, as it must, to actually bring about the change that it indirectly demands. This film is a site of contestation but never its solution. It is in its refusal to say anything in particular that *Medium Cool* finds its strengths, as well as its weaknesses. It speeds up the process of ordering tragic events in the hopes of letting us see how these orderings might be reductive and otherwise support the rising authoritarian tide, but it does nothing to produce a counterplatform, for to do so would be take part in the very process that it rejects. In this way, as with the other films discussed here, it is messianic. Its resolution can only arrive from the outside, and attempting to prefigure this forthcoming solution would only undermine it. *Medium Cool* makes itself powerless in the hopes of making room for another power altogether, one that it cannot quite predict.

*Medium Cool*'s own capacity to reproduce order is disavowed in the name of an opening to potential but—apart from the failings of saying nothing in particular—this approach always also leaves available the possibility for a new authority to approach, to rise from the darkness or take hold of these openings.

For radical openness, despite all its rejections, always provides the room for the very thing it rejected to re-emerge, for negative forces to find new shapes and to take hold of the ambiguities to which films like *Medium Cool* cling. Within its eternal openness and adamant hope is to be found radical difference, but also the repetition of the same and indeed perhaps also something worse. *Medium Cool* is a film about and enacting *force*, but what it lacks is *faculty*. This is its major problem: in order to say what it wants, it must say nothing at all; it must be adamant in its ambiguity, and in this way it must always fail. Its attempts to render politics, to chart a course through all this tumult and unrest and to provide something like a précis for these events, something that might make them understandable and manageable, and which might point toward something else, must always come up empty. It must fail, fail at coherence, fail at narrative, fail at filmmaking, and fail at politics. For to not fail would be to do exactly what the film resists. This is the impossible bind of *Medium Cool* and the impossible bind that this brand of antiauthoritarian art cinema broadly defined: it must all always fail, and in doing so open up the possibility for something else, something new.

# Coda

## Political Modernism and the Possibility for Action

Each of the films discussed in this book rejects authority in the name of a radical opening to change. As I have shown, by rejecting all authority, even and primarily the filmmakers' own, these films must turn to ambiguity. The difficulty of these films is constituted by this turn, because the embrace of ambiguity as politics means that there is no guarantee that anything new will arise. The positive outcome of this gamble is that these films might result in thought, thought about politics and about the possibility of realizing something different; the negative outcome is that these films might remain absent of meaning, and that on the rare occasion that meaning does arrive, they offer no mechanism for universalization. There are therefore risks involved in these undertakings: the risk of irrelevance, the risk of inaction, the risk of appearing to say nothing at all.

In *Germany Year Zero*, when Edmund finally gently hangs up his coat and jumps from the opened side of a bombed Berlin building to his death, openness is extended to its limit. The impossibility of his situation, the unbearability of his available avenues for action, has exhausted him and us, and the only system that can leave open the possibility for something new is to be found in the film's refusal to make a decision as to the responsibility and orientation of his violent acts and the status of his punishment. So he must jump, and thanks to this jump this film makes its refusal; with anger it declares that it will not resolve the political future of Edmund's world. Edmund's future is closed, but the possibility for different political outcomes remains open. In *Sátántangó*, when the Doctor finally boards himself up completely inside his home, he too makes the decision to preserve openness; here, ironically, he accomplishes this by confining himself to his drab house, resigning himself to inaction. Alone in his mud-soaked town, the Doctor demands that we act just like him, that we watch as the denizens of this town slowly leave, and then that we watch as he finally closes out all light. Alone in his, and our, inaction, the film asks whether refusal is a path toward change, but it refuses, as it must, to answer this question. Indecision, or perhaps the raging against decision, is complicated by *Woman on the Beach*, because Jung-rae's model for how the world might engage differently with knowledge and decision is directly stated. But this film's ambivalence toward Jung-rae's claims, as examined through the possibility that he might just be using them as avenues for escape, complicates their validity. When this film ends, Mun-suk points her car toward what might be a positive horizon. But in so doing, she gets stuck in the sand and, as a result, heads back the way she came. The film likewise traces this path between the appeal of openness and the possibility for decision, now with palpable frustration as to how openness to change can be manipulated. Finally, at the end of *Medium Cool*, when John and Eileen's car is abruptly destroyed in a wreck and the twin cameras turn on each other with such fury, this openness as refusal is once and for all codified. The dueling cameras, which bring into question the capacity of media to withstand and represent refusal, finally find in each other only a black screen, thus signaling the possibility for difference that relies on the absolute negation of the means and methods for representation. In this most extreme dedication to openness, this mode of antiauthoritarian cinema finds its limit: a dedication to difference that blocks its ability to say anything at all.

The chapters of this book have been arranged to broaden the scope of rejection as each proceeds. First, authoritarianism is rejected, then the economic corollaries of capitalism and communism are dismissed, and, finally, even democracy is put aside. These rejections signal toward some kind of positive alternative, but, as each of these endings makes clear, these films always refuse to picture it, with some refusing to picture anything at all. Each less declarative than the last, these films all come near to meaning but never quite arrive. This is the fulfillment of their antiauthoritarian wish, but it also amounts to a position of indecision. This ambiguity renders any reading of these films unstable.

My project here therefore shares a number of connections to the broad grouping of theorists from the 1960s and 1970s that loosely fit into the category of "political modernism." These thinkers, arising at first in relation to the French publication *Tel Quel*, had a major impact on English and North American film studies, starting in the 1970s. *Tel Quel* pulled together a diverse group of theorists including Julia Kristeva, Jacques Derrida, Jean-Louis Baudry, Roland Barthes, and other significant French theorists of the period. The ideas deployed in this journal later filtered into the *Cahiers du Cinéma*—most notably impacting the era of the journal known for ideological critique rooted in Althusserian Marxism—and subsequently into the English journal *Screen* via the significant work of film theorists such as Stephen Heath, Colin McCabe, and Laura Mulvey. As D. N. Rodowick notes, the theorists associated with this era of *Screen* and *Cahiers du Cinéma* were organized broadly by their interest in critiquing the dominant ideology, which they often achieved by exploring the ways that pernicious ideas are coded into the basic configuration of commercial cinema. These theorists embarked on this project by contending that commercial narrative films function in most cases to reconstruct and furthermore promote dominant modes of seeing by virtue of their supposed "apolitics"—which are of course deeply political because they reproduce "normalcy" and in so doing present reductive avenues for seeing the world. As Rodowick notes, "By offering narrative based on principles of unity, continuity, and closure, the argument goes, Hollywood films efface the materiality of the film medium and through this transparency of form promote an identification with, and unquestioning acceptance of, the fictional world offered by the film."[1] This is to say that by reproducing an uncritical realism based on an ease of seeing, commercial films ask us to accept their world as normal, and therefore they function not just to entertain us but also to convince us of the proper place of things in the recognizable world that the spectator and film seem to share.

For theorists like Jean-Louis Comolli and Jean Narboni—major figures in the ideological critique period of the *Cahiers du Cinéma*—the task of film criticism became the categorization of films in relation to their unique connections to ideology. In "Cinema/Ideology/Criticism," their seminal text on the methodology of ideological critique, they deploy seven categories for categorizing the cinema they encounter. These categories map the various ways of thinking about cinema and its relationship to politics, particularly as it pertains to ideology. The categories range from "those films which are imbued through and through with the dominant ideology in pure and unadulterated form"[2] to cinema that "attacks the basic problem of depiction by giving an active role to the concrete stuff" of a film.[3] Comolli and Narboni's essay is therefore largely concerned with proposing a method for thinking about the politics of cinema in a general sense.

Among the seven categories proposed, one became the focus of much of this style of criticism. The category that Comolli and Narboni most clearly lionized was that of

> films that attack their ideological assimilation on two fronts. Firstly, by direct political action, on the level of the 'signified', i.e. they deal with a directly political subject. 'Deal with' is here intended in an active sense: they do not just

> discuss an issue, reiterate it, paraphrase it, but use it to attack the ideology (this presupposes a theoretical activity which is the direct opposite of the ideological one). This act only becomes politically effective if it is linked with a breaking down of the traditional way of depicting reality. On the level of form, *Not Reconciled*, *The Edge* and *Terra em transe* all challenge the concept of 'depiction' and mark a break with the tradition embodying it.[4]

This category is particularly valuable as it proposes a "countercinema" in which the spectator is removed from the stability of normalcy and asked to encounter the film in a new kind of way. This cinema, along with that which relied on formal disruption but without the direct representation of political content, became the major cause of those dedicated to ideological critique. It was indeed this new style of cinema—a cinema that champions formal innovation in the name of defamiliarization—that came to constitute political cinema as a category of filmmaking. For Rodowick, "Political modernism insisted firstly on a 'politics of representation' in the assumption that foregrounding the process of signification would draw the spectator's attention to the materiality of the image through the disruption of the unity and transparency of film form."[5]

For the thinkers of *Screen* and *Cahiers du Cinéma*, all cinema was political, but a radical, politically minded cinema could only be constituted via a form of ideological critique that relied on practices of alienation, on making a viewer aware of their attention and the fact of their position in relation to a film. What this criticism called for was a cinema that turned the attention of the viewer away from narrative order and instead toward the materiality of the images on display. What is constituted by this argument is then a dichotomy between commercial cinema (what is often referred to as "realist cinema" but what I would call "continuity cinema," so as to separate it from the "realism" that founded so much of art cinema) and a modernist cinema predicated on disruption and alienation. One of the major tenets of this divide pertained to the capacity and potentials of narrative. As one of the major sites of readability, narrative can serve as a system to reinscribe ideology through comfort, or conversely can serve as an easily available space for disorienting an audience.

This divide is intimately related to the subject of this book. Narrative disruption plays a major role in the way that the films in this analysis function to provide openings to reconfiguration, and delays in narrative progression are therefore an important element of how the films I have discussed achieve an emptying of authority via an opening to new meanings. The difference between the approach to antiauthoritarian cinema here and the ideas that fit into the category of political modernism, however, emerges when I consider the goals of a political cinema.

Rodowick titles his book *The Crisis of Political Modernism*, and the crisis under discussion is what author sees as the incommensurate wishes of these theorists. For Rodowick, this crisis stems from the faulty pairing of Marxism and deconstruction, as these two modes of analysis have wildly different relationships to ideology, and indeed to critique. "In many respects the predominance of ideological criticism in the discourse of political modernism engendered, as the very condition of its logic, a series of oppositions that required the effects of illusion and falsity as epistemological categories in order to validate the theoretical project conceived for the film avant-gardes. . . . In its attempt to reconcile Althusser and Derrida for a political aesthetic, this opposition served to construct questionable epistemological valuations according to criteria of textual forms."[6] The problem, then, is a product of too much determination, or too little, depending on one's stronger allegiances. That is, for those dedicated to the task of deconstruction, the appeal of this formal alienation is its capacity to break apart systems for seeing, but there is no mechanism for reordering, as the very structure of this process serves to unearth and dismantle illusory ways of understanding the world. For the Marxists, however, the problem is the opposite: the ordering mechanism is the central concern because the reconstituting of an emptied-out and alienated viewer in the name of a particular political project is the goal.

This is Rodowick's crisis: if a making aware of the constructedness of things is the goal, and the process by which this goal is achieved is built on disorientation and unreadability, then there can be no subsequent realization that is not also subject to this same process. There is no system for reforming things that is not also susceptible to deconstruction, and the projects associated with Marxism are therefore always sowing the seeds of their own demise as well. As Rodowick neatly summarizes, "Political modernism's particular delimitation of the text as a site of 'political' activity can now be understood as naïve. Once the criteria devolving from the formal self-identity of the text are challenged, the required epistemological judgment—which decides between ideological and theoretical or illusionist/idealist and materialist films—is rendered inconclusive."[7] Rodowick's solution to this problem is to propose a *discursive* method for analyzing films, and he subsequently focuses on the task of locating the meaning and use of a film within a larger spectrum of how it has been taken up and otherwise activated.

My own analysis has been more clearly aligned with the deconstructionist pole of Rodowick's dichotomy, and I have argued throughout that the hope of these films is not necessarily Marxist, nor aligned with any other particular political solution. I have argued that the hope here is *messianic*, which is to say that these films put their faith totally in the hands of an undrawable exterior force that might ameliorate the needs they voice. But by eliminating some of the determinative qualities present in political modernism, I do not contend that I have found a solution. Indeed the susceptibility of this messianic approach has been addressed throughout this discussion, and remains the major obstruction that these films face. Unreadability has been accelerated here, muting some of the turmoil of political modernism, but creating new and striking barriers to use.

The dark rejoinder to the refusals these films make is to be found in the possibility that their hope for a positive future might never be fulfilled, for ambiguity not only renders these films without content, it also presents opportunities for co-option. A dedication to total openness is not only ineffective, it also makes these films available for unforeseen actors to take as their own. That is, the forces of power in the world today, in particular the forces of neoliberal democratic capitalism, can point to just these fixations on ambiguity and say "this is us too"—they can claim also to maintain a radically open status, and can take ownership of the creative powers of contingency and ambiguity. The dynamic that allows for this co-optation on the part of powerful and in particular market-oriented forces is particularly pernicious given the likelihood that in moments of openness the prevailing forces of power will be the first things to fill these openings, so long as the piece fits.

The task of the forces of contemporary authority and control is to create a dominant ideology that is as malleable and aleatory as the avenues of ambiguity and antiauthority that might critique it. As a result, the structure of the ideology that accompanies neoliberalism proposes a worldview open to inclusivity, but one that also takes for granted the unassailability of capitalism and the market, a rationale whereby all methods of thought are judged by their closeness and similarity to the market. It is perhaps the capacity to render an antiauthoritarian critique silent and ineffective by beating it to its own arguments that has made neoliberalism so effective—we simply have no system by which to reject it.

These four films thus fight against authority, but they present no rejoinder for the new kinds of authority that have taken root in our post-1989 world. This is not to say that these films failed in their objectives, but to question whether their methods are the right ones for today. What now remains for a cinema dedicated to combating the rise of unchecked authority? Is authority even the problem anymore? And, finally, if these films are representative of global art cinema broadly defined—particularly in regard to their embrace of ambiguity and its failings—what is the role of this tradition of cinema in any attempt to combat the forces of inequality and injustice in our world? To conclude, I think it is perhaps valuable to move to another model for political cinema—that of direction.

Throughout the course of my writing this analysis, much has changed in the world; paramount has been the perception of a new form of authoritarianism, and the conditions we now face are not altogether different from those of 1968. The election of Donald Trump as president of the United States has poked holes in illusions pertaining both to the functioning of American democracy and to faith in democracy in general. The rejoinder of openness and undecidability seems particularly inappropriate in this moment, and indeed the calls for direct critique have started to resound much more loudly. As a result, I think it is best here to conclude not by avoiding these calls, but by thinking of the politics of ambiguous cinema from another vantage, that of its potential for voicing political concerns directly. These concluding remarks will proceed by following a different path in evaluating the potentials for the style of cinema addressed here: what I contend is that where these films find their use is not in their capacity to produce meaning, but in their ability to serve as a catalyst for producing thought. But the kind of thought they produce is of particular value; it is a style of thinking that provides, ideally, the space for a unified political project, one that is not aleatory but rooted in a general claim for the well-being of a society. What these films might potentially do is provide the grounds by which thinking might arise, thinking that might also find its way into action anchored by a unified politics—in these contexts a politics built around the needs of the dejected, misguided, or otherwise imperiled characters that each film presents.

For Hannah Arendt, the traditional relationship between thinking and action has been reversed in the modern world, leading to myriad problems in the relationship between thinking and politics. Traditionally, Arendt notes, "Thought was conceived as the most direct and important way to lead to the contemplation of truth. Since Plato, and probably since Socrates, thinking was understood as the inner dialogue in which one speaks with himself . . . and although this dialogue lacks all outward manifestation and even requires a more or less complete cessation of all other activities, it constitutes in itself a highly active state."[8] In this arrangement, thought functions as a personal interchange in which different avenues and options are considered and, through an inner dialectic, the thinker prepares to behold truth, despite its possible nonarrival.

If these films strive to create a window upon events in the hopes of opening the possibility to see something anew, and if their ambiguity refuses any artificial conclusion that might disrupt this process of renewed vision, then one way to look at them is as serving to provide avenues for thought. That is, they offer up a series of familiar-looking but otherwise difficult-to-order images and ask that the audience arrive at some understanding in the absence of a readily available meaning; in this way *they ask for thought*. They ask that a viewer reconcile these images with their understanding of the world, an interchange that relies on the hope that the viewer might find in them some new idea or perspective. The particular subject of each film here is the topic of political transition, and ideally each provides the space for a dialectic that can yield to some conclusion.

Thinking in this way is not distinct from action but is in fact a specific form of action, one that calls forth a whole category of subsequent actions, those known as "work." As Arendt explains: "Thinking and working are two different activities which never quite coincide; the thinker who wants the world to know the 'content' of his thoughts must first of all stop thinking and remember his thoughts. Remembrance in this, as in all other cases, prepares the intangible and the futile for their eventual materialization; it is the beginning of the work process, and like the craftsman's consideration of the model which will guide his work, its most immaterial stage."[9] This cinema of transition asks us to think and hopes to serve as the beginning of what might later be called work, or rather the rebuilding of things that results from thought and that can help turn these insights into material change in the world.

But in the modern world, which for Arendt is the world after Galileo, the function of thought, and of philosophy in particular, has been radically altered: "After Descartes based his own philosophy upon the discoveries of Galileo, philosophy has seemed condemned to be always one step behind the scientists and their ever more amazing discoveries, whose principles it has strived arduously to discover *ex posto facto* and to fit into some over-all interpretation of the nature of human knowledge."[10] In the modern world, for Arendt, the domain of truth is thought to be addressed only by science, and philosophy is left either to attempt to understand or critique the epistemological underpinnings of science or to attempt to address current conditions with clarity but without any appeal to any overall solution. As Arendt notes, speaking again of philosophers, "In both instances, whether they looked upon nature or upon history, they tried to understand and come to terms with what happened without them. Obviously, philosophy suffered more from modernity than any other field of human endeavor; and it is difficult to say whether it suffered more from the almost automatic rise of activity to an altogether unexpected and unprecedented dignity or from the loss of traditional truth, that is, of the concept of truth underlying our whole tradition."[11]

For Arendt the process of thought leading to material change has been seriously diminished in the modern world. This is because in order for thought to *work*, to bring about anything in terms of change, there must still be the possibility of truth, the possibility for an idea to be found that holds within it some claim for a universal solution to the problems that the world faces. The value of thought is further illuminated in its difference from contemplation. For Arendt via Plato, thinking is a highly active process, but it is also the preparation for beholding truth, whereas contemplation is the stillness that accompanies truth's arrival, the state of being with the universal.[12] But without a claim to truth, this system loses its motor; the work that might arise from thought fails to materialize, or materializes only as personal creative endeavor, as hobby.[13] Thought in the modern world can never become work because work must hold within it a reason for its being that carries some claim for its worth in society; today only science can make this claim.

Without a claim to a universal truth, the work that derives from thinking cannot find purchase, cannot be justified as a project undertaken for a general good. The thinking provoked by these films has, under Arendt's views, no possibility for finding its way out of the cinema and into the world. Ernesto Laclau, in his essay "What Do Empty Signifiers Matter to Politics?," offers a possible way out of this bind. Speaking of Rosa Luxemburg's model for how class struggle finds unification in moments of intense opposition, Laclau posits that "in a climate of extreme repression any mobilization for a partial objective will be perceived not only as related to the concrete demand or objectives of that struggle, but also as an act of opposition against the system."[14] In this way politics built around the struggle against an oppressive system finds its unity not through compromises between competing ideas, but by virtue of their common identity as oppositional. For Laclau, this relationship allows for unity where it would otherwise be unavailable, and not as solidarity with other issues, but as the formation of a unified struggle that does not distinguish between its constitutive parts. Laclau continues, "Luxemburg's argument is that a revolutionary mass identity is established through the overdetermination, over a whole historical period, of a plurality of separate struggles. These traditions fused, at the revolutionary moment, in a ruptural point."[15] In this way, a revolutionary program builds a unified platform not in spite of its differences, but because these differences no longer appear to be differences at all. A natural-seeming process that covers over difference in the formation of a unified category, such a process makes the need for a general truth irrelevant as unity is taken for granted in a process that "simultaneously asserts and abolishes its own singularity."[16]

For Laclau, this process is built around the capacity of what he calls "the empty signifier" to aid in unification. The role of the signifier in this scenario is to serve as the fulcrum for fusing different ideas and platforms, and the reason it must be empty is because the less it holds the more valuable it is as a vessel for a unifying principle. These empty signifiers appear at the outset to be fully formed—if perhaps vague—words or concepts, but they have the capacity to be refilled with a promise that overcomes difference and in fact serves as a nodal point. Terms like "liberty," for instance, which call forth a set of ideals but provide no particular map or discrete set of principles, are thus taken up and reauthored by a cause, and in this way they serve as unifying forces that propel a movement forward. They can do this because their relationships to their signifieds are adrift, because they are, in the first place, ambiguous.

The films discussed here share many qualities with these empty signifiers. Necessarily empty of meaning, they take the form of an empty vessel that can be pushed in any number of directions. Like an empty signifier, *Germany Year Zero* maintains a link to the world of recognizable things and occurrences, but this link is tentative because the film at times complicates, as I have discussed, its relationship to its spaces and events. It resists comment and disallows particularity; it cannot be said to "have any form of representation of its own," as Laclau puts it.[17] Emptied of meaning, it waits to see what might happen in or to its ambiguous aesthetics, and waits to see who might take them up and why. All the while it asks for thought, thinking that might turn successfully into work because its truth claim, its universalizing principle, has been restored by way of its ambiguity. In moments of transition, when these films ask for us to think, they do so at a moment when their empty status also enables them to be used for the cause of the opposition. Like "liberty," *Germany Year Zero* is vague enough to be a catalyst for the unification of a cause. The plight of Edmund, for instance, is capable of speaking to different groups in different ways, but the general need to alleviate his misery is just enough to potentially allow for divergent approaches to be unified. In this way, and in the right context, differing approaches to politics can find their unifying point, their commonality as opposition, their claim to truth. This is a film that can ask for a form of thought that has the possibility for unification, and it can do so because of its combination of narrative and aesthetic ambiguity with verisimilar photography. This is the possibility of art cinema.

The proposal I have presented here is speculative, and the possibility of these films engendering this renewed form of thought is slim. But this potential is nonetheless valuable in examining the work that these films can do, and furthermore for examining what the art cinema form has to offer to politics. For Laclau, empty signifiers, in addition to being filled up, can also be used up: "If 'workers' struggle' becomes the signifier of liberation as such, it also becomes the surface of inscription through which *all* liberating struggles will be expressed, so that the chain of equivalences which are unified around this signifier tend to empty it, and to blur its connection with the actual content with which it was originally associated. Thus, as a result of its very success, the hegemonic operation tends to break its links with the force which was its original promoter and beneficiary."[18] Through this process, the empty signifier fills with meaning in moments where it takes on this universalizing project, but in the long term regains its empty status once more. Once the groups that it had brought together have lost their unification point and have fallen apart again, the fulcrum of their unity starts to appear different, or even irrelevant, to each now distinct grouping. Antiauthoritarian cinema of this type can slip into and out of a cause. What appears to have lost any link to action can find its claim to truth again, and just as quickly lose it once more. The films discussed here are not stable in their resignation to inaction. The thoughts they encourage can again find their purchase, and this is because they so clearly reject meaning, because they are so resigned to emptiness.

These four films, of course, were each made at exactly the wrong moment to find use as empty signifiers. Each, with the exception of *Medium Cool*, was made after their oppositional moment, immediately after their makers' might have stood opposed to a centralized power and found unified potential in the concerns of those who resisted that power. But, as with the empty signifier, it is always a surprise what concepts are taken up to speak to newly unifying forces. This is a cinema of waiting; it is a cinema that finds its politics not through its own actions but through a spurring of thought that might generate action. Ultimately, for it to be political, ambiguous cinema must place its hope in the possibility that one day the thoughts that it encourages will find their use in the world. That these films will find their universalizing functions is another messianic wish, and its arrival is always unexpected.

The antiauthoritarian cinema I have discussed in this book thus holds within it two potentials: first, it is a space of thought, an object through which ideas can be measured and weighed. It demands a dialectical mode of interaction because it refuses to ever verify any particular set of ideas. It provokes us with verisimilar images that are at once locatable and escape location, and speaks of particular events without ever exactly commenting on them. In this way it incites thought and, later, remembrance. The specifics of the thinking that these films encourage are likewise of value. Each is dedicated to thought in times of change, and in this way strives to prepare viewers for the possibility of a new politics, a new cause that can arise from the thoughts that are provoked. Whether this thinking will find its way into work, however, is in question: for these thoughts to find their outlet, they must be justified by a claim to truth.

This is where the second potential of this mode of antiauthoritarian cinema steps in: as ambiguous, empty objects these films open up the possibility for renewed unification. They provoke the viewer to think, but also provide the possibility that their emptiness might be taken up, filled, so to speak, and used to bridge difference in pursuit of a unified claim. This combination of propelling thinking while also remaining empty is a product of ambiguity, and is central to the history of art cinema. The capacity to reproduce images that claim a relationship to reality—images that might be called verisimilar—but to also remain ambiguous is what makes art cinema political. Its emptiness, its refusal of meaning, is why it is valuable. Here, in these moments of transition, art cinema is most adamant in its rejections, and as a result finds its most radical form of hope. Provocations for thought without the structure for molding it, emptied husks that hope for renewal, these films are antiauthoritarian by virtue of the fact that they offer nothing at all.

# Acknowledgments

This book began, years ago, as a dissertation project undertaken at the University of Wisconsin–Milwaukee (UWM). I am deeply indebted to the range and depth of support I have received throughout its development, particularly by way of the Media, Cinema, and Digital Studies program at UWM as well as the Center for 21st Century Studies.

Along the way I received insights and support from a wide array of thinkers, including EJ Basa, Mike Beebe, Allain Daigle, Bridget Kies, Scott Krzych, Molly McCourt, and Chris Williams. This project additionally benefited greatly from the community arranged around a conference organized by the journal *World Picture*, and so I would like to thank its organizers Brian Price, Meghan Sutherland, and John David Rhodes.

I am grateful too to Rutgers University Press, who has been very supportive all throughout the writing and revision process. Lisa Banning has been a wonderful and supportive editor, and I thank her for her patience and contributions to this work.

I additionally had the privilege of receiving thorough feedback from a selection of thinkers the quality of which this book surely does not deserve. These included Kennan Ferguson, Ivan Ascher, and Peter Paik. Adam Cottrell, Adam Ochonicky, Alison Sperling, and Gordon Sullivan were also essential to this project, and indeed to my life over the last few years. Eric Herhuth's and Mark Heimermann's weekly contributions for years kept me afloat, and I am particularly grateful to them.

The three scholars most important to this project, and indeed my work in general, are Elena Gorfinkel, Brian Price, and Patrice Petro. I truly did nothing to deserve such a thoughtful group of supporters, and I cannot thank them enough. Elena Gorfinkel was a key influence on this work, and her guidance is plainly obvious in what follows. Among these scholars, I have known Brian

Price the longest, and his work (and the style thereof) continues to impact my own. Patrice Petro, of course, deserves special thanks; her substantive and insightful advice and attention are surely responsible for whatever this book has to offer. I am so happy to have had the support of this unique group of thinkers, and I thank them all immensely.

I would like to thank my family for their unwavering support, and finally, of course, Mary Clinkenbeard, for everything.

# Notes

## Introduction

1 Douglas Martin, "Barney Rosset Dies at 89; Defied Censors, Making Racy a Literary Staple," *New York Times*, February 22, 2012.

2 The distinction between authoritarianism and totalitarianism is important here, and will be discussed in depth in chapter 1. It is for the moment sufficient to note that I think of these as related but different systems of governance, and that these differences are to be found primarily in their respective relationships to authority.

3 This will be discussed at length in both chapters 1 and 3, but I am thinking here of Zygmunt Bauman's argument pertaining to liquidity operating as the new form of authority: Zygmunt Bauman, *Liquid Modernity* (Cambridge: Polity Press, 2000).

4 David Bordwell, "The Art Cinema as a Mode of Film Practice," *Film Criticism* 4, no. 1 (1979): 56.

5 Ibid.

6 Ibid., 59.

7 Ibid.

8 Ibid.

9 Ibid.

10 Ibid., 60.

11 Ibid.

12 Ibid., 61.

13 Ibid.

14 Bordwell contends that the more extreme category of "modernist" cinema was beginning to disrupt the otherwise stable category of art cinema. I must contend that this is where I depart from Bordwell regarding this topic; the differences between these categories evade me and I think of it as much more useful to think of art cinema as a broader category, albeit one still defined by a tradition of ambiguity. For a thorough explanation and taxonomy of art cinema and its relationship to modernism, see András Bálint Kovács, *Screening Modernism: European Art Cinema, 1950–1980* (Chicago: University of Chicago Press, 2007).

15 Mark Betz, *Beyond the Subtitle: Remapping European Art Cinema* (Minneapolis: University of Minnesota Press, 2009), 10.

16 Ibid., 13. Betz focuses on the legacy of the 1960s, particularly the tumultuous period surrounding 1968.

17 Ibid.

18 Ibid.

19 Ibid., 38.

20 Rosalind Galt and Karl Schoonover, "Introduction: The Impurity of Art Cinema," in *Global Art Cinema: New Theories and Histories*, ed. Rosalind Galt and Karl Schoonover (Oxford: Oxford University Press), 3.

21 Ibid.

22 These qualities are most famously outlined in André Bazin's essay, "The Evolution of the Language of Cinema," in *What Is Cinema?*, trans. Hugh Gray (Berkeley: University of California Press, 1967), 1:23–40.

23 Rosalind Galt and Karl Schoonover, "Introduction: The Impurity of Art Cinema," in *Global Art Cinema: New Theories and Histories*, ed. Rosalind Galt and Karl Schoonover (Oxford: Oxford University Press), 6.

24 It is notable here that both and all forms of authority return in remarkable ways. Authorial intention returns in deviation and, as per Bordwell's dynamic, actually becomes the major tool of analysis for these films, and political authority returns in these absences of meaning as a kind of suspended force that can finally put an end to all this seeming indifference, its significance kind of growing in its absence.

25 Galt and Schoonover, "Introduction," 8.

26 For an in-depth account of this process of "witnessing" and its relationship to global art cinema, see Karl Schoonover, *Brutal Vision: The Neorealist Body in Postwar Italian Cinema* (Minneapolis: University of Minnesota Press, 2012).

27 Danielle Celermajer, "Unsettling Memories and the Irredeemable," *Theory & Event* 19, no. 2 (April 2016).

28 Ibid.

29 Ibid.

30 Ibid.

31 Ibid.

32 Ibid.

33 Chapter 4, which maps a possible turn toward authoritarianism by way of the film *Medium Cool*, is the only exception here.

34 See, for instance, the essays in Tiago De Luca and Nuno Barradas Jorge, eds., *Slow Cinema* (Edinburgh: Edinburgh University Press, 2016).

35 Martin Jay, "'The Aesthetic Ideology' as Ideology; Or, What Does It Mean to Aestheticize Politics?," *Cultural Critique*, no. 21 (1992): 44.

36 Astradur Eysteinsson, *The Concept of Modernism* (Ithaca, NY: Cornell University Press, 1990), 41.

37 Theodor Adorno, *Aesthetic Theory* (London: Continuum, 2002), 19.

38 Angelos Koutsourakis, *Politics as Form in Lars von Trier* (New York: Bloomsbury, 2013), xv–xvi.

39 Ibid., xvii.

40 Ibid., 2.

41 This dynamic between particularity and the possibility for something totally new—and its relationship to political film theory—will be discussed at length in the coda, which takes up what has been called the crisis of political modernism directly.

42 Siobhan S. Craig, *Cinema after Fascism: The Shattered Screen* (New York: Palgrave Macmillan, 2010), 2.
43 Ibid., 2.
44 Richard Rushton, *The Politics of Hollywood Cinema: Popular Film and Contemporary Political Theory* (New York: Palgrave Macmillan, 2013), 8.
45 Ibid.
46 Ibid., 9.
47 Ibid., 16–17.
48 This argument is well represented by Cavell's book *Pursuits of Happiness: The Hollywood Comedy of Remarriage* (Cambridge, MA: Harvard University Press, 1981).
49 Richard Rushton, *The Politics of Hollywood Cinema: Popular Film and Contemporary Political Theory* (New York: Palgrave Macmillan, 2013), 25.
50 Ibid., 29.

## Chapter 1 Authority Year Zero

1 Quoted in Rainer Stollmann, "Fascist Politics as a Total Work of Art: Tendencies of the Aesthetization of Political Life in National Socialism," *New German Critique* 14 (1978): 47.
2 Stollmann, "Fascist Politics as a Total Work of Art," 47.
3 Susan Buck-Morss, "Aesthetics and Inaesthetics: Walter Benjamin's Artwork Essay Reconsidered," *October* 62 (1992): 38.
4 Marsha Landy, *Fascism in Film: The Italian Commercial Cinema, 1931–1943* (Princeton, NJ: Princeton University Press, 1986), 3.
5 Ibid.
6 Angelo Restivo, *The Cinema of Economic Miracles: Visuality and Modernization in the Italian Art Film* (Durham, NC: Duke University Press, 2002), 24–25.
7 Ibid., 27.
8 Ibid.
9 Ibid., 32.
10 Geoffrey Nowell-Smith, "North and South, East and West: Rossellini and Politics," in *Roberto Rossellini: Magician of the Real*, ed. David Forgacs, Sarah Lutton, and Geoffrey Nowell-Smith (London: BFI Publishing, 2000), 8.
11 Ibid.
12 See, for instance, André Bazin, "In Defense of Rossellini," in *What Is Cinema?*, trans. Hugh Gray (Berkeley: University of California Press, 1971), 2:93–101.
13 Geoffrey Nowell-Smith, "North and South, East and West: Rossellini and Politics," in Forgacs et al., *Roberto Rossellini*, 11.
14 Sandro Bernardi, "Rossellini's Landscapes: Nature, Myth, History," in Forgacs et al., *Roberto Rossellini*, 55.
15 Karl Schoonover, *Brutal Vision: The Neorealist Body in Postwar Italian Cinema* (Minneapolis: University of Minnesota Press, 2012), 111.
16 Ibid., 112.
17 Ibid., 147–148.
18 Hannah Arendt, "What Is Authority?," in *The Portable Hannah Arendt*, ed. Peter Baehr (London: Penguin, 2003), 467.
19 Hannah Arendt, *The Origins of Totalitarianism* (San Diego: Harcourt, 1973), 259.

20 Ibid., 460.
21 Arendt, "What Is Authority?," 468.
22 Ibid., 492.
23 Ibid., 501.
24 Ibid., 496.
25 Ibid., 502.
26 Walter Benjamin, "The Storyteller," in *Illuminations*, ed. Hannah Arendt (New York: Shocken, 1968), 108.
27 Ibid.
28 Ibid.
29 Arendt, "What Is Authority?," 502.
30 Svetlana Boym, "Ruinophilia: Appreciation of Ruins," *Atlas of Transformation*, http://monumenttotransformation.org/atlas-of-transformation/html/r/ruinophilia/ruinophilia-appreciation-of-ruins-svetlana-boym.html.
31 Walter Benjamin, *The Origin of German Tragic Drama*, trans. John Osborne (London: Verso, 1998), 177–178.
32 Ibid., 178.
33 Georg Simmel, "The Ruin," in *Essays on Sociology, Philosophy and Aesthetics*, ed. Kurt H. Wolff (New York: Harper and Row, 1965), 262.
34 Ibid.
35 Ibid., 266.
36 Ibid.
37 Karl Marx, *Capital: A Critique of Political Economy* (London: Penguin, 1990), 1:899.
38 Ibid.
39 Ibid.
40 Ibid.
41 Ibid.
42 Ibid., 896n.
43 Zygmunt Bauman, *Liquid Modernity* (Cambridge: Polity, 2000), 25.
44 Ibid.
45 Ibid., 29.
46 Ibid.
47 Ibid.
48 Ibid., 87.
49 Ibid., 4.
50 Ibid., 13.

## Chapter 2 The Image That Waits

1 Dina Iordanova, foreword to *A Companion to Eastern European Cinemas*, ed. Anikó Imre (Chichester, U.K.: Wiley-Blackwell, 2012), xv.
2 Ibid.
3 Ibid.
4 Manohla Dargis, "Finding Beauty in the Miserable and the Mundane," *New York Times*, January 11, 2006, http://www.nytimes.com/2006/01/11/movies/11sata.html?_r=1&.
5 David Bordwell, "TANGO Marathon," *Observations on Film Art*, October 22, 2006, http://www.davidbordwell.net/blog/2006/10/22/tango-marathon.

6 Phil Ballard, "In Search of Truth: Béla Tarr Interviewed," *Kinoeye* 4, no. 2 (2004), http://www.kinoeye.org/04/02/ballard02.php.
7 André Bazin, "The Evolution of the Language of Cinema," in *What Is Cinema?*, trans. Hugh Gray (Berkeley: University of California Press, 1967), 1:27.
8 Ibid., 29.
9 Ibid., 35.
10 Ibid., 36.
11 Ballard, "In Search of Truth."
12 Bordwell, "TANGO Marathon."
13 Peter Hames, "The Melancholy of Resistance: The Films of Béla Tarr," *Kinoeye* 1, no. 1 (2001), http://www.kinoeye.org/01/01/hames01.php.
14 Dargis, "Finding Beauty in the Miserable and the Mundane."
15 Bazin, "Evolution of the Language of Cinema," 1:36.
16 John Cunninghamm, *Hungarian Cinema: From Coffee House to Multiplex* (New York: Wallflower Press, 2004), 143.
17 Ibid., 195.
18 Ibid., 151.
19 Ibid., 143.
20 Ibid.
21 Alexei Yurchak, *Everything Was Forever, until It Was No More* (Princeton, NJ: Princeton University Press, 2005), 4.
22 Siegfried Kracauer, "Those Who Wait," in *The Mass Ornament: Weimar Essays*, trans. Thomas Y. Levin (Cambridge, MA: Harvard University Press, 1995), 135.
23 Ibid., 129.
24 Ibid., 135.
25 Ibid., 137.
26 Ibid., 138 (emphasis in original).
27 Ibid.
28 Ibid., 139.
29 Ibid.
30 Ibid.
31 See, for instance, the discussion of Tarr's long takes in András Bálint Kovács, *The Cinema of Béla Tarr: The Circle Closes* (New York: Wallflower Press, 2013), 56–59.
32 Kracauer, "Those Who Wait," 140.
33 The character, Estike, echoes throughout the torture sequence the words that, presumably, her father speaks as he beats her.
34 The domestic disinterest in Tarr is relatively well documented. See, for instance, Bálint Kovács, *Cinema of Béla Tarr*, 172.
35 Elizabeth Goodstein, *Experience without Qualities: Boredom and Modernity* (Stanford, CA: Stanford University Press, 2005), 1.
36 Ibid.
37 Ibid., 10.
38 Ibid., 398.
39 The topic of messianism was discussed in the introduction and will be returned to later in this chapter.
40 Patrice Petro, *Aftershocks of the New: Feminism and Film History* (New Brunswick, NJ: Rutgers University Press, 2002), 57.
41 Ibid., 57–58.
42 Ibid., 66.

43 Quoted in ibid., 66.
44 Ibid., 66.
45 Bálint Kovács, *Cinema of Béla Tarr*, 97.
46 Ibid., 173.
47 Ibid., 172–173.
48 Ibid., 63.
49 Ibid., 175.
50 Ibid.
51 Jacques Rancière, *Béla Tarr: The Time After*, trans. Erik Beranek (Minneapolis: Univocal, 2011), 4.
52 Ibid., 7.
53 Ibid., 8.
54 Ibid., 9.
55 Ibid., 49.
56 Ibid., 49.
57 Jacques Derrida, *Specters of Marx*, trans. Peggy Kamuf (London: Routledge, 1994), 144 (emphasis added).
58 Ibid., 81.
59 Ibid.
60 Pier Paolo Pasolini, "Observations on the Long Take," *October* 13 (1980): 5.
61 Ibid.
62 Mary Ann Doane, *The Emeregence of Cinematic Time: Modernity, Contingency, the Archive*. (Cambridge, MA: Harvard University Press, 2002), 224.
63 Ibid., 162.
64 Ibid., 162–163.
65 Ibid., 163.
66 I toyed with placing another comma in this sentence, so that it would read: "The doctor waits with us, in the dark and without hope, for any particular outcome." I deem both versions accurate and valuable.
67 Rancière, *Béla Tarr*, 61.
68 I will return to the topic of death, and its relationship to hope, in chapter 4.

## Chapter 3 The End of Authority, the End of Democracy

1 Excepting of course the return to authoritarianism, the possibility of which will be discussed shortly.
2 The Hallyu should not be confused with the realist and politically minded strictly film-based New Wave of the late 1980s.
3 Kyung Hyun Kim, *Virtual Hallyu: Korean Cinema of the Golden Era* (Durham, NC: Duke University Press, 2012), 11.
4 Ibid., 125.
5 Acquarello, "Where Are the Snows of Yesteryear?: Hong Sang-soo Searches for Lost Time in *Woman Is the Future of Man*," *Senses of Cinema*, October 18, 2004, http://sensesofcinema.com/2004/feature-articles/woman_future_man.
6 Kim, *Virtual Hallyu*, 125–126.
7 David Scott Diffrient, "South Korean Film Genres and Art-House Anti-Poetics: Erasure and Negation in *The Power of Kangwon Province*," *Cineaction* 60 (2003): 62.
8 Akira Mizuta Lippit, "Hong Sangsoo's Lines of Inquiry, Communication, Defense, and Escape," *Film Quarterly* 57, no. 4 (2004): 22.

9 Ibid., 23.
10 Ibid., 24.
11 Ibid.
12 Ibid., 25.
13 Ibid.
14 Ibid., 26.
15 Ibid., 27.
16 Ibid., 22.
17 Ibid., 29.
18 Darcy Paquet, *New Korean Cinema: Breaking the Waves* (New York: Columbia University Press, 2009), 20.
19 Ibid., 21.
20 Ibid.
21 For much more on the politically minded cinema of the 1980s and its unsteady partnership with mainstream politics, see Young-a Park, *Unexpected Alliances: Independent Filmmakers, the State, and the Film Industry in Postauthoritarian South Korea* (Stanford, CA: Stanford University Press, 2014), chap. 1.
22 Michael Robinson, "Contemporary Culture Production in South Korea: Vanishing Meta-Narratives of Nation," in *New Korean Cinema*, ed. Julian Stringer and Chi-yun Shin (Edinburgh: Edinburgh University Press, 2007), 24.
23 Ibid.
24 Ibid., 28.
25 Ibid., 29.
26 Park, *Unexpected Alliances*, 3–4.
27 Ibid., 13.
28 Ibid., 14.
29 Hye Seung Chung and David Scott Diffrient, "Forgetting to Remember, Remembering to Forget: The Politics of Memory and Modernity in the Fractured Films of Lee Chang-dong and Hong Sang-soo," in *Seoul Searching: Culture and Identity in Contemporary Korean Cinema*, ed. Frances Gateward (Albany: State University of New York Press, 2007), 116.
30 Ibid., 129.
31 Ibid., 132.
32 Ibid., 133.
33 This distrust of authoritarianism is particularly true for figures like Hong Sang-soo, whose political ideas were forged in the fight for democracy in the 1980s. Authoritarianism, of course, for others continues to haunt South Korea in a different way, and returned with force of late thanks to the election and subsequent disastrous presidency of Park Geun-hye, Park Chung-hee's daughter.
34 Chung and Diffrient, "Forgetting to Remember, Remembering to Forget," 133–134.
35 Moon Jae-cheol, "The Meaning of Newness in Korean Cinema: Korean New Wave and After," *Korea Journal* 46, no. 1 (2006): 40.
36 Ibid., 40–41.
37 Kyung Hyun Kim, *The Remasculinization of Korean Cinema* (Durham, NC: Duke University Press, 2004), 18.
38 Again, the election and subsequent scandals of Park Geun-hye come to mind.
39 Kim, *Remasculinization of Korean Cinema*, 19.
40 Ibid., 20.

41 Ibid., 131.
42 This translation is based on the subtitles provided in the film.
43 J. Hoberman. "Sea Change: Sand, Surf, and Everything Comes Undone in Hong Sang-soo's Woman on the Beach," *Village Voice*, January 1, 2008.
44 Gilles Deleuze and Felix Guattari. *A Thousand Plateaus: Capitalism and Schizophrenia*, trans. Brian Massumi (Minneapolis: University of Minnesota Press, 1987), 486.
45 Stephen L. Gardner, "The Eros and Ambitions of Psychological Man," in *The Triumph of the Therapeutic: Uses of Faith after Freud*, ed. Elizabeth Lasch-Quinn (Wilmington, DE: Intercollegiate Studies Institute, 2006), 228.
46 Ibid., 232.
47 Ibid.
48 Ibid., 230.
49 Zygmunt Bauman, *Liquid Modernity* (Cambridge: Polity Press, 2000), 5 (emphasis in original).
50 Ibid., 5.
51 Ibid., 25.
52 Ibid., 236–237.
53 Juliet Flower MacCannell, *The Regime of the Brother* (London: Routledge, 1991), 11.
54 Ibid., 17.
55 Ibid., 26.
56 David Harvey, *A Brief History of Neoliberalism* (Oxford: Oxford University Press, 2005), 2.
57 Market-restricted neoliberalism, I should add, is an equally significant concern, if not the topic of this discussion.
58 Harvey, *Brief History of Neoliberalism*, 3.
59 For a particularly useful explanation, see Mark Blyth, *Austerity: The History of a Dangerous Idea* (Oxford: Oxford University Press, 2013).
60 Harvey, *Brief History of Neoliberalism*, 185.
61 Jesook Song, "Between Flexible Life and Flexible Labor: The Inadvertent Convergence of Socialism and Neoliberalism in South Korea," *Critique of Anthropology* 29, no. 2 (2009): 141.
62 Ibid., 143.
63 Ibid., 152.

## Chapter 4 Force, Hope, and Death

1 Ethan Mordden, *Medium Cool: The Movies of the 1960s* (New York: Knopf, 1990), 241.
2 Ibid., 239.
3 Ibid., 241.
4 Roger Ebert, "Medium Cool," *Chicago Sun-Times*, September 21, 1969.
5 Ibid.
6 Ibid.
7 Wexler went on to make a variety of politically minded documentaries.
8 Vincent Canby, "Real Events of '68 Seen in 'Medium Cool': Haskell Wexler Wrote and Directed Movie," *New York Times*, August 28, 1969.
9 Ibid.
10 Ibid.

11 Ibid.
12 Ibid.
13 Christophe Menke, *Force: A Fundamental Concept of Aesthetic Anthropology* (New York: Fordham University Press, 2012), 9.
14 Ibid., 5.
15 Ibid., 6.
16 Ibid. (emphasis added).
17 Ibid., 11.
18 Ibid. (emphasis added).
19 Ibid.
20 Ibid., 12.
21 Ibid.
22 Ibid.
23 Ibid.
24 Ibid.
25 Ibid., 40.
26 The subject of messianic hope was explored in depth in the introduction, and touched on again in chapter 1. It is key to my understanding of political ambiguity in art cinema.
27 Menke, *Force*, 44.
28 Ibid.
29 This subject is discussed at length in chapter 2.
30 Ibid., 90.
31 Jean Baudrillard, *Symbolic Exchange and Death*, trans. Iain Hamilton Grant (Thousand Oaks, CA: SAGE), 3–4.
32 Ibid., 4.
33 Ibid.
34 Ibid.
35 Ibid.
36 Ibid., 162.
37 Ibid., 4.
38 Ibid.
39 Ibid., 5.
40 Ibid.
41 Kristin Ross, *May '68 and Its Afterlives* (Chicago: University of Chicago Press), 3–4.
42 Ibid., 6.
43 Ibid., 6–7.
44 Ibid., 7.
45 Ibid., 15.
46 Alain Touraine, *The Post-Industrial Society*, trans. Leonard F. X. Mayhew (New York: Random House), 89.
47 Ibid., 90.
48 Ibid., 90–91.

## Coda

1 D. N. Rodowick, *The Crisis of Political Modernism: Criticism and Ideology in Contemporary Film Theory* (Berkeley: University of California Press, 1994), xiii.

2 Jean-Louis Comolli and Jean Narboni, "Cinema/Ideology/Criticism," in *Cahiers du Cinema*, vol. 3: *1968–1972: The Politics of Representation*, ed. Nick Browne (London: Routledge, 1990), 61.
3 Ibid., 64.
4 Ibid., 62.
5 Rodowick, *Crisis of Political Modernism*, xiv.
6 Ibid., 275–276.
7 Ibid., 287.
8 Hannah Arendt, *The Human Condition* (Chicago: University of Chicago Press, 1958), 291.
9 Ibid., 90–91.
10 Ibid., 294.
11 Ibid., 294.
12 It is for this reason that I think that the current category of contemplative cinema is a bit of a misnomer. This is a cinema that demands an active mind, a mind engaged in thought rather than the passivity of contemplation.
13 Arendt, *Human Condition*, 128.
14 Ernesto Laclau, "Why Do Empty Signifiers Matter to Politics?," in *Emancipation(s)* (London: Verso, 1996), 40.
15 Ibid., 41.
16 Ibid.
17 Ibid., 42.
18 Ibid., 45.

# Index

Page numbers in italics indicate figures.

## About the Author

KALLING HECK is an assistant professor of screen arts and English at Louisiana State University.